38 Specks

Gerard Catherin
and Jennifer Sinclair

38 Specks

The Proposition

To the memory of Madame Paul Nicolas my beloved Taty (née Catherin 1910–2012) and to my dearest friends Jean Claude Villeneuve (1947–2017) and Col Ribaux (1937–2018)

38 Specks: The Proposition
ISBN 978 1 76109 066 0
Copyright © Gerard Catherin and Jennifer Sinclair 2021

First published 2021 by
Ginninderra Press
PO Box 3461 Port Adelaide 5015
www.ginninderrapress.com.au

Contents

The Proposition		7
Prologue		9
Introduction		13
1	Rennes-le-Château, 14 April 2003	17
2	Three weeks earlier, Sydney, 6 a.m. 25 March 2003	23
3	How I got into gold: Brisbane Valley Creek, NSW, 1986	28
4	France, June 2006	36
5	Salsigne and the revelation, 10 June 2006	43
6	Return to Rennes-le-Château, 2006	50
7	How I got into diamonds: Sydney, New South Wales, 1995	60
8	Brisbane Valley Creek, New South Wales, 1997	63
9	Kandie Peak, New South Wales, 1998	66
10	New deal going nowhere	71
11	France, November 2010	74
12	Four little specks	80
13	Thirty-eight specks	83
14	Gold dust or bulldust	88
15	Just because of a little book	93
16	A story to tell: Adelaide, 2014	101
17	The documents	107
18	The information	111
19	Anticlines and synclines: Adelaide, 2014	114
20	'One day I will make you very rich'	120
21	Secrets and lies	126
22	Lunch at number 18	130
23	The coded parchments – fake or real?	137
24	What would you do?	142

25	'I have no more money…'	147
26	The ecclesiastics	150
27	A pain in the derrière	154
28	Elizabeth Van Buren	157
29	Close encounters: Sydney, 1972	161
30	Gremlins in the Go-Devil: Good Forest, NSW, 1989	165
31	Geometry and the goddess	169
32	A rose for a lady	178
33	Fractals, portals and pine cones 'kissing noses'	181
34	White Lady Rock	185
35	Out of the blue	192
36	Gold and roses: Norwood	198
37	Mining the French archives	206
38	'There's gold in them hills'	209
39	Alchemy and demons	214
40	Devils, demons and dragons	217
41	The counterfeiters of Bezu	220
42	Fouquet's letter	223
43	The best-laid plans: Canberra, November 2014	227
44	Mungo Lake	230
45	Bloodlines and bones: Adelaide	232
46	A sign of good fortune ahead: Adelaide, March 2015	238
47	The Hand of Faith	241
48	Change of fortune: Mount Airly, New South Wales, 2015	247
49	Fortune flips	252
50	The wilderness and the White Lady	256
51	Dead man's bones: Adelaide	261
52	The new gold rush	269
53	The 'stone' of Avols	274
54	The search continues	279
	Epilogue	282
	Bibliography and further reading	284
	References	296

The Proposition

Reputations have been made and lost in the quest to find the truth about the millionaire priest of Rennes-le-Château.
Gold is the ultimate product.
It has no boundaries, no nationality and no fixed address.
It can be carried in your pockets.
It can take you from poor to rich overnight.
It can be found and sold leaving no trace of the transaction.
Millions of dollars' worth of gold still lies undiscovered in the ground.
The truth is out there and up for grabs.

Once you eliminate the impossible, whatever remains, no matter how improbable, must be the truth.

Sir Arthur Conan Doyle

Gold! Gold! Gold! Gold!
Bright and yellow, hard and cold,
Molten, graven, hammered and rolled;
Heavy to get and light to hold;
Hoarded, bartered, bought and sold,
Stolen, borrowed, squandered, doled;
Spurned by young, but hugged by the old
To the verge of the churchyard mould;
Price of many a crime untold.
Gold! Gold! Gold! Gold!

Thomas Hood (1799–1845)

Prologue

Somewhere on the old Strzelecki desert track on the way to Birdsville, Queensland. Late winter 2011.

For a long time, the only sound was the crackle of timber in the campfire. A light breeze spun spirals of smoke into the cold night air. I turned up the collar on my jacket, looked up and scanned the blue-black night sky, clear as crystal. Years ago, I had seen strange lights – reported them even, but tonight the stars of the Southern Cross sparkled like diamonds and everything was as it should be.

'Great country,' I said to my mate.

'Yeah, mate. *Gold* country. How much further to Birdsville, do you reckon?'

'About four days' worth. If everything goes according to plan.' I poked the fire with a stick and watched a burst of embers rush upwards as if trying to escape the flames. I settled by the fire and lit a cigarette with the end of the stick. 'Funny you mentioned gold,' I said. 'Makes me think of that priest in France.'

'A priest, you say.'

'*Oui*, a French priest, lived in a village called Rennes-le-Château, not far from where I lived as a boy. Money started to smile at him around 1892. If you knew how many books have been written about this bloke, you would have a fit.'

My mate flicked his cigarette butt into the flames and took another beer from the esky. 'So what do you reckon? I mean, how did he get the cash?'

'They say he found some old documents in his church that led him to a treasure and after that he had no problem with cash,' I said. 'To get cash, you need to give something in exchange. There are plenty of theories, mate, but no one has been able to prove anything. There must be a catch and the more I think about it, the more I feel the answer is simple. Since my last trip to France, I have this theory and I can't get it out of my head. It's driving me nuts. I think I could be onto something.'

'Yeah, and what's that?'

'Mate, I think he found real gold.'

'Yeah, and why's that?'

'Imagine you're walking into a pawnshop with a coin from the treasure of Lava or a piece of ancient jewellery.'

'Lava, where's that?'

'A small gulf in Corsica. One of my cousins lived there in the eighties when some guys discovered a treasure – ancient gold coins. If you sold one coin from that find, you would be richer by about one hundred big ones. Anyway, you're in the pawnshop and the guy behind the counter looks at the coin – then he looks at you and asks you to wait a minute while he goes out the back and comes back with the boss. The boss looks at the coin, exchanges a knowing glance with his employee, then says something like, "Sorry, mate, we don't deal with this gear, but if you leave your name and phone number, I could find out for you." So naturally you walk out empty-handed because I don't think you would leave your details, would you?'

My mate thought for a moment. 'Depends how smart I am, right?'

'Right. Then you could look up a numismatic shop and try your luck again.'

'Numis– what?'

'Numismatic – a shop that specialises in coins, but I know you would walk out empty-handed again. Then again, if you're silly enough to leave your name and number, don't be surprised if a cop knocks on your door next morning just to ask few questions – you with me.'

'So where did these coins I'm trying to sell come from?'

'Let's just say it was a lucky find,' I said.

'OK, so what about finders keepers?'

'Not in France, mate – the state owns it all. Now think about this. If you walk into the same pawnshop with ten small gold nuggets in your pocket – let's say each nugget weighs one ounce – that's around thirty grams, not much really, but at $1,200 an ounce, you have $12,000 worth of gold in your pocket. Even if the guy only offers you $1,000 an ounce, you take it and walk out with a smile. No one will ask you where it came from because it can never be traced.'

'So what are you saying?'

'I think the priest found a gold vein or a reef. When he needs cash, he creates a decoy, goes and gets some more gold from a hidden location, then, no worries, he sells it anywhere he can find a buyer, and believe me, there are plenty of them. Bob's your uncle, he just got some cash – no questions asked.'

'You're starting to sound like bloody Lasseter and his lost gold reef, mate. Do you know where this gold vein is?'

'Maybe.'

'Now you've really got me hooked. When do we go?'

'I'm thinking about it. Now let's hit the sack. We need to get to Birdsville in time for the races.'

Introduction

I remember the day I became a Rennie.

It was 2006, the middle of the high season in the South of France, a perfect summer's day. The sort of day you read about in the travel brochures. Blue sky, another small village just a few kilometres away; a glass of wine, a baguette and a Camembert cheese waiting for me.

However, I was facing a two-and-a-half-metre-high fence, a locked gate with a heavy padlock and a large sign that read, 'Entry to the mine prohibited, trespassers will be prosecuted'. A fence is not a deterrent to anyone willing to trespass. However, I could not find a way to get in, no matter how strong my curiosity was.

The mine of Salsigne was at one time the biggest-producing opencast gold mine in Western Europe – but I didn't know that then and I didn't know that my discovery could just be an answer to one of France's greatest unsolved mysteries.

The tiny village of Salsigne is in the Languedoc, about forty-seven kilometres (twenty-nine miles) north of Rennes-le-Château (as the crow flies) in the south-west of France. If you too are a Rennie, the mention of that name may send a tingle down your spine. A Rennie is someone who is hooked by the unsolved mystery of Rennes-le-Château and its priest Bérenger Saunière, who at the end of the nineteenth century became rich way beyond his station. Rennies have read all or most of the books written about the mystery, estimated at over five hundred. They have trawled the Internet for information – they may have joined a blog or one of the many Rennes-le-Château societies, or participated in one of the many guided tours to the village.

Rennies have read and reread *The Holy Blood and the Holy Grail,* by

Michael Baigent, Richard Leigh and Henry Lincoln, published in 1982, the book that sparked the mystery internationally, and which is still in print. It was one of the main source books for Dan Brown's infamous novel *The da Vinci Code,* estimated by some to have sold over eighty million copies. They have probably seen the *The da Vinci Code* film and either loved or hated it.

Over time, the mystery of the 'millionaire priest' has attracted all sorts of theories, endlessly debated in the Rennie literature. They may have a particular favourite. Did the priest uncover a great secret and find a hidden treasure? Was he paid by certain noble families to find important documents confirming the existence of a sacred bloodline? Did he find the mummified bodies of Jesus or Mary Magdalene, or was he working undercover for a secret society? Was he engaged in a simony scam – selling thousands of masses? Had he discovered the Ark of the Covenant and got it to work? Was he travelling through different dimensions or dealing in a death cult? On the other hand, was he just an educated and clever man who knew how to fool the villagers and the Church and exploit the riches in the land?

Google 'unsolved mysteries' and it's almost certain that listed amongst the pyramids, the monsters, alien encounters and the conspiracy theories you'll find an entry for Rennes-le-Château. Over the years, the story has become a veritable paradise for conspiracy theorists. However, most of the theories rely on hearsay and circumstantial evidence – there are very few verifiable facts.

In 1965, when stories were appearing in the French media about the 'millionaire priest', I was working as a *motard de presse,* tearing through the streets of Paris on my motorbike, delivering newspapers all over the city. It would take a head-on collision, a hankering for adventure and an affair of the heart for me to make the decision to emigrate from France to Australia seventeen thousand kilometres away.

That is where I learned about gold.

Rennies are committed to the quest – they haven't given up on finding the truth. If you are not a Rennie now, maybe you will be when you turn to the last page of my story.

Two thousand and six was my 'ah ha' moment, but it all started in 2003 when I returned to France for a family holiday after an absence of twenty-eight years. I wasn't a Rennie then and I wasn't looking for gold. Sometimes things just come together in unexpected ways.

1

Rennes-le-Château, 14 April 2003

That was when I saw the red earth.

A rich ochre-red like the earth in outback Australia, or the old goldfields near Bathurst in New South Wales. But this was the south of France and even though I was born in Paris and had lived in the Languedoc for several years as a boy, I had never seen this colour soil in France before, or, if I had, I'd never noticed it.

My partner Lesley, my daughter Nathalie and I were in the last week of our holiday, staying with my aunt Taty in Aussillon, a suburb of Mazamet. We were about five kilometres out from Couiza on the road to Rennes-le-Château, the little village with a big reputation, perched on top of a mountain. It is a relatively short distance from Couiza to Rennes-le-Château, an easy drive, but the road snakes its way up the mountain, making it tedious.

I slowed the black Mercedes I had hired for our vacation and pulled over to the verge.

My daughter Nathalie looked up from her mobile phone. 'Why are you stopping?'

We had just enjoyed a delicious lunch at Carcassonne, and were on the way to check out Rennes-le-Château before heading back to my aunt's house.

'Can't you see something unusual?' I said.

'No.'

'Look, the red earth. Can't you see it?' I said, pointing to a rough patch of earth next to the road, about ten square metres in size. 'It's red like in Australia around Bathurst.'

'So what?' said Nat, fixing her attention back onto her mobile phone. My partner Lesley had been snoozing in the back seat. 'What's happening?' she said, stifling a yawn. 'Are we there yet?'

'Papa saw some red earth so he stops. You know Dad, he's probably looking for diamonds.'

'Or gold,' said Lesley stretching. 'He drives everybody crazy with his rocks.'

'Listen, you two: I know a lot more about gold than you do. I just want to have a quick look at something – anyway, we're nearly there, give me a break. Look, I'll buy coffees, OK.'

'Come *on*, Papa.'

Most people sail through a landscape observing the big picture. Prospectors train their eyes to see the detail. We have an instinct – call it a sixth sense. Some seem to be born with it – others develop it over time after years of experience.

I got out of the car and looked around. It was definitely unusual. I hadn't noticed any red earth before and, looking at the countryside, this seemed to be the only patch. I squatted down, picked up a few rocks and rolled them round in my palm; definitely quartz, and some little pebbles that looked like ironstone. Quartz and ironstone can be indicators of the presence of gold; but it was the colour of the earth that really struck me. It was red, like the soil in the goldfield region around Bathurst, an area I knew very well. Iron-rich, red earth can be an indicator of gold if associated with quartz, hematite and magnetite.

Bathurst was the location of Australia's first gold rush in the 1850s and it was where I had found my first gold. The only thing missing here were the gum trees.

'Are you coming, for God's sake? We're dying for a coffee,' Nathalie shouted. 'Let's go.'

I checked my watch and headed back to the car.

Nathalie watched me with her head out the window. 'Did you find anything?'

'Yes, quartz and ironstone – they call quartz the mother of gold.'

'Yeah, yeah,' said the girls in a perfect chorus. 'Get in.'

I got back in the car and headed for Rennes-le-Château. As we entered the village, Nathalie pointed to a sign: '*Les fouilles sont interdites sur le territoire de la Commune de Rennes le Château. Arrete du 28.07.65.*'

'What does that mean, Papa?'

'Fossicking is prohibited on the territory of the village of Rennes-le-Château.'

'Did they know you were coming?' she said with a wink.

I edged the car through the narrow streets looking for a car park. The houses were constructed of a creamy white stone, echoing the colour of the limestone cliffs that characterise the geology of the south. I pulled up to a low stone wall that bordered what appeared to be the only car park. At the end of the wall, a neo-gothic tower jutted out across the edge of the mountain. A splash of yellow broom caught my attention and momentarily took my memory back to the Australian bush.

We sat in silence on the wall, like three lizards enjoying the warmth of the sun, unusual for that time of the year. The view across the valley was breathtaking. If you arrived in Rennes-le-Château knowing nothing about its strange reputation, you might be excused for thinking it was just another tiny isolated French village, strange and desolate – nothing special, not worth the trip. But this view would make up for it. It was panoramic, extending across the great sweep of the valley of the Aude to the Pyrenees Orientales, which mark the border with Spain. At night, you can see the lights of many small villages across the valley.

The Celts, Romans and Visigoths had occupied this part of France since ancient times. I could understand why they established fortified centres here; the vantage point across the valley was fantastic. Some people believe that the remains of Rhedea, a Visigoth city of some 300,000 people lay beneath Rennes-le-Château. But as far as I could find, no one has conducted an extensive archaeological dig to support this theory. It was one of the many unverified 'facts' of the mystery. In the late nineteenth century, Bérenger Saunière, the village priest, put this information on one of a series of postcards he produced to promote the village. If it wasn't for books like *The Holy Blood and the Holy Grail* and *The da Vinci Code*, this village would probably have remained a forgotten place.

Nathalie's voice broke through the magic. 'Well, are we going to sit here all day? What about that coffee? A warm cuppa wouldn't be bad, don't you think?'

We walked around looking for a café but nothing was open. Everybody is dying to go to Rennes-le-Château, but the place was like a cemetery – deserted.

'Let's check out the church,' I said, as we crossed the square.

According to the story, this was where Bérenger Saunière discovered some parchments, a hidden tomb, and documents that revealed an 'explosive secret' that led him to a fabulous treasure and great wealth. It sounded like the standard plot of a fictional treasure story, like something out of *Raiders of the Lost Ark*. Then again, I had to admit that treasures had been found in this region – not surprising with its long history of conflict and battles over land. The problem for treasure seekers in France nowadays is that under French law the finders have no rights to the find. If the finder wants to convert the treasure into cash, it must be sold on the black market – which can be a dangerous business. Eventually, items from 'the find' make their way onto the open market and the treasure hunters are found out.

There is one commodity that can be sold, exchanged or converted into cash anywhere in the world with no questions asked – native gold. That is of course unless you're selling a nugget like the seventy-one-kilo Welcome Stranger, found by James Deason and Richard Oates in 1869 just under the surface within the roots of a stringybark tree near the mining town of Moliagul in Victoria. How lucky can you be? At the time, it was the world's largest-ever recorded nugget.

There is an old prospectors' saying that 'gold is where you find it'. In 1980, an amateur fossicker using a metal detector discovered the Hand of Faith, a nugget weighing twenty-seven kilos, only fifteen centimetres beneath the ground, behind the Kingower state school in Victoria. The school is about forty-eight kilometres (twenty-nine miles) from where the Welcome Stranger nugget was found. Bought a few years ago for one million dollars by the Golden Nugget Casino in Las Vegas, the nugget now graces the casino's lobby. It would be worth about US$3 to $4 million in today's money. Some of the largest nuggets in the world have been found in the Victorian goldfields.

The church was smaller than I had imagined. As we walked inside, we were shocked by a statue of what looked like a devil to the left of the entrance. He was supporting a font in the shape of a shell above which stood four angels, each making a sign that together formed the sign of the cross. At the angels' feet, an inscription read, '*Par ce signe tu le vaincras.* In this sign ye shall conquer him'. I thought that was a bit odd as this well-known phrase usually reads, 'By this sign, ye shall conquer'. The addition of *le* changes the meaning to conquer 'him'. The verb *vaincre* can also be translated: to 'outdo', to 'win' or to 'be the victor'. Conquering could mean winning or taking possession after a battle for land, for example. I asked myself, conquering what or who, and winning what? Curiously, the letters 'BS' sat below this inscription. Was it the devil that needed to be conquered, or perhaps Bérenger Saunière?

Leaving the church, we wandered about for a bit and discovered that the Atelier Empreinte, one of the two bookshops in the village, was open. There was that strange devil again at the shop's entrance, a replica of the statue in the church, for sale at 35,000 euros. I wondered who would buy such an ugly thing.

I browsed the titles on Rennes-le-Château and Bérenger Saunière. I had read some of them, like *The Holy Blood and the Holy Grail* and *L'Héritage de L'Abbé Saunière* by Claire Corbu and Antoine Captier, published in 1985. I tried making conversation with the bookseller, asking him which were the best books. He simply pointed to the shelves with a curt 'They're all there.' I spotted *The Tomb of God: unlocking the code to a 2,000-year-old mystery* by Richard Andrews and Paul Schellenberger, published in 1996. The authors claimed to have applied mathematical logic to the mystery of Rennes-le-Château and the alleged treasure. The promise of a healthy dose of archaeology, geometry, surveying and plain common sense appealed to my practical nature.

I noticed the girls talking in hushed tones and giving me sideways glances; a little conspiracy seemed to be taking place. As we walked out, I discovered what the conspiracy was all about. Nathalie had bought *The Tomb of God* for me for my birthday. It was 14 April, three days before I turned sixty-one. I was a happy man.

'Now let's get a coffee,' said Lesley.

'We'll try Limoux on the way back,' I said.

It was late afternoon when we left Rennes-le-Château, acting like real French citizens, talking about the dinner we knew would be waiting for us in Mazamet. On 17 April, Nathalie walked into town alone and returned one hour later with a bunch of flowers for Taty and a beautiful birthday cake. The end of April was fast approaching. Lesley and I would return to Australia and Nathalie to Ireland.

The geological indicators I found on the way to Rennes-le-Château were an unexpected and intriguing find and something I planned to follow up on my own. France is a long way from Australia and, as is the way of things, the practicalities of life back home took precedence over dreams. The red earth, quartz and ironstones became another holiday memory. From time to time, I picked up *The Tomb of God*, but it would be another three years before the next piece of the Rennes-le-Château puzzle fell into my lap. One thing was certain, though I probably did not realise it at the time: the Rennes-le-Château game had just invited me to play.

2

Three weeks earlier, Sydney, 6 a.m. 25 March 2003

A man and a woman going to Paris, the city of love, where I was born in 1942. Life could not have been better. Lesley and I were on the footpath at the front of her house in the inner-city suburb of Paddington, waiting for the cab that I had booked the day before and wondering why we had to be at Sydney International airport so early. Our flight was leaving at ten a.m.; three hours waiting seemed a bit much. I was returning to France to see my family after twenty-eight years. It was an *incredible* feeling, tremendous excitement mixed with apprehension; the butterflies in my stomach were out of control.

The whole family was there to greet us when we arrived at Charles de Gaulle airport. Uncle Henry, my mother's brother, his wife Mireille, my cousin Sylvie and her husband Michel, who we called 'The Corsican'. What a reunion after so long; smiling faces, everybody talking at once, crying, laughing, it was an emotional volcano. The last time I had seen Sylvie she was a girl of thirteen, now she was married with two children – hard to imagine. I also had two children, Nathalie and Dominic, from my marriage to my first wife Suzie. It made me realise that I was not getting any younger.

We picked up the little black Mercedes at Montparnasse. My family lived twenty-eight kilometres away in the commune of Pontoise in the north western suburbs of Paris. Out of the airport, the new world hit me – the noise, the traffic. If you have ever driven in France, especially Paris, you will understand. The French drive like maniacs – pedestrians watch out. Nobody seems to care, but then everybody is happy – that is the French way for you. I had expected things to change, but this was incredible. In twenty-eight years, the suburbs of Paris had become so large, spreading over many kilometres. I lost my sense of direction and could not even remember how to get out of the city. I nearly had a panic attack – had I completely lost the plot? Mireille and the kids went in their car. Luckily, my uncle was in ours; he was our salvation.

As a young man living in Paris, I had worked as a *motard de presse,* making deliveries all over the city for Moto Presse at 13 rue Paul Lelong – mainly newspapers, films from TV stations, horse racing newspapers and the like. My best friend's father, Monsieur Croize, the weatherman with the newspaper *Le Figaro,* got me the job in 1963, just after my release from compulsory national service. Being young and mad about motorbikes, I loved it. It was like Formula 1 in the streets of Paris every single day and night. I had a BMW 600cc with sidecar – the biggest motorbike available at that time. Everything was somehow permitted for the powerful *Service de Presse*: speeding, going through red lights, riding on the footpath, riding on the left – you name it. Every Monday, there was a special delivery of free newspapers to *le Petit Palais,* where driving infringements were sorted, with the exception of the driving infringements given by cops unaware of the unwritten 'rule': *motards* are not fined; they work, they ride and they speed for *La Presse.* The computer age has changed all this, though.

In 1965, on a delivery run for the newspaper *Combat,* my luck ran out. I had to pick up the papers near the stock exchange at midnight and deliver them on the platform at Austerlitz station. A head-on collision with a car resulted in three months in hospital. That's when I decided to immigrate to Australia. That and an affair of the heart with my first love, Odette, a French woman who I met in the air force – but that's another story.

We were all looking forward to the coming weekend. Uncle Henry had booked a small hall for a big family reunion. All of us, plus at least thirty friends, would spend two nights in the hall equipped with sleeping facilities, just like a holiday camp. My daughter Nathalie joined us on the Friday, flying in from Ireland, where she worked as a chiropractor. For the first three days, all we did was eat, sleep and talk. Every day we would hear 'what's for lunch', 'what's for dinner'. The table was being reset for dinner even before lunch was finished – it was overwhelming. French people have only one thing in mind – food – but surprisingly they do not really put on weight.

One glorious afternoon, we were sitting outside in the garden after a meal of roast horse, green beans and flageolets – small beans that are so tasty that some people call them the caviar of beans – delicious and very healthy, when the conversation turned to treasure hunting.

'Found any diamonds lately?' said Michel.

I had gotten into diamonds back in the 1990s after leaving my job as catering manager at Jenolan Caves House in the Blue Mountains, west of Sydney.

'Plenty of indicators,' I said. 'But no one to back me up with the finances to take it further. But I'm positive something will come up.'

The indicators were so good that in 2001 I signed a deal with Chuck Fipke. Chuck and his mate Stewart Blusson were famous for discovering the diamond-rich area in the north-west of Canada, which led to Chuck staking the multi-billion dollar Etaki diamond claim in 1998. His company, Dia Met Minerals Limited, had a ten per cent stake in the mine. BHP Billiton Canada Incorporated, part of the BHP Billiton Group, the world's largest diversified resources company, was the operating company. In the end, Chuck decided that our venture was too small and pulled out of the project. He was happy for me to keep the site, but to take it to the next stage I needed to apply for an exploration licence, and that was expensive. Diamond exploration in Australia was at its lowest and nobody was taking any risks; but I hadn't given up on the search.

'If you know someone who's interested in putting up some finances, let me know,' I said.

Then out of the blue, the little Corsican said. 'Why don't you do what my dad did?'

'What's that?'

'Look for treasure. Dad found one by pure luck in the gulf of Lava off the west coast of Corsica.'

Michel told us how in 1985 his father and two of his father's friends were walking in the shallow water near the shore searching for sea urchins when they spotted something sparkling in a rock – it was an old coin. After many enquiries, they discovered that it was an extremely old and rare coin, and very valuable. All up, with the help of three other guys, they found about four thousand gold coins and a gold plate dating from the third century AD, the time of Claudius II Gothicus.

'From poor to rich overnight,' said Michel. 'Imagine those guys, diving for treasure by day, and then spending their evenings living it up in nightclubs, a little too conspicuously. People started to talk, even thought they were part of a gang of armed robbers. The guys tried to claim they had inherited it and began selling it to dealers on the black market. Of course, a flood of rare Roman coins on the market eventually raised questions among collectors. Then they started overspending and eventually the state found out. The French navy cordoned off the area with nets, and installed large signs, warning people not to swim near the area because of 'great danger'. What was the danger? They anchored small patrol boats day and night preventing anyone from getting close. The problem is that Corsica is a French territory under French law. Submerged treasure is a maritime cultural asset and belongs to the state; they call it 'cultural patrimony'. Now, if it had been discovered off the coast of Great Britain, the find would have been declared a treasure trove and the finders would have at least received a reward for their efforts. But here you'd be lucky to get even a thank you.'

'What happened to finders keepers?' said Lesley.

'Under French law, the finders have no rights to the find,' I said. 'There's no incentive for treasure hunters in France, they may as well leave it in the ground – it's not worth the trouble.'

'So what happened to them?' said Lesley.

'Eventually the party soured,' said Michel. 'In 1994, eight people were sentenced to between six and eighteen months in prison for illegally making money from the find.'

'So did they give up all the treasure?' I said.

'Now that's something I don't know,' said Michel with a smile. 'Actually, when you go down to see Taty, you should visit Rennes-le-Château. It's not far from Carcassonne. That place is a big treasure mystery all of its own. Do you know about it?'

'Yes,' I said. 'I've heard about it. The priest who became a millionaire.'

I had already made plans for the week ahead. Nathalie, Lesley and I planned to stay with Taty, my ninety-three-year-old aunt in Mazamet. We were keen to visit Albi to see the cathedral made of red bricks in the ancient Roman style. Then I wanted to see my old school in Saint Pons de Thomières and after that, we had to see Béziers. As a boy, I had heard the story of the slaughter of the inhabitants of Béziers during the Albigensean crusade against the Cathars, a Gnostic Christian sect, labelled by the pope as heretics. The town had been one of the strongholds of Catharism in the region. Carcassonne and Rennes-le-Château were definitely on the itinerary.

'You must have read my mind,' I said. 'There's no way I'd travel in the south of France without going to Carcassonne and Rennes-le-Château.'

The discussion about the treasure at Rennes-le-Château reinforced my desire to go there. It was an interesting mystery, and it would have been silly not to go being so close. The drive from Mazamet to Carcassonne takes less than an hour, and then it's about another hour to Rennes-le-Château. It would also give us a chance to buy some bottles of one of my favourite wines, the region's famous sparkling white, La Blanquette de Limoux.

Two days later, we were on our way to Mazamet, as happy as Larry. Arriving at Taty's house we were tired, but in good spirits. Taty greeted us with a huge smile.

Another day in Arcadia; *aux anges*, as we say in French, feeling like angels.

3

How I got into gold: Brisbane Valley Creek, New South Wales, 1986

When I said goodbye to France in 1967 at the age of twenty-five, I was happy to see the back of it. For a young French guy full of spirit and *joie de vivre*, Australia was a real adventure. My decision to emigrate was easy. Odette, the love of my life at that time, was going to follow me. I felt that I could climb mountains and I would have gone to the end of the earth with her.

We lodged our applications at the Australian embassy and within two weeks, my application was accepted. We decided that I would go first to test the ground. It was hard not being able to speak English, but youth and a sense of adventure were on my side. However, as is often the way with *les affaires du coeur*, it did not work out. The authorities rejected Odette's visa application because she was still married at the time; *c'est la vie*. Two years later, I met Suzie, a blonde-haired, blue-eyed Aussie girl. We were in a Sydney café one afternoon, both sitting at a table with friends, her playing with the salt shaker, giving me the opportunity to ask her if she was in need of pepper. That was the beginning of our relationship. We married in 1973, our two children came along – life was good.

Finding a job as a chef in Sydney was easy. I was young, experienced and well qualified, having trained at Le Grand Balcon hotel in Mazamet and completed my training during my compulsory national military service in Germany from 1960 to 1963. In those days, the additional qualification of being a French chef in Australia was a great advantage. French chefs were highly valued in Sydney and restaurants were paying good money to hire us. We were a small group, well aware of what the market was offering and we took advantage of it, moving to who paid the most.

I got my first break working for Michel Ray, a French guy who owned the Ozone 2 restaurant in Potts Point in Sydney and the Ozone restaurant at Watsons Bay, a prime waterfront position. It would later become the famous Doyles seafood restaurant on the beach. Michel was the first restaurant owner to introduce outdoor dining in Sydney, having the courage to put tables outside on the pavement facing the sea, quite a radical move in those days.

Travelling around Australia became part of the program, working in Port Headland in Western Australia as head chef for the Walkabout motel chain, which went broke about six years later, then in Adelaide, South Australia.

In 1987, the New South Wales Tourism Commission advertised the position of food and beverage manager at Jenolan Caves House. The Jenolan Caves, in the magnificent Blue Mountains, are the oldest discovered open caves in the world and a popular tourist attraction. Bushranger James McKeown is reputed to have discovered the caves in around 1835, using them as a hideout. Built in the 1800s, Jenolan Caves House was one of the few first-class hotels in the area outside Sydney and Katoomba. It is part of a stylish complex of buildings that reminded me of Switzerland, or the eastern part of France like Alsace. The architecture and the décor is magnificent, but the catering was lacking. Visitor numbers had dropped drastically and the business was rapidly deteriorating.

My good friend Michel Laroche happened to be the assistant manager and he convinced me to apply for the position. Within three weeks, I received a pleasing notice – my application had been successful. At the time, I was working as head chef at Le Trianon Restaurant in Potts Point, one of the two top restaurants in Sydney. I suppose working there contributed in my favour in securing the position. People used to say among other things that my soufflés were better than the ones at the famous La Tour d'Argent, one of the most expensive restaurants in Paris – it must have been for good reasons.

Suzie was working in the city at that time. She and the kids stayed in our house in Sydney until the Old Police Station in Jenolan, which was in need of renovation, was finally transformed into a three-bedroom house to accommodate the four of us. Until then, I made the eight-hour round trip each week to visit my family. The job was a big challenge; another adventure waiting to be experienced and one that I knew I would relish.

Jenolan Caves is a very spiritual place to the Gundungurra nation, the Indigenous people of that region, who know it as 'Binomil' or 'Bin-oo-mur'.[1] They believe that the cave water has healing properties and that the crystals possess healing powers, especially for spiritual well-being – much the same as many non-Aboriginal people believe today. Their culture is a living culture today. At that time, like most non-Indigenous Australians, I knew nothing or very little about Aboriginal spiritual beliefs, but I could feel that there was something very special about the location – magical even. Little did I know that several years later a fascination with crystals would become a large part of my life.

After six months, business had picked up dramatically. The place was booked out every day. Weekends and school holidays were frantic – we were overwhelmed with buses, up to ten per day. Eventually a new car park was constructed. The road leading from the highway to Jenolan was narrow and winding. We could not risk having two buses meet face to face. We needed a plan B – a two-way radio was the answer.

Managing three restaurants was a huge challenge. We were on a three-thousand-hectare reserve in the middle of nowhere, 182 kilometres from our main source of supplies in Sydney and with a workforce close to 160 people who had to be fed three times a day. To put it simply, the place was buzzing with excitement.

So there I was, right in the middle of one of the world's most famous geological and spiritual treasures and right in the heartland of the old gold rush, which began in 1851 near Bathurst, the largest town in the region, about sixty kilometres from the caves. Plenty of gold can still be found in this region today. Within a radius of 150 to 200 kilometres, nearly every creek carries gold, but unless you know how to find it, you might live for a century in the region and know nothing of its existence. That's where my mate Peter Donahue came in.

Peter was the night security guard at Jenolan Caves House, and the perfect image of an old-time gold prospector. Not overly tall, at 1.7 metres, with a beard, wild hair and hands roughened by hard work and years of prospecting. His handshake could break your fingers. He might have looked rough, but he had a heart of gold. Peter did other jobs too, like breaking in horses for a guy near Oberon who owned land about fifteen kilometres away near Native Dog Creek. Further on is Black Spring, where people find sapphires. Peter was not so much into sapphires; the work is harder as it involves a lot of digging. Gold prospecting was his passion – and it was about to become mine.

I bought a 1942 Willys, an old army jeep I found as a wreck in a paddock near the town of Mudgee. In 1941, the Go Devil, as the manufacturer called it, won the US Army tender for a four-wheel drive reconnaissance vehicle. It took me nine months to restore, strictly by the manual with no modifications – then my toy became my workhorse. It was the perfect vehicle for treasure hunting trips into the countryside, through mud, snow, thick bush and across creeks. Just driving it gave me a lot of pleasure. On my days off, I drove to Sydney for the day to see Suzie and the kids and arrived back at Jenolan about two a.m., tired and hungry. Peter and I would go into the kitchen, make coffee and a bite to eat and talk about the thing that interested us most – gold.

The first time I went panning for gold was with Peter. He took me to Brisbane Valley Creek, about forty kilometres from Jenolan. He said that we would get more there and it was easy access. We took off at about six a.m. arriving at the creek by six-thirty a.m. We each had a shovel, a pan, a sieve and a plastic jar. Peter showed me how to dig gravel from a depth of at least thirty to sixty centimetres, the deeper the better, then put the sieve on the pan, throw the gravel onto the sieve and shake the sieve vigorously so that the fine gravel fell into the pan. What was left, we tipped out onto the ground and checked for sapphires. Then we started panning – it wasn't rocket science.

'Now you must move the outer lip of your pan five centimetres under water till all the light stuff is gone from the pan. It takes about five minutes and always move the pan clockwise unless you're left-handed, got it?'

There is an old saying amongst prospectors that goes something like this. If you are a novice and see something twinkling in your pan and you say to yourself I think this is gold, then you can be almost certain that it won't be; but if you think, wow, look at that gold, you can be almost sure that it is. Seriously, after only three pans, I could see some gold specks in the top left-hand side of the pan. Seeing the glitter of real gold flakes in my pan for the first time was an incredibly energising feeling, not because of the monetary value that the gold represented, but knowing the gold had been in the earth for millions of years, and there I had some in my pan. It's hard to explain if you haven't experienced it. For me, it was a feeling extraordinaire, almost magical, a feeling that took hold and has never left me.

Exploring the old gold rush region, I met fossickers who told me stories of the time when people were literally tripping over gold nuggets and of the towns that sprung up almost overnight as new deposits were discovered and diggers from all over the world flocked to Australia to make their fortune. Towns like Sofala, the area's most successful gold-mining town and the oldest surviving in that area, now a relic of its former glory. Years ago, you could buy a small bag of the river sand and be guaranteed that you would find a speck of gold in it. Where in the world could you find such marketing strategy?

Walking the main street of about two hundred metres, I understood why the town's dystopian atmosphere made the perfect setting for Peter Weir's film *The Cars That Ate Paris*. Relaxing with a beer outside the pub showing the wear of time, watching the locals some of whom looked pretty much the mirror image of the old gold prospectors of the nineteenth century. Buying lunch at the coffee shop with it's classic

Aussie menu of a pie floater – a beef pie covered with peas and gravy or fish and chips; egg and bacon rolls; peas, mashed potato and gravy – tomato or barbecue sauce twenty cents extra. There was something about this land and its people – the laidback lifestyle, the she'll be right attitude and a sense of fair go that fueled my optimism and spirit of adventure.

That is how it all started – I was hooked.

By 1989, business at Caves House was booming. Our average number of meals per week was reaching eight thousand. Gross profit had risen seventy-four per cent; not bad for a business that had been going broke a few years earlier. Two hundred and sixty thousand visitors had gone through the doors in that year and the hotel was back to its former glory. We became the second-busiest tourist resort in Australia after the Great Barrier Reef.

The premier of New South Wales visited frequently, telling staff that the state government did not intend to sell the business. Well, it seems that it was performing too well, because that is exactly what the government did, without even a thank you. Looking back, we who worked at Caves House – the farmers' wives, the backpackers, the locals from the town of Oberon thirty-five kilometres away, and all the guides working for the reserve – we deserved a medal for a job well done.

At midnight on 3 July 1990, I switched off the lights in the Caves House restaurant for the last time, locked the doors, and surrendered the keys to the CEO of the Jenolan Reserve. Then in my little three-cylinder Suzuki Mighty Boy, packed with my belongings and Sam, my black kelpie, I drove to Sydney, out of a job and about to end my marriage of seventeen years with Suzie. To make things worse, the next day I had to be in court for my divorce. It was 4 July, Independence Day in America, quite ironic really.

When I thought about the diggers moving from Sydney over the Blue Mountains on their way to the goldfield around Bathurst, a distance of two hundred kilometres, I felt more equipped. The car heater was working well; I had money from my redundancy and a friend in Sydney. Nothing was lost; this was only a bad period.

I lost interest in gold prospecting for a while, but did not forget what I had learned, especially the three most important rules in gold prospecting: find a friendly farmer; observe (look outside the square); and, most important of all, secrecy. It is paramount that the rule of secrecy is understood at all costs. Unfortunately, for some that is not always the case.

I found share accommodation easily and work the same week for a temping agency; all I had to do was to keep working. After six months, I rented a flat by myself and not long after I received payment for my share of our house, which allowed me to buy a two-bedroom flat with a garage in Balgowlah. I was now downgraded from Balgowlah Heights to Balgowlah, but it didn't bother me, I had a nice roof over my head, it was mine and I was ready for a new adventure.

Near the end of 1991, I was sent to work for Alan Bond at the Watsons Bay Hotel, on the prime waterfront position at Watsons Bay. Bond was the infamous Western Australian millionaire who won the America's Cup in 1983. He bought the pub from the Doyle family. I had been working there for less than three weeks when Bond filed for bankruptcy and the pub got a new owner, the Doyle family again. The family already owned several restaurants in the area: the restaurant next door, the one on the jetty, the one at Circular Quay and another at the fish market. Everybody called it Doyle's Peninsula. John Doyle, one of the five brothers, ran the pub. From the moment we met, we got on like a house on fire. When he asked me if I wanted to be the head chef, I did not hesitate to say yes; it was a stable job in a beautiful location. I was still keen on gold prospecting but life was about to take a new turn.

After returning to Australia from France in 2003, I was back at work at Watsons Bay Hotel, pleased to be earning money, but my heart wasn't in it any more. There were some compensations – the good food, fabulous location and the wonderful kitchen staff, my A team – but I had been in the same job since 1991. I loved so many things about the Australian bush life, especially Jenolan, and I missed it all.

Working as a chef was an obstacle to my main passion – my diamond exploration project. I felt I was onto something, and that if I played my cards right, it could bring me quite a bit of money. I was determined to learn as much as I could about diamonds. However, I could not get the image of the red earth I saw on the way to Rennes-le-Château out of my head. Rennes-le-Château was miles away from Sydney but it was as if the old Australian goldfields and the land around Rennes-le-Château were linked in some way. Something about the red earth, quartz the mother of gold, and the little ironstones was certainly playing tricks on me.

I planned to return to France in 2006, this time alone.

4

France, June 2006

'Hey, bushman! You look like a real Aussie. How are you?'

Jean Claude's smiling face beamed out from the crowd at the international arrivals lounge of Charles de Gaulle airport.

His partner Monique gave me a big hug. '*Oui*, you look like a bushman, my man!'

I guess I did look pretty much like a stockman from the Australian outback. I was wearing my ten-year-old dark brown Driza-bone raincoat, my Blundstone elastic-sided leather boots, which are very comfortable for travelling, and a pair of jeans. Driza-bone coats are designed to do exactly what the name sounds like – keep the wearer as dry as a bone. Need is the mother of invention: Edward Le Roy originally designed them in the late 1800s for sailors. He immigrated to New Zealand and teamed up with T.E. Pearson, whose father started Pearson soap.

Pearson took a consignment of Leroy coats to Australia, and then adapted the design, working in the backyard shed of his home in Kangaroo Street in Manly, the same street where my children went to kindergarten. The coat has become an iconic Australian fashion statement. I felt like Crocodile Dundee or the Man From Snowy River – except that I am afraid of horses.

'I'm fine and happy as you can see. You haven't changed, Monique.'

'Well, it's only been twelve months.'

The previous year, Jean Claude and Monique had stayed with me in Sydney for five weeks. We went four-wheel driving, mostly in the rugged country of the Blue Mountains National Park. We followed the fire trail from Jenolan Caves to Oberon, a sixty-kilometre, seven-hour trip through the Great Dividing Range in the Kanangra Boyd National Park. It is wild country, very hilly, rough and dry. Thirty kilometres after Bathurst, the Great Dividing Range climbs to an elevation of 1,200 metres. This is gold country – you can almost smell it.

For four days, we had the time of our lives, sleeping under the stars, Lesley and me in the back of the ute, Jean Claude and Monique in a double swag on the ground.

This is an ancient land of stark contrasts. Freezing in winter when the countryside is covered with snow, and boiling in summer with temperatures sometimes reaching 50°C. Eucalyptus trees blanket the hills creating a tapestry of colours, shapes and sizes. Ancient creek beds, dry most of the year, cut their way through the valleys. Dead trees litter the ground, not having survived the searing summer heat. They make perfect sanctuaries for some of the deadliest snakes and spiders in the world; nature is in control here.

Bushwalking can be a death trap for an unprepared novice. Within a hundred metres, it is easy to lose your sense of direction, as everything looks the same; but the rewards are great and there is an immense feeling of peace. Experienced bushwalkers come prepared with plenty of water and always tell someone the exact coordinates of their route. Thousands of kangaroos live in the bush. At night, sleeping in your swag, they come near, nearly touching you. In the mornings, a deafening chorus of birds will wake you.

The five days I stayed with Jean Claude and Monique in the fourteenth arrondissement near Alesia went like a flash. We visited the Louvre and climbed to the top of the Eiffel Tower, which was pure luck, as usually you can only go to the second floor. I understand now why my city of Paris is called the 'city of lights'. A dinner cruise along the Seine on *Les Bateaux Mouches* was expensive but had to be done. It is one of the most desirable night tours of Paris; the food is good, the wine even better and the service first class. The smallest house in Paris is a curiosity on the Left Bank; a single-storey dwelling only 1.1 metres wide, sandwiched between two buildings six floors high.

We spent a lot of time in the Quartier Latin, my favourite location in Paris, especially the ancient Rue de Bievre, which appeared on maps as early as 1250. François Mitterrand, the former president of France, lived there from 1972 to 1995 and the famous poet Dante lived there during his stay in Paris. At number 30, there is a great little Algerian restaurant, Restaurant La Bievre. My best friend Jean Pierre and I hung out there in the 1960s after my release from the military; the street was part of our headquarters. Jean Pierre was not a *motard de presse* but he rode with me every single night on my midnight run. Every evening, for over two years we went to Restaurant La Bievre for dinner – always choosing the couscous. I used to tell Suzie that one day I would take her to a special little restaurant to eat the best couscous in Paris. Eventually, we made the trip in 1975.

Nothing had changed. When Suzie and I walked through the door, the first person to see me was the owner. 'Gerard, how are you?' he said, pointing to a table where Jean Pierre and his new girlfriend were sitting. I could not believe it. I had left France eight years earlier, having no contact with the owner or Jean Pierre or anyone else, and out of the blue there was Jean Pierre, as if he had been waiting for me to arrive. It was as if the owner was simply telling me that I was late, to take a seat and wait for the couscous 'same as usual'. I did not even need to order. For a moment, it felt like I was dreaming. The strange thing is that there was one night when Jean Pierre refused to come with me on the Combat run and he could never really explain why. It was the night I crashed the bike and ended up in hospital.

It was time to head south to Mazamet to see aunt Taty. Jean Claude and Monique dropped me off at Austerlitz station after wishing me bon voyage. I had time to treat myself to a cup of coffee, served in a thin glass, which in my view definitely gives a better taste, with the croissant dunked in of course. It was a great feeling to hear people speaking French all around me, but a little strange. I had been living in Australia for so long that sometimes I forgot that I was French.

It was the first time I had travelled on the TGV. My destination was Toulouse, the capital of the cassoulet, a kind of bean stew. The train was quiet, clean and very comfortable. Normally it travels at a speed of three hundred kilometres an hour, but because the track was not completely finished all the way to Toulouse, we were only travelling at a speed of around a hundred and seventy kilometres an hour. Still, it was very fast. Around five hours later, I arrived at Toulouse station where I changed trains for Mazamet. The local train travelled at a speed I was more familiar with, and an hour and a half later, I arrived at Mazamet station, the end of the line.

Continuing by car takes you through Labastide-Rouairoux; Saint Pons de Thomières; Saint Chinian, known for its red wine by the same name; Puisserguier; and Béziers situated above the river Orb. The names of many of the creeks, rivers and towns in the south are derived from *or*, the French word for gold, or *aurum*, the Latin word for gold, like Auriac, Auroux and Les Aurières, to name a few. Was there gold around Béziers? I couldn't resist asking myself that question.

I did not know much about the history of the region at that time; but I did know that there was a connection between Mazamet and Australia – believe it or not, because of Australian wool. From the 1850s to the 1970s, Australia sent wool and hides to Mazamet for processing, simply because of the extreme softness of Mazamet's water. For a time, Mazamet was among the fifteen wealthiest towns in France and had more millionaires than you can think of. Nearby towns like Castres, Labastide-Rouairoux and Saint Pons de Thomières also benefited. The only downside was the stench that pervaded the town from the processing. The connection between the two countries is evident today in the street names like Rue d'Australie, Adelaide, Brisbane, Melbourne and Sydney.

The train journey gave me plenty of time to reminisce about the old days. There is an exodus out of Paris in the summer months –

Parisians heading south for their *vacances*, glad to be out of the capital for a few weeks, as the tourists pour into the city. I was no exception. It was 1964 and for two weeks, I was staying with Taty in Mazamet. Riding on my BMW R60 motorbike along the A20 L'occitane autoroute was a real adrenalin rush. The trip from Paris took me about seven hours.

One day, feeling a bit bored, I decided to take the bike for a spin up the steep forested road that leads to the small village of Hautpoul perched on a hill about two kilometres from Mazamet's market square. It is a favourite of mountain bikers and hikers. At the top of the hill, there is a Mary statue, Notre Dame d'Hautpoul. I rode through the Arnette valley, and then gunned the bike up the hill. When it came time to go down, I jumped onto the bike, but the gradient was so steep that I could picture myself going head over heels, with the bike landing on top of me. It was a crazy idea, even for me, so I jumped off, lay the bike on its side, sat on my backside and held on for dear life. With one push, the bike and I took off, sliding all the way down. Needless to say, my bike, and the seat of my trousers, were the worse for wear – you can imagine the scratches and the damage.

As the train approached Mazamet, I thought of seeing Taty again and my heart started beating faster. I was born out of wedlock at Neuilly sur Seine, a commune in the western suburbs of in Paris in 1942, which in those days was not 'acceptable', but I was very welcome as a new member into the family. Taty immediately registered my birth and on the same night, she and her friends celebrated at the La Tour d'Argent, well known for *le canard à la presse*, pressed duck. Later in life, I was told that on that night she got very intoxicated indeed. In 1945, sadly, my mother died and my grandmother and my uncle Henry cared for me.

Charles de Gaulle announced the end of World War II on 8 May 1945. France was in chaos and my uncle and grandmother wanted to leave Paris. A construction and public works company, Les Grand Travaux de Marseille, was desperate for engineers and my uncle secured a job in Haiti, returning to Paris in 1956, when the notorious dictator Papa Doc came to power. The family decided that I would live with Taty in Saint Pons de Thomières. In 1959, we moved a few kilometres west to Mazamet, where Taty taught at the music college. I lived with her until 1960, when I was called up to do compulsory national military service.

Taty was a talented musician and singer, and a great beauty. She often sang at weddings and funeral services in l'Eglise de la Madeleine in Paris. At the age of eighteen, she was awarded first prize for violin by Le Conservatoire National de Musique de Paris. In 1928, she received her diploma with honours from the Conservatorium, and in 1936, she was offered a position as a member of the orchestra on the luxuriously appointed French transatlantic liner the SS *Normandie*. She declined the job offer, however, and married the sculptor Deglesne, who worked with gold and ivory. She told me that he was well known in Paris and London, where apparently he did some work for the British regent. Money was flowing, but he was spending twice the amount of his earnings and there was never any money at home. She divorced him two years later. In 1953, she married musician Paul Nicolas. With Taty on violin, Paul on piano, and their friend Mr Bourget, a wealthy businessman from Labastide Rouairoux, on cello, they formed the 'happy trio'. Every two weeks, the trio played for Mr Bourget's friends.

Arriving at Taty's house, I was delighted to find her in good health, good spirits and very happy to see me again. Walking through the door, I could tell that she had had a little cry. Putting my arms around her, we stayed like that, hugging each other for a couple of minutes. Those minutes were priceless for us both. I will never forget, as they will never return. We both settled after a while.

'What would you like to eat tonight?' said Taty.

'Here we are again: all you think about is food,' I replied with a smile.

'Well, we need to eat, don't we?' she said.

'OK, Taty, I'll see. Tomorrow I need to be at Mazamet train station by nine a.m. to pick up the rental car I booked from Paris. I was thinking of asking Michel next door to come with me. What do you think?'

Taty's neighbours, Michel and his wife Annie, were wonderful caring people, always asking her if she needed anything. They even opened and closed the shutters of her house every day.

'That's a good idea, yes. He will be pleased to see you again. Yes, do it, but right now I need to lie down for a while. All these emotions are wearing me out. I hope you understand.'

'Of course, Taty, take as long as you need. I'm going to watch the French news.'

The next day, I picked up the rental car, but did not drive anywhere for four days, wanting to spend as much time as I could with Taty.

On the fifth day, another piece of the Rennes-le-Château puzzle was about to drop into my lap.

5

Salsigne and the revelation, 10 June 2006

I was just about to knock on Michel's door when it opened – he had seen me coming. The smell of something delicious wafted from the house.

Suddenly I felt hungry. 'Gosh, something smells nice. What is it?'

'Annie's making cassoulet for tonight. We're having friends over to play French Tarot. We play every week, not for money, just for fun.'

'I haven't played French Tarot since my national service days – we used to play every day. I wouldn't mind joining you before I return to Sydney,' I said. 'I'm thinking of going for a drive to Albi. What do you think?'

'Why don't you go and see the old gold mines of Salsigne instead?'

'You're joking. What gold mines?' I could not believe that I had never heard of the gold mines of Salsigne. To say that I was flabbergasted would be an understatement. Immediately, I imagined the landscape around Bathurst, which is dotted with small diggings dating from the time of the gold rush in the 1850s.

'My God, yes, that's better than going to Albi,' I said. 'How do I get there?'

'Take the road to Carcassonne, go past the turnoff to Les Martys, then about fifteen kilometres out from Carcassonne there's a turn-off to the left which takes you to the village of Salsigne and on to the mines.'

Following Michel's directions was easy. When I reached the turn-off to Les Martys, I stopped, got out of the car and lit a cigarette. It was a perfect day – warm and sunny. I kept thinking about the old gold diggings at Hill End in New South Wales, a location I knew like the back of my hand. The cigarette finished, I got back in the car and drove off, wondering where I would find the diggings, thinking they must be very small since I had never heard about them – but then, I had left France in 1967.

I saw the sign to Salsigne and continued on the D41. A short time later, I entered the little village of Villanière. All I could see was a café, a few shops and a tourist information centre. I entered the café, and sat at a table near the window waiting for the waitress to appear – I was the only customer. The waitress looked rough, but then the place being so 'busy', she probably did not feel like dressing for the occasion.

'*Bonjour, monsieur*, what would you like?'

'A *café au lait* but please, not too hot. Can you smoke inside?'

'Hey, why not? Since when can't we smoke inside?'

It did not take long for her to reappear with the coffee.

'Could you tell me how to get to the gold mines of Salsigne?'

'The gold mines?' she said with a look that could scald.

'Yes, the gold mines.'

'Bloody Australians. They should all go back to where they came from. They should take their pollution with them and leave us in peace. We can no longer go fishing in the river – the fish are dying, it's a mess everywhere and you want to know where the mine is.'

What was she talking about, out of the blue, swearing like a trooper, calling Australians bastards? What did Australians have to do with the mines? She certainly did not like Australians; lucky she did not know where I was from – she probably would not have served me. Unbelievable, it was like an angry tornado of words. Obviously, there was a strong feeling in the town about the mine.

'What's your interest? Are you working for those guys?' she said.

'Oh no, I'm just here from Paris to see my aunt who lives in Mazamet. I heard about the mines and thought I would go for a drive.'

She started to calm down, so I asked her how many mines there were.

'Only one. How many do you want? Don't you think that one big hole in the ground is enough? How many do you need?' she said, throwing her hands into the air. 'It's been closed since 2004 – my God, they finally closed it, but now we have to make them pay, and we will. Good luck if you want to see it – walk four hundred metres that way.' She waved her hand in the direction of the mine. 'You can't miss it.'

I finished my coffee in record time, walked out of the café and took a deep breath. I looked in the direction the waitress had indicated but couldn't see any sign of the mine, so I walked round the corner to avoid being observed, looked around a bit then ducked into the tourist office. On display were a few books, some local road maps, lots of photos and DVDs about the history of the Cathars, but nothing about the mine. I headed back to the main street and walked in the direction she had indicated – it did not take long to reach the mine. I came upon a flat piece of ground facing a wire fence about two metres high, a locked gate with a heavy padlock and a large sign: '*Defense d'entrer sous peine d'amende*. Entry to the mine prohibited, trespassers will be prosecuted'. A fence is not a deterrent to anyone willing to trespass. However, I could not find a way to get in, no matter how strong my curiosity was – not my lucky day. From where I was standing, I could only see the top of the mine, but I was stunned – clearly this was a huge opencast mine, nothing like the diggings around Bathurst.

The only thing to do now was to return to Taty's house, where I had no doubt that a good French dinner would be waiting for me. I would ask Michel in the morning to use his computer so I could find out more about the background of gold mining in the area.

I spent a sleepless night in Mazamet.

Morning could not have come sooner. I was up early and made myself a typical French breakfast of *tartines beurrees*, a rich sweet bread, which I buttered and dunked into a big cup of strong black coffee – not too hot. Time seemed to be moving slowly – Michel would not be up for a few hours yet. I had always been an early riser – years of working on the breakfast shift. I gave him until ten o'clock then knocked on his door.

'Gerard, good morning.'

'*Bonjour*, Michel. May I use your computer?'

'Yes, of course. How was your trip to Salsigne?'

'Good, really good. I'll tell you all about it in a minute, after I log into something.'

'OK, take your time. I'm going to Carcassonne. I'll be back in the afternoon.'

I jumped onto the computer, Googled 'gold mine Salsigne', and instantly got back hundreds of entries. The first on the list was an article written in 1996 by Lucien Trueb, a graduate of the Physical Chemistry Department of the Swiss Federal Institute of Technology in Zurich, Switzerland. I was stunned by what I read. The Salsigne gold mine is in the Montagne Noire, the Black Mountain Range, which is located at the south-western end of the Massif Central* and bordered by three departments: Tarn, Herault and Aude. It is about twenty kilometres north of Carcassonne and sits between the villages of Salsigne and Villanière. Gold was discovered near Salsigne in 1892. It was the most productive opencast mine in Western Europe, and the last in France. As at 1996, the cumulative production was approximately a hundred and twenty tonnes. With a current value of around US$1,200 per ounce, this would be worth US$4.6 billion today – incredible.†

Photos showed the size of the mine and just as I had imagined, it was huge. The ore body consisted of two adjacent auriferous formations, with a totally different geological and geochemical history. Both opencast and underground mining technologies were used. The elliptical

* The Massif Central is a highland region in the middle of Southern France, consisting of mountains and plateaus. It covers about 15% of mainland France.

† Gold and precious metals are valued in Troy ounces (t oz), a quaint unit of imperial measure that dates back to the Middle Ages (AD 476–1453). One Troy ounce of gold weighs about 31.1g. (One regular ounce is 28.35g.) There are 32.15 t oz in 1 kg (1,000g). (1,000g ÷ 31.1g = 32.15 t oz). One hundred and twenty tonnes (120,000kg) of gold is equal to 3,858,000 t oz (120,000kg x 32.15 t oz = 3,858,000 t oz). The approximate selling price today for 1 t oz is US$1,200. Therefore 120 tonnes of gold would be valued at US$4,629,600,000 or US$4.629 billion (3,858,000 t oz x US$1,200 = US4.629 billion). (https://goldprice.org/)

opencast mine, *la carrière* as the French call it, measured eight hundred by four hundred and fifty metres and was opened in 1983. In 1996, it was being extended to both the north and south. Good ore was also available to the west, where an old underground mine had been intercepted and cleaned out. Further extension in that direction was hindered by a dump of waste rock of about thirty million tonnes. At the beginning of the operation, the ore was hand-picked, which means it must have been close to the surface.

The Mine d'Or de Salsigne had different operators until 1992, when two Australian companies bought it: Eltin Minerals Pty Ltd, one of the major mining contractors down under and Orion Resources, a Western Australian gold mining company.

The mine had a fascinating history going back two thousand years. The Romans mined iron ore around Salsigne and the area of the Aude Department for about three hundred years, until the third century AD. The iron ore was contained within sulphide-rich quartz veins and seams containing finely disseminated arsenopyrite and pyrite veins. These veins were exposed at or near the surface forming *chapeaus de fer*, 'iron hats', called gossans. Naturally, they are red in colour because of the oxidised iron minerals. The presence of an iron hat is usually a key indicator of gold. The Romans smelted the iron ore using charcoal and wind power. The ruins of three granite blast furnaces ten to fifteen metres high were found on the tops of nearby hills. Long stone walls on two sides funnelled prevailing winds blowing either from the Pyrenees to the south, or from the Atlantic to the north-west into the furnace mouths. Over time, the ore smelting produced eleven million tonnes of slag. According to Trueb, with the technology at their disposal, the Romans did not discover that the gossans also contained gold. It is highly unlikely that this gold will ever be recovered since the village of Les Martys has been built on top of the slag heaps. With today's technologies, this huge amount of slag could produce an estimated twenty-five tonnes or 800,000 ounces of gold. I imagine the Romans would have been very happy to find the gold, but they didn't. I wondered how many people in Les Martys knew they were actually *marchant sur l'or* – 'walking on gold'.

Before the discovery of gold, Salsigne was once the world's largest producer of arsenic, which occurs naturally in the soil and in the ore. Incredibly, farmers dusted the fine-ground ore liberally on the vineyards to fight fungal diseases, causing the entire region to become a geochemical arsenic anomaly. Clicking on several more recent references, I discovered that the mine was closed in 2004 for cleaning. With arsenic and other heavy metals polluting the watercourse and soil for over a century, it was one of the most polluted sites in France. No wonder the fish were dying and the waitress was so angry.

At the end of the article, Trued noted that the fortified castles around Salsigne 'testify to the strategic importance of the site'. Throughout this region, their crumbling remains appear like jagged teeth on the top of the limestone ridges. The presence of gold would certainly account for the area being considered strategic.

Over the centuries, the rich and powerful, including the Church, have fought over two key resources – land and the precious minerals it contains. The south of France has seen its fair share of conflict and competing interests. Could the existence of a source of native gold, thought to have been exhausted years before, be the explanation, or part of the explanation, underpinning the legend of a 'great secret' in this region? Rennes-le-Château is about forty-seven kilometres west of Salsigne, as the crow fliers. In geological terms, that is extremely close. My mind was working overtime.

The next day, I took the same route to Rennes-le-Château that I had with Lesley and Nathalie in 2003. My first stop was for lunch at Carcassonne, then about forty-five minutes to Limoux through the Roufiac d'Aude, and about the same again to Rennes-le-Château via Alet les Bains and Couiza.

Travelling through France is a delight for the senses. The small villages each with their own unique character, the chateaux and restaurants with their specialities. Markets alive with eager customers tasting cheeses, sampling wines and small-goods. Trestle tables groaning under the weight of colourful arrays of fresh seasonal produce. Cakes and pastries tempting the tastebuds. A good Camembert, a baguette and a glass of red is a real feast for lunch sitting in a park.

They say that when you first approach the old city of Carcassonne it is like approaching a fairy-tale castle. With its conical towers rising above the city wall and a drawbridge over the moat, it really does look like something out of a Disney movie.

I took a table inside La Taverne du Château on a corner of the first square that you come to in the heart of the old city – it was packed, which is always a good sign. A vine covered in fiery red flowers clambered up the front wall; red and white checked tablecloths continued the folkloric theme. I ordered a salad niçoise and a glass of La Blanquette de Limoux, a perfect accompaniment to salad. They say that Benedictine monks created the wine in 1351 in the abbéy of Saint Hilaire long before champagne was produced. In fact, this is the oldest sparkling wine producing region in the world. Apparently, the monks were making a still wine from le Mauzac grapes and found some bottles going into secondary fermentation and voila. *Blanquette* means 'small white' in the local Occitan language.

The last thing I expected to come across in France were indicators of gold. The red earth, quartz and ironstone I found on the road from Couiza to Rennes-le-Château in 2003 are all indicators, interesting clues on their own, but now that I knew there was a known source of gold in recent history, and that it was in close proximity to Rennes-le-Château, the evidence was mounting.

6

Return to Rennes-le-Château, 2006

Around two o'clock, I stepped out of the café and headed to the car park. The sky had cleared to bright blue with hardly any clouds. I took a photo of the drawbridge. It was difficult to imagine what life was like for the inhabitants of Carcassonne in those terrible years in the twelfth and thirteenth centuries during the Albigensian Crusade, when the French king joined forces with the pope to destroy the Cathars and their supporters. One by one, towns, villages and castles fell to the crusaders commanded by Simon de Montfort, a baron from the Ile de France. Carcassonne fell in 1209 and became his headquarters.

To encourage knights to join the crusade, the pope had announced that God would grant them total absolution from all sins – both present and those to come. In 1095, the pope had made the same 'offer' to encourage the French nobility and gentry to join the first crusade to reconquer Jerusalem. Many believe that the real motive behind the Albigensian Crusade was to break the power base of the southern barons, and acquire land and the riches it contained. Today, man's brutality is still being justified in the name of God.

Now there were children playing on a merry-go-round near the car park and tourists admiring the magnificent stone walls and turrets that had been restored with such care.

About forty minutes later, I was passing the sixteenth-century Château des Ducs de Joyeuse on the way to Couiza. Like many of the surviving medieval castles and chateaux, it was now a boutique hotel and restaurant. Not far from the chateaux, there is a junction between two rivers: the Aude and the Sals, the 'salt' river, which flows through the heart of Couiza. I crossed the bridge over the river. Take a right here and you will end up in Montazels, the village where Bérenger Saunière was born on 11 April 1852, the eldest of seven children. Heading southwest, I took the left turn up the winding road to Rennes-le-Château. This time, I did not stop at the red earth; I was too eager to get to the village and have a closer look around. Entering the village, past the sign forbidding fossicking, I edged through the narrow streets to the parking lot with the magnificent view looking south across the valley.

Twenty-eight years was a long time to have been away from the land where I was born and raised. As a young man, I was too busy riding motorbikes around the streets of Paris. I had no idea about the beauty of the countryside, the history and the people. I know more about the history and the geology of Australia. It felt like I was rediscovering my own country. I got out of the car and scanned the plateau below. My eyes rested for a moment on Mount Cardou, the White Mountain, which according to Andrews and Schellenberger was the location of a mysterious tomb situated about halfway up the mountain.

I knew that in the late 1800s, Bérenger Saunière had allegedly discovered something hidden in the village church that resulted in him becoming very rich, far beyond his station as the priest of a ramshackle village in the middle of nowhere – a village so small that it wasn't even on some maps. With money that seemed to be at his disposal, he completely renovated the village church, purchased land in the name of his housekeeper Marie Dénarnaud, built several impressive structures on his estate, including the Villa Bethanie, bought Paris fashions for Marie, gave money to villagers and lived the high life – fine wines and spirits, good food and entertaining.

I walked across the car park, glancing up at the Tour Magdala, which jutted out from the edge of the hill. With its crenellated top, it reminded me of the rook in a chess set. This is where Saunière housed his extensive library of books, magazines and newspapers, along with a huge collection of stamps. He also gave lectures on the history of the village, and sold postcards which he designed, featuring photographs of the village and historical notes. According to one theory, he wanted to cash in on the tourist trade enjoyed by towns like Lourdes and nearby Rennes les Bains, famous for its hot springs and mineral-rich waters, by promoting Rennes-le-Château's ancient past as a Visigoth city and the church dedicated to Mary Magdalene. Saunière was certainly enterprising.

I cut across to the gardens where the Belvedere, a stone terrace, connected the Tour Magdala to the Orangerie, a summerhouse where Saunière kept exotic plants. He even kept monkeys in a cage at one time. I passed the Villa Béthanie, originally called Villa de Marie. Its classic Renaissance-style architecture stood in stark contrast to the humble village houses.

There was no doubt that the building works were substantial. It was one thing to see photos of the estate, but to see it in real life, even though time had tarnished the edges, was extraordinary. The stone masonry in the construction of both the Belvedere and the Tour Magdala was impressive – in fact, the whole structure was impressive. It reminded me of the flamboyancy and extravagant spending of the nouveau riche.

I headed towards the church across the public square and noticed the Calvary in the centre of the garden next to the church entrance, strategically facing a Visigothic pillar and statue of Our Lady of Lourdes. Unfortunately, the church was locked, a deterrent to the many attacks by vandals over the years. I could never understand this sort of wanton vandalism. Regardless of the treasure stories, the church was of great historical significance. In 1059, it was consecrated to Mary Magdalene and some believe its foundation could date as early as the ninth century. Others believe that it was built on an ancient site of worship and a crypt beneath the church may contain the relics of martyrs or saints who died for the Christian faith. This would make it a reliquary church and explain why the lords of Rennes specifically wanted to be buried there. If this was the case, the crypt would be one of the oldest in France, dating anywhere from the fifth to the eighth centuries, with a seigniorial tomb beside it built sometime after that.[2] There have been various digs – both official and unofficial – in and around the church. The church is a listed building belonging to the state and the French authorities have not allowed any significant archaeological excavations.

When Saunière arrived in Rennes-le-Château in 1885, the village church was a wreck. It was in such a state of disrepair that in 1853 a local architect had advised that it would be better to rebuild it from scratch rather than to restore it. The village was poor and Saunière's stipend was less than a hundred francs per month, nowhere near enough to even consider renovations, which in 1879 had been costed at close to three thousand francs.

From the outset, Saunière had made himself unpopular with the republican authorities. The political debate at the time was whether the country should continue as a republic, or once again return to a monarchy. It was nearly a hundred years since the French Revolution (1789–1792), but the wounds were still raw. Like most priests at that time, Saunière was a monarchist and in October 1885, on the eve of the general elections, he preached a blatantly political sermon, urging his mainly female congregation to vote against the republic. As punishment, Saunière was labelled a 'militant reactionary', his stipend was suspended, and he was sent to teach at the junior seminary at Narbonne. During his time in Narbonne, Saunière visited his brother Alfred, also a priest and a monarchist. Alfred was editor-in-chief of *La Croix du Sud*, a Catholic magazine that published articles critical of the republic. He was also employed nearby as a tutor to the Marquis de Chefdebien's children. The marquis had been one of the prime movers behind the plan to have the monarchy reinstated. Henri de Bourbon, the Comte de Chambord, was the heir to the French throne, but he died in 1884.

In 1887, Saunière returned to Rennes-le-Château with a thousand francs, courtesy of the Comtesse de Chambord.[3] It was common for the nobility to donate to the Church. In 1857, the comtesse had donated four thousand francs to Louis de Coma, the priest of Boulou, a small village to the south of Rennes-le-Château. De Coma also built a magnificent estate, which he named Gethsemane. Saunière would later inflate this amount to three thousand francs in a 1910 report.[4] This would seem to indicate that he needed to account for an amount of two thousand francs obtained from an undeclared source.

Saunière began repairing the church, starting with the replacement of the altar and the old stone floor. The repairs continued over the next several years. There were major structural works, which even included the construction of a dividing wall between the original walls and the church interior. The internal fit-out was extensive. There are statues of saints and decorative paintings on the walls, a bas-relief above the Confessional depicting the Sermon on the Mount, fourteen stations of the cross around the walls, an ornate baptismal font and that infamous statue that looked like the devil holding up the holy water stoup.

The records show that Saunière funded the initial renovations with the money from various grants, donations, loans and money received for delivering masses. Then around 1891 something happened that enabled him to take the church renovations to a new level and to begin building the estate and live a lifestyle way beyond the means of a small village priest. According to the modern versions of the story, during the renovations Saunière found documents or parchments that contained important information that led him to a 'treasure'. Some researchers believe that one of Saunière's predecessors, Abbé Antoine Bigou, priest of Rennes-le-Château from 1774 to 1792, created clues as to the location of these important documents and hid these clues in and around the church. Eventually, Saunière's spending came to the attention of the Church. Following an investigation, the Bishop of Carcassonne accused him of funding his excessive expenditure from money he made from trafficking in masses. Priests could legitimately receive money for saying up to three masses a day, with the surplus passing to the bishopric; any more than this was viewed as suspect. As punishment, Saunière carried out a ten-day period of penance in the Monastère de Prouille. However, it appears that on his return he continued with his spending.

In 1911, the Bishop of Carcassonne set up a commission of enquiry under the direction of the vicar general, Jean Saglio, who undertook a detailed examination of Saunière's accounts. The charges included trafficking in masses and lavish spending. Saunière's account of his income included gifts from unnamed benefactors; money from collection boxes; his salary and the sale of postcards, old stamps and wine. However, the limited information he provided could not account for his expenditure.

Many researchers believe that Saunière financed his lavish lifestyle and building projects by committing simony, receiving money for hundreds more masses that he could ever say in a year, let alone in a day. Another theory suggests that Saunière was involved with *La Sanche*, the Cult of the Dead, a network of penitent priests who secretly conducted costly rituals and private mortuary masses designed to ensure that a person's soul went to heaven regardless of the life they led. The priests practised trepanation, which involved opening the deceased's skull with a special instrument in order to facilitate the soul's escape. The Church outlawed the practice but priests were still practising it in nearby Limoux up until the seventeenth century. *La Sanche* still exists in some form today as evidenced by an annual procession in Perpignan each Easter, when hooded penitents proceed in a procession through the city.

If the bishop had accessed more of Saunière's accounts, he might have been able to piece everything together, something it seems Saunière wanted to avoid at all cost. However, the examination of Saunière's accounts by the commission of enquiry produced nothing. Saunière resigned in 1909 and died in 1917. I asked myself how a poor parish priest in a tiny forgotten village could acquire enough cash to undertake an extensive building program, live an extravagant lifestyle, entertain celebrated political and cultural figures, as well as incur travel and other personal expenses, which apparently he never recorded.

The interesting thing about Saunière's money is that it was available intermittently. There were periods when he spent like a very rich man, spending up to fifty thousand francs a month. This was sometimes followed by a period of drought, sometimes lasting for several months, when the cash seemed to dry up. Sometimes he recorded debts, and at times he even borrowed money to pay his bills. Either his income stream was not steady, or his access to money was not assured. This is understandable during World War I, when movement within the country was dangerous and access to accounts held in other countries was almost impossible. Then again, was the periodic lack of money a deliberate ruse? Saunière kept the source of his income a secret to the end. Who or what was he protecting and why?

The old saying 'gold is where you find it' might give the impression that it is easy to find; it is not. However, there are some famous stories of people coming across lumps of gold just lying on the ground, or not far beneath the surface. In the early days of settlement in Australia, an amazing amount of gold was found on the surface; people had no idea they were literally 'walking on gold'. On 19 July 1851, the year before Bérenger Saunière's birth, the *Bathurst Free Press* reported that a man travelling on horseback found forty-five kilos of gold in three lumps just lying on the ground. Hard to believe, but it's true. The gold must have come from a reef somewhere. After so many millions of years, how lucky can one be?

Gold commonly occurs as a native metal, but sometimes it forms compounds with tellurium, sulfur or selenium. The Golden Mile is a massive gold deposit in Kalgoorlie, Western Australia. Gold-bearing tellurides were first discovered in the Golden Mile in 1896. Before 1896, rocks containing tellurides were not recognised as rich gold ores. People took them to be pyrite, commonly known as 'fool's gold', and the rocks were used on cart tracks, walkways and as building stone. Incredibly, for a short time, the streets of Kalgoorlie-Boulder had indeed been paved with gold.

The authorities often hushed up the early finds in Australia. They were afraid that gold fever would take hold and 'unhinge people's minds', and everyone, including servants, soldiers, even shopkeepers would stop work and head for the goldfields. In fact, that is exactly what happened. Some of the early explorers were convinced that there was no gold at all. They described the countryside as flat, hot, harsh, rocky and inhospitable. In other words, nothing of great interest or value. They made assumptions and overlooked the signs.

Perhaps the solution to the mystery of Bérenger Saunière's 'treasure' was so simple, so obvious, that it had been overlooked. Could Saunière or someone close to him have discovered native gold somewhere in the surrounds of Rennes-le-Château? Possibly – but what kind of gold was it, and how did he find it? Taking into account the price of gold at that time, there is no way that simple panning for flakes could account for that amount of money. Considering what was known about prospecting and mining in those days, the timing of the find, and what I had read about the priest's behaviour, it was much more likely that if Saunière found native gold, it had to be from a vein. Perhaps from a source that had remained hidden over the centuries, possibly from an ancient abandoned mine, or from an undiscovered source – it was a tantalising proposition.

After 1892, Bérenger had access to a lot of money. There is great speculation about the true amount of Saunière's expenditure. Estimates of his wealth vary anywhere from US$5 to 10 million in today's money and some people believe that is only part of it. Just how much gold would you need to convert it to US$10 million? People may visualise Saunière carrying tons of rocks in order to make that amount and wonder how he could have transported it without being seen. You would be surprised at how little gold is needed to make that kind of money – only thirteen and a half one-litre bottles. With a weight of about two hundred kilos, the load would easily fit in the back of my Suzuki and I would have no problem driving it to my secret location for further use, if you know what I *mean…voilà*.*

* All measures of weight are based on the density of fresh water, which is 'one'. The density of gold is 19.3, almost 20 times heavier than water. Therefore, if you could fill a one-litre bottle with gold, it would weigh almost 20kg. Our one-litre bottle of gold weighing 19.3kg holds 620.5 t oz of gold (32.15 t oz x 19.3kg = 620.5 t oz). In today's money, one Troy ounce (t oz) of gold is worth approximately US$1,200. To make US$10 million from the sale of the gold, you would need 8,333 t oz (10 million ÷ 1,200 = 8,333 t oz). Our one-litre bottle of gold weighs 620.5oz, therefore you need 8,333 ÷ 620.5 = 13.429. In other words, 13.5 one-litre bottles of gold are needed to get US$10 million.

If the gold came from a reef or a vein, it would have taken no time to fulfill the equation. Compared to what the Aussie diggers collected during the gold rush, this amount is laughable; and compared to the production of the gold mine of Salsigne, it's a tiny drop in a very large ocean. To put it simply, it would have been a walk in the park. Could it account for Saunière's wealth? Absolutely.

I had no doubt that there was native gold around Rennes-le-Château and I was now working on the assumption that Bérenger Saunière found a gold vein – in other words: there's gold in them hills. The only way to prove it was to find some, but I was leaving France for Australia the next day and would be back at work the following week. In the meantime, I needed to do some research: dates, names, when, how and why. I needed to learn more about the geology of the Languedoc and the history of gold mining in France. Most of all I needed to find native gold around Rennes-le-Château.

I hate departures, but what can we do. Jean Claude, Monique and I headed for Charles de Gaulle airport, none of us saying a word. I felt sad about leaving France and I knew that my 'chauffeur' and his half of the 'darling couple' were sad to see me go. But in the back of my mind thoughts of the beautiful sunshine of the Sydney summer I was returning to cheered me up. I still call Australia home.

Parking was the usual headache. I checked in with Qantas and picked up my boarding pass. We shared a last drink, hugs and kisses, 'goodbye guys, be good, don't cry, tomorrow is another day and hope to see you soon'. Alone in the departure lounge, mentally preparing myself for the two-hour wait and the long, tiring flight, my head began to fill with questions. When would I be back? Definitely in 2010 to celebrate Taty's hundredth birthday. I imagined her birthday cake ablaze with all those candles – hard to believe. That was four years away and anything could happen in the meantime, but I trusted that she would stay healthy and happy, and that nothing would go wrong.

Not long into the flight, nearly everybody on the plane was sleeping, with the exception of a few, as I could see lights shining on some of the head panels. With my nose against the small window, I tried to see the clouds, but the moon had gone for the night and it was pitch black. A little conundrum was going around in my head, thirty thousand feet up on the way to Australia. There is a well-known puzzle about a prisoner who is locked in a cell with two doors and a prison guard at each door. One of the doors will lead him to freedom – but which door? To select the right door, he must ask each guard a question – the same question. The guards can only answer yes or no. He knows that one guard always tell the truth and the other always lies; the question is how will the prisoner find the door to freedom? What question will he ask?*

When I left Jenolan back in 1990, I had put gold prospecting on the backburner; all of my efforts went into learning as much as I could about diamonds. Now it seemed I had two doors before me. One led to an undiscovered diamond pipe somewhere in New South Wales, the other was leading me back to France and to gold.

---

* The answer is available at http://puzzling.stackexchange.com/questions/2188/two-doorswith-two-guards-one-lies-one-tells-the-truth. Accessed 15 January 2020.

7

How I got into diamonds: Sydney, New South Wales, 1995

There is one way to captivate a prospector's attention – tell him or her that there has been a big find in the past, that it hasn't been exhausted and that the source can't be located.

It was 1995, five years since I had left Caves House. I walked into the Department of Mineral Resources in Sydney to look for maps and information about fossicking for gold. On the way to the main office, I noticed an ugly wooden bookshelf with about ten books for sale; one title caught my attention: *Diamonds in New South Wales* by Tony Mac-Nevin, a geologist who worked for the department. I flicked to the imprint page: published in 1977 – turns out it was the last copy in print, so I bought it for $20.

I was fascinated by what I read. There had been many diamond finds in New South Wales since the turn of the nineteenth century, around two million carats, but nobody had found the source since. That did not surprise me; diamonds are rare and finding them is not easy. I was hooked, but knew nothing about diamonds – I needed to find out more. It was my lucky day and the start of a whole new adventure in minerals exploration, my hunt for diamonds. I had to learn as much as I could – and fast. I bought Eric Bruton's book *Diamond*. It was even more fascinating than Tony's book. Bruton described how Kalahari Desert ants tunnel underground and bring all sorts of mineral grains to the surface, even Ballas diamonds, which are like little marbles, unusual and quite rare.

Later, I discovered that Chuck Fipke proved that this theory was wrong;

but hey, if ants were connected with diamonds, I was going to find out for myself.

I knew where I could find anthills – I had seen lots of them on my twice-weekly trips on the road to Jenolan. Over two weekends, I sampled them all. I took one small bag of gavel from each anthill mound. Let me tell you, those ants bite like hell.

Back home, examining the samples under the binocular microscope, I discovered some microspheres which looked like Ballas diamonds. However, I had never seen a real-life diamond in the raw before, only photos. I had to be sure, so I took the microspheres into Gem Studies, a laboratory on the corner of Park and Pitt Streets in Sydney. They were willing to show me some rough diamonds, but they could not tell me what my spheres were with any certainty unless I paid for analysis. This would have set me back at least AU$2,000. Bad luck, I had to find another way; I needed someone who could tell me what I was looking at.

I decided to send some of the spheres to my cousin Thierry in France, asking if he could find someone knowledgeable enough to give me some answers, hoping free of charge. I packaged them in a small envelope secured with sticky tape and sent them by airmail. Several weeks later, Thierry rang me; he had made contact with a geologist in the Bureau de Recherches Geologiques et Minieres (BRGM), Bureau of Geological and Mineral Research, who agreed to look at my samples. Pierre Jezequel was the chief geologist in charge of the department Les Mineraux en Grains in Orleans. I faxed Pierre, asking him what it would cost. His reply was simple – expensive, between one and two thousand dollars, depending on the number of grains. He ended his letter with a question: why do you need to know? The next day I rang him, telling him that I could not afford the cost, but he asked me again why I needed to know. It was not why I wanted to know, but why I needed to know. Everybody wants something, but not everybody needs something – I had to show a need for it. I thought it would be obvious why I needed to know.

'Well,' I said. 'I'm looking for diamonds.'

He laughed and asked me if I knew anything about diamonds. At that point, I felt like the village idiot and, when I look back, I probably was. I knew enough about gold, but nothing about diamonds, and I told him. He told me what I should learn, what I should know and what books I needed to read. That was our first meeting, seventeen thousand kilometres away by phone. From then on, Pierre became my mineralogy and geology teacher, by fax, then by email; we developed a solid and trusting relationship. In 2003, Lesley, Nathalie and I enjoyed a memorable lunch with Pierre in Orleans. He is retired now but we still keep in touch regularly. What I did not know then was that Pierre had a professional interest in the area around Rennes-le-Château.

Dominic and Nathalie were attending Macquarie University and, until they got their driver licences, I was their taxi driver. After I dropped the kids off, I spent hours in the university library, reading and photocopying anything of interest. Four days a week, I read and learned, trying to grasp everything at once. The new earth sciences of geophysics and geochemistry have created a completely new geological frontier that the prospectors of old could never have dreamt of.

Chuck Fipke once said that the best graduate school was not found in academia but in the field, where mining companies worked daily on their problems and did their own research. Their secrets were only made public to be taught at universities when they had no more competitive value. I planned to choose a location from Tony MacNevin's book, take a drive, and most of all bring back some samples. In the meantime, I kept going back and forth to the Bathurst-Jenolan area on my days off.

8

Brisbane Valley Creek, New South Wales, 1997

Oberon is one of the locations mentioned in Tony MacNevin's book about diamonds. It is not far from Brisbane Valley Creek, the small stream where I got my first taste of panning for gold with Peter Donahue back in 1987. I knew the grounds very well – it is one of my favourite sites for gold panning. The creek runs through the pine forest, a great spot for hiding the car. Jumping the fence was easy and I always found specks of gold. There are stories that gold prospectors had found diamonds there, but this is hard to prove. A technique called salting, planting gold flakes or diamonds at a location, was a common practice used by unscrupulous prospectors to fool unsuspecting investors into buying a lease. One technique involved the seller concealing some gold flakes on the edge of his hat. At an opportune moment, he would tip his hat down making sure the flakes fell into the pan. Usually, the one intending to buy the lease never noticed the trick. All his eyes could focus on were the gleaming gold flakes in the pan.

I figured that this was as good a place to start as any. I decided to test my knowledge as well as my panning skills, and try my luck – panning for gold and diamond indicators. That day, I was getting a lot of zircons and black grains. I easily recognised the zircons but was not sure about the black grains; to me they looked like ilmenites, one of the main indicators of kimberlite, a diamond-bearing rock. Thanks to my reading, I was now more knowledgeable but still guessing. Well, the samples stayed in the drawer for some time.

I remembered that in one of my conversations with Pierre he had discussed ilmenites and mentioned that the bureau had published a book in 1974. Written by Dr A. Parfenoff, one of their geologists, it was a bible of minerals and mineralogy related to diamond exploration. I wrote to Pierre asking him if I could buy the book. Not long after, I was delighted when it arrived in the post. Of course, it was in French – I understood about a tenth of it, but I found what I needed to know.

I had collected well over a thousand black grains and was reasonably sure that they were ilmenites, and that I could be on the right track to finding diamonds. I decided to send some of them with an attached letter to Larry Barron, head geologist in the Diamond Department of Mineral Resources in Sydney, located in St Leonards at that time. The parcel sat on his desk for ten days – he was on holidays. Larry rang me on his first day back. We were having a good solid conversation – 'yes but this, yes but that, don't you think that' and then I mentioned Parfenoff's book.

'What,' he said as if a bomb had landed. 'Do you have Parfenoff's book?'

'Yes, I'm looking at it.'

'Bloody hell, where did you get it?'

'Well, from BRGM. I know someone there. Why?'

'There were only a few copies printed. I worked for two years for BRGM in Orleans on a project. When I left, I asked to buy the book but unfortunately it was no longer available. Can you believe it?'

'Well, if you want the book, you can have it, but I need a copy.'

That day was the beginning of a wonderful relationship. From then on, I went to Larry's office every Monday on my day off. He was generous with his time, teaching me about geology, mineralogy and petrology. I think he figured that I had a natural talent for the subjects. I learnt how to use a polarising microscope to examine rocks and minerals in thin sections and I had the opportunity to meet with other geologists in the department. It was fantastic, a real privilege, so much knowledge and equipment – I learned a lot. I told Larry about my first conversation with Pierre Jezequel and we laughed about my innocence and lack of knowledge at that time. I started to take photographs of diamonds both for my personal pleasure and also managed to take some for the department.

Finally, I bit the bullet and got cracking, picking a location to test out my newly acquired knowledge. I chose Kandie Peak, the first site listed in Tony MacNevin's book. It was a two-day drive north-west of Sydney – it would be a challenge and I could not wait. Several mining companies had explored the site previously – Stockdale back in 1977 and CRA Exploration in the 1980s – but very little had been done. Larry and I discussed what I could expect and what type of rocks I should find and bring back. He told me that Macquarie University was interested in the site, but he did not think they had done any work.

I asked my best friend Frederic Brard if he wanted to come with me to collect samples from my 'secret location'. Frederic owned the Menage a Trois hairdressing salon in Cremorne, a suburb on the north side of Sydney. He did not know much about prospecting, but he loved going on trips with me, especially when a four-wheel drive was involved – we were like brothers. We would hit the road in my Suzuki Sierra, a reliable four-wheel drive. We dumped the back seats to accommodate two twenty-litre water cans, a jerrycan of fuel plus one more next to the spare wheel at the back, another spare wheel inside the car, tools for emergency, sleeping bags, an esky for food, a crowbar, pick, shovel, and bags for the samples. In other words, we were loaded to the teeth and ready for action.

9

Kandie Peak, New South Wales, 1998

Frederic was lying on the ground. He looked like a balloon ready to explode. Hands, feet, lips, even his ears were like a mix of cauliflower and sausages. He kept falling asleep, even though he could not close his eyes. He looked like the Michelin man and I was getting worried. There was one thing we had forgotten – the Aerogard, a strong insect repellent.

It was a two-day drive to the location. Half the way was sealed road, and then we hit the rough unsealed road and the dust. Overnight, we slept somewhere on the ground for five hours. Up at six a.m. the next morning, it was already 28°C and rising. It did not take long before we were ambushed – billions of mozzies, unbelievable. If we had to stop, we could only last a minute outside the car. When we arrived at our destination, the temperature had risen to around 35°C and Fred was in bad shape. I considered turning back, but he insisted that I get the samples. Using a wire brush, a dustpan, and a sieve to screen out any grains above four millimetres, I ended up with two bags of sand nearly fifteen kilos each.

I had just finished filling the first bag when a guy appeared on a motorbike – the station manager. This could mean trouble, but luckily, we were off the property by about ten metres from the dirt road. Still, I was anticipating questions about what business we had on the land and why we were sampling. But when he saw the condition Fred was in, he immediately told us to wait there until he got back with some Aerogard. He returned ten minutes later. We asked Fred to stand up then gave him a mega spray. That afternoon we headed back to Sydney, me happy, Fred sleepy and both of us exhausted. The doctor we saw on arrival was worried about Ross River virus, but lucky for Fred it was just a severe allergic reaction to the mosquito bites. Still, it took him three weeks to get better.

We brought back the two bags of sand. Thirty kilograms does not sound like much, but I had to sort it by hand, wash it to get rid of light stuff and anything magnetic, leaving only interesting grains of sand. From a fifteen-kilo bag, I ended up with maybe less than half a kilo. For three hours, every night after work, I sorted through that half-kilo of sand, checking every single grain under the microscope; hand-picking the interesting ones and dreaming about the next find. Every time I picked up an indicator, my heart beat a little faster and I kept on working and dreaming. I never enjoyed something so much. It was like a treasure hunt into the microscopic world – the colours and the geometric shapes of all the different minerals was fascinating. One month later I had some good stuff, especially garnets and chrome diopside, a few black grains, mica (phlogopite), some zircons and perhaps some chromites – I wasn't sure. There were also some very interesting pieces of broken eclogites – diamonds are found in eclogites.

Back in Larry's lab, I showed him the results. He suggested I get in touch with Rondi Morgan Davies, who was doing her thesis at Macquarie University on the characteristics and origins of alluvial diamonds from eastern Australia. We had an instant rapport and from then on I went to Larry's office every Monday and to Rondi's office every Tuesday. I was having a ball. Rondi was more than impressed, telling me that she had never seen such results from an exploration program. She introduced me to the person in charge of the thin sections in the university laboratory and arranged for a thin section to be made from a piece of eclogite I provided. A thin section is a slice of rock, about 0.03 millimetres thick, attached to a glass slide with epoxy and covered by another glass slide. It can be used for analysis under a polarising microscope. It was ready within a week at no cost. The person giving it to me said, 'Let me know when you find your first diamond.' Now I knew for certain that I had found some diamond indicators. I mailed some to Pierre Jezequel in France. He could not believe it; from knowing absolutely nothing, I could now enter into a semi-professional discussion about diamond exploration. I was willing to send some samples for further investigation, but not in Australia. I was not being paranoid: the world of minerals exploration is fast paced and cut-throat – secrecy is paramount. It is not a matter of discourtesy or deceitfulness; one simply does not give away secrets, especially to a potential competitor.

By pure luck, I had picked up a copy of one of the bibles of diamond exploration in Larry's office: *Diamond exploration techniques emphasising indicator mineral geochemistry and Canadian examples*, a report written by Chuck Fipke, J.J. Gurney and R.O. Moore and published in 1995. Chuck was a true adventurer, known in the mining world as a modern-day Indiana Jones. He was familiar with Australia, having worked at Broken Hill and Lightning Ridge in the 1970s. He had developed a new technique for sampling and analysing earth samples. It went beyond simply analysing the sample for the presence of certain indicators, to analysing the exact elemental composition of all the indicators to know whether their combined chemical signatures indicated the presence of diamonds. This technique saved the mining industry millions. Chuck knew nothing about my samples, or me, so I decided to send the samples to his lab in Kelowna, Canada. I did not expect to hear anything back for weeks or months, if at all. It was a long shot. Two weeks later, at three a.m., my phone rang. Half groggy, I stumbled out of bed, hoping like hell that something hadn't happened to one of the kids.

'Is that Gerard Catherin?' said a woman with a Canadian accent. She introduced herself as Agnes Fung, working for Chuck Fipke.

They had received my samples and wanted to send one of their representatives to meet with me here in Australia. I was trembling from head to toe. I could not believe it – Chuck's people wanted to meet with me. I had to get up in two hours to go to work, so I told Agnes that I would write to her. Then I went back to bed and just lay there wide awake, brain ticking over, unable to sleep. I do not know how I got to work and how I coped during the day; work was now definitely in the bloody way.

I had no computer, only a fax machine, so I handwrote a letter and faxed it through to Agnes. She replied that they had found good indicators within the samples and they wanted to test the site. Well, my samples did not come from private land or property; I had taken them from the verge between the road and the fence of the private property at Kandie Peak.

I started to correspond regularly with Agnes, seeking to find out what they had discovered in my samples that sparked their interest. After about two months of back and forward faxes, I woke one morning to find pages of data analysis hanging from my fax machine. It had come through in the middle of the night and I had not heard it. Now I would be able to find out what was so interesting and why they were so eager to see me. I studied the data for two weeks, not finding the secret. It did not matter what I said, Agnes would not give me an answer – she drove me nuts.

One morning on my day off, after three cups of coffee and quarter of a packet of cigarettes, the answer hit me: the sodium content in some of the garnets – ah, got you. The sodium content in some garnets is indicative of pressure/temperature (P/T) ratio. High sodium indicates a stability field corresponding to the stability field of diamonds. I told Agnes that I had found the answer and she agreed. If they had told me earlier, we would have saved a lot of time.

The following week, Chuck and I signed a confidentiality agreement by fax. The week after that, Chuck arranged for Peter Gregory, a geologist from Perth, to meet with me in Sydney. Late the same afternoon, we were on the road to the site for two days of sampling. The first thing Peter did when we arrived was a due diligence loam sampling at the spot where I had collected the indicators. Peter asked me to be at least four hundred metres away from him while he took the samples, then immediately sealed the bag and guaranteed that the sample had not been salted. Peter and I continued sampling all afternoon until late, then erected our tents, started a fire, made ourselves a cuppa, cooked dinner and hit the sack. The next day, we were on the road back to Sydney, loaded with sixteen bags of twenty kilos and a hundred kilos of rocks. My poor little Suzuki will never forget the treatment.

Peter sent the samples by plane to Chuck's laboratory. It took a while for them to arrive – problems with customs in Hawaii. Within five weeks, the results from the electron microprobe analysis were ready. They were equally as promising as my first samples, but there was still no evidence of actual diamonds, only indicators. Peter returned to the site from Perth on his own as I had to work. The second analysis still did not find any diamonds. At the time, Chuck was heavily involved with the Ekati mine and, unfortunately, he decided that the site was too small for him to get involved; he suggested that I take over.

A minerals exploration licence is granted for two years. It would have cost me $22,000 – unfortunately, I did not have that kind of cash. To my great disappointment, things died off. I was not bitter, but eager to pursue the whole project. I was convinced that there was a diamond pipe out there and I was not about to let all those years of research and exploration go to waste. On the upside, I had the data from Chuck's analysis – in anyone's estimation, that was gold.

Then I met Lesley.

10

New deal going nowhere

It was nine years after my first wife Suzie and I had divorced. I used to see Lesley on my way to work at Doyles around the same time each morning. We were both buying the daily newspaper at the local newsagent. Lesley went jogging just around the corner in Centennial Park – I had a real crush on her. One day, getting a bit more courageous, I asked the owner of the shop about her and the next day I gave him a greeting card to give to her – her response was nearly instant. I let my apartment on Sydney's North Shore and moved into her little terrace house in Union Street, a beautiful part of Paddington. Life could not have been better.

Lesley and I saw Larry Barron every Monday and I still visited Rondi at Macquarie University every Tuesday. I had given Larry the results of Fipke's analysis of my samples. He introduced me to Tony MacNevin, whose book I had found so fascinating. I discovered that Tony lived in Manly, just five minutes from me when I lived in Balgowlah. The four of us went for an agreeable lunch and established a firm friendship.

Not long after that, Larry introduced me to another geologist, Peter Temby. Peter's credentials in the world of diamond mining were impressive. He was part of the team that discovered the diamond pipe about a hundred kilometres south of Kununurra in the East Kimberley region of north-west Australia. This discovery went on to become the Argyle diamond mine, world famous for pink diamonds. Larry suggested that I show Peter the data from Fipke's analysis of my samples; I had nothing to lose, so I thought why not.

Peter studied the data for a moment. His response stunned me. 'Mate, this data has been fabricated.'

'Mate, you've got to be joking,' I said. 'Fipke did the electron probe analysis in his own lab, I received the data by fax and, yes, I know it looks good, but this is no fabrication, trust me.' It took a while to convince him. I told him that the only thing holding me back was lack of finance. All I needed was someone who could back me financially – did he know anyone? I told Peter that he could keep the data.

Some eight months later, he introduced me to Barry, his solicitor, who became a very close friend.

Time went by slowly. I did a few trips back to Kandie Peak, but only for pleasure. Without the necessary finances to obtain a minerals exploration licence, that was all I could do. Finally, Barry introduced me to Joe, a developer, who agreed to back me financially. Not long after, we applied for three exploration licences covering nine hundred square kilometres at a cost of AU$33,000. We assigned Tony to the project, as a geologist must do all reports to the department. Then we hit the road – a two-day drive back to Kandie Peak in a Toyota ute. Tony and I spent ten days sampling and brought back sixty bags of twenty kilos each, which we took to Joe's place. Unfortunately, there was a disagreement, the deal fell through and the samples were dumped. The partnership dissolved and, once again, it was back to the drawing board. I was very disappointed and considered getting in touch with one of the big mining mobs, but would they take notice of a chef? I figured they would probably laugh at me. However, I was not defeated and remained positive that something could eventuate.

Minerals exploration is a cut-throat business involving big money. It is hard to think of an endeavour that would be more fraught with deceit, backstabbing and con artists than the hunt for precious metals – maybe espionage comes the closest. Two more tries at signing deals failed; the diamond project was on hold once again. However, I could not go through life trusting no one and I was not about to give up on finding finances for the project to go ahead. For the moment at least, plan A, diamonds, became plan B, and Rennes-le-Château became plan A. All I needed was time, money, maps, a good pair of boots and of course my panning dish.

Twenty-ten was fast approaching. I was still working at the Watsons Bay hotel. John Doyle had retired and things were no longer the same. The pub was now run by the 'three ugly sisters' famous for their chardonnay of the same name. Quite amazing selling a wine with a large label bearing such a name – not appealing, if you ask me, but that is the way they liked it and so be it. Taty would reach the ripe old age of a hundred on 22 December. Her birthday fell at the busiest time of the year for me, with all the end of year functions and parties at work, so I decided to return to France at the end of October.

My fare was booked for Saturday 27 October. I would go alone, spend three days at Jean Claude's place then head down to Mazamet on the TVG. Taty was now living in a nursing home in Mazamet, so I booked accommodation nearby at the Charlarn Grande Rue du Pont de l'Arn, a secluded little bed and breakfast only four minutes' drive to Mazamet. My trip started to take shape. I planned to explore the surrounds of Rennes-le-Château, walk the countryside and test some of the creeks. It did not matter how small they were, as long as I got some colour in the pan. Just thinking about the buzz I got when I saw the gold mine at Salsigne and realised the implications of its proximity to Rennes-le-Château made my head spin. I sent an email to *la mairie*, the town hall of Limoux, asking if it was possible to buy a topographic map of the area. I was disappointed when they did not reply, but not surprised. Maybe they thought I was another nutcase searching for treasure. In a way, they were not wrong, but that did not make things easier. However, my disappointment was brief. I downloaded simple, readable maps from the Internet, showing the roads and creeks around Rennes-le-Château and Rennes les Bains – very basic, but it was all I needed. I knew what I was looking for. It was not an esoteric secret, but something much more tangible. I could not wait.

11

France, November 2010

Sydney airport customs. The prospector's pan in my carry-on luggage put me in a category requiring further investigation; that and the ten thousand dollars pocket money I declared I was carrying. Luckily, my prospector's pick was in my luggage. The authorities took me into an interview room, where I filled in a form stating that the money was mine, which was no problem. I explained that the pan was for gold panning and that Australian pans were the best because they have a groove at the top, which is perfect for catching gold specimens.

'Is there gold in France, mate?' said the customs guy.

'Yes, mate, without any doubt. Wish me good luck.'

'Well, have a good trip, enjoy the holidays and good luck. I hope you find plenty.'

The Sydney–Paris flight was long and boring. Forty-five minutes in Seoul was just enough time to grab a bite, and then change planes. The airport was magnificent but the food not so good. I had no problems at Charles de Gaulle airport – no one asked about the pan.

Three days spent with Jean Claude and Monique went like a flash. They thought I was a crazy Frenchman when I told them that I needed to buy a small shovel. I picked one up for just €12 at the fantastic Porte de Clignancourt flea market and killed two birds with one stone.

I took the TGV from Paris to Toulouse then hopped onto the local train to Mazamet, where Kevin Wilkinson, the English owner of the B&B, was waiting for me. The next day, I picked up a rental car and visited Taty in the nursing home. Kevin and I got on like a house on fire from the moment we met. Every morning at six a.m., we shared some of our thoughts for the day ahead over a breakfast of coffee and croissants. Like so many other British expats, Kevin, his wife and two children had been drawn to the mild weather and relaxed lifestyle in the south of France. He had bought the hotel three years earlier and maintained it beautifully. I could not have found a better place. I was in a fantastic mood every single day. Each night, the staff at Taty's nursing home set up a table for us to enjoy dinner together. I spent some of the evening watching TV with Taty, who went to bed early; then I went back to the B&B and did the same. No one knew my plans, not even Taty. As the French would say, '*Il ne faut pas vendre la peau de l'ours avant de l'avoir tué*. Never sell the bear skin until you kill the bear.'

Every prospector dreams of finding the mother lode, the original source of gold deposited millions of years ago within a molten quartz vein by volcanic activity. When you see gold sparkling in a quartz vein, you have hit the mother lode, or you are not far from it. You and your descendants will be living in luxury for generations; that is, if you keep your mouth shut and no one sees you. Over time, bits of the vein break off by the action of erosion. Eventually, gold will find its way into rivers and streams and become alluvial gold. That is where my search would start; but always in the back of my mind was the thought of finding a vein or reef.

My equipment was minimal – my Aussie pan, the little shovel, my pick, a plastic jar for the day's takings – plus supplies: a whole camembert cheese, a baguette, apples and a packet of cigarettes. Everything fitted nicely into a small backpack. I was thinking that I should have brought some cigars to celebrate, but maybe that was tempting fate.

It was the beginning of winter; the days were getting cooler and shorter. The best time to pan was between nine-thirty a.m. and two-thirty p.m. I was usually at Rennes-le-Château before eight a.m. and back at the hotel by four-thirty p.m., then at Mazamet five minutes later to join Taty for the evening meal. I never went for lunch or coffee at a public place. Going into a café with mud-stained boots and trousers would have attracted unnecessary attention. People are curious, wondering what this stranger is doing, thinking you must be one of those silly treasure hunters, which is not good for your image or perhaps even your safety. Undertaking a field trip is not without its risks, even if it is only a swarm of mosquitos. Over the years, Rennes-le-Château had become a mecca for virtually every type of treasure seeker and investigator you could imagine: prospectors; dowsers; spiritual seekers and ufologists to name a few. The town had benefited financially from the international attention, but there was also a deep suspicion of strangers and, over the years, there had been a string of unusual deaths associated with the mystery. The authors of *The Tomb of God* considered proximity to the 'secret' to be dangerous, as the list of those murdered or meeting a sudden or 'accidental' death seemed to be out of proportion to the natural law of averages. The treasure of Rennes-le-Château was not called 'accursed' for nothing – the risks were real.

The two main rivers in the area are the river Aude that begins in the Pyrenees and the river Sals, which feeds into the Aude as it passes by Montazels and Couiza. Numerous tributaries and creeks run off these rivers; it would take weeks to sample them all, considering the precautions that would be necessary. The river Sals has a strange origin, appearing to bubble up from beneath the ground near Mount Bugarach, about thirteen kilometres south-east of Rennes-le-Château. It is also salty. Rainwater infiltrates the limestone and loads itself with salt while crossing an important deposit of crystal salt. At times the river contains sixty grams of salt per litre – twice that of the Mediterranean. The Sals flows north-west through Rennes les Bains, providing the town with its amazing mineral waters. People have been coming to Rennes les Bains since Roman times to benefit from the water's healing effects. The river Blanque reinforces the Sals shortly before it enters Rennes les Bains. Immediately to the west of this spot are three curiously named natural landmarks: L'Homme Mort, the Dead Man, is an area of land that allegedly contains an entry into a tunnel system leading to a sacred site.[5] The Fauteuil du Diable, the Devil's Armchair, is a large boulder, which has been fashioned into an armchair overlooking the expansive view and Les Roches Tremblantes, the Trembling Rocks, huge boulders that can literally move in the wind and when touched. Beside the road that follows the curve of the river Blanque and immediately south of these three strange landmarks lie the ruins of a very ancient mine. From Rennes les Bains, the Sals flows almost due north snaking its way westward between the foot of Mount Cardou, and the high slopes, which hide the ruined Château Blanchefort to the east. A local landmark known as the Roc Nègre, the Black Rock, is located beneath the ruined Château Blanchefort between Rennes-le-Château and Rennes les Bains. Another landmark known as the White Rock stands halfway up the side of Mount Cardou. According to Andrews and Schellenberger, this is the location of a 'mysterious tomb'.

On the first day of my exploration, I drove to Carcassonne, and then headed south towards Rennes-le-Château, never parking the car in the same spot. I pulled the car over to the side of the road, checked the map and traced the path of the river Aude as it skirted the town of Espereza on its way to Montazels. The D118 roadway, La Route des Pyrenees, almost mirrored the river in its path. I noticed that at a spot about halfway between Espereza and Montazels, a tributary, Le Ruisseau de Couleurs, flowed eastwards towards Rennes-le-Château, about three kilometres away. It looked like the Aude was only about a hundred metres from the D118 at that spot. A pathway, Le Chemin de Couleurs, followed the tributary and ended about a kilometre north-west of Rennes-le-Château. I guessed it would be an easy walk.

On the eastern side of the Aude around this location was an old gypsum mine, situated on private property, La Mine des Encantados. I imagined that as a boy growing up in Montazels, Bérenger Saunière would have heard stories about the old Roman gold mines and treasure finds in the area. He may have even explored the old mines and caves. According to one story, when Saunière became the priest of Rennes-le-

Château, the locals reported that he walked the countryside within a radius of around five kilometres of Rennes-le-Château. I figured that he must have walked the Chemin de Couleurs following Le Ruisseau de Couleurs.

I looked on the map for the junctions where two or even three rivers met. If each river contains gold, these are great spots to pan. Due to its high density, gold travels from the highest point to the lowest points of the riverbed. If the speed of the current either slows down or changes direction suddenly, the gold will drop out of the flow and settle in a calm part of the river or on the riverbed. It will usually dig all the way down to bedrock along with other heavy elements like silver, tin and platinum. It can also be stopped on its way down by rocks well encrusted in the local geology, or by tree roots.

I chose my spot, parked the car where it could not be seen, then got out and walked for about a hundred metres along the road. Then I left the road and headed for the creek, mentally preparing my alibi in case anyone spotted me. Well, tough luck, I thought. Hey, I had my camera – I was just an Aussie tourist taking photographs. My heart was pounding. I needed to relax and study the environment, so I sat down in a peaceful spot with a view of the creek, always keeping my back against a tree.

When I am prospecting alone in Australia, I usually leave a note on the car windscreen saying something like 'John, mate, don't forget the cigarettes, waiting for you at the normal spot, don't take too long'. It is a deterrent to anyone with bad intentions – one never knows. But here it did not matter, because clearly I was just a 'photographer'.

I remembered an incident near Milparinka in New South Wales when I went alone to collect petrified wood from a creek, intending to collect well over two hundred kilos. From the main dirt road, a small track took me to the creek, a distance of around five hundred metres. I parked the ute and started collecting – the creek was full of it. After about twenty minutes, I saw a small plane overhead. It flew low a couple of times – I waved. I knew it was the farmer and I knew he would radio his homestead. I jumped in the ute and drove off, and then stopped at the turn-off, waiting for someone who I knew would be coming to check on me.

In less than ten minutes, a young guy driving a ute showed up, with two kelpies in the back. 'G'day, mate, what's up?' he said, jumping out of the ute. 'Need any help?'

'No, mate, just came to collect a bit of petrified wood from the creek – my friend from Kandie Peak told me I would find some here. Was that your dad flying the plane?'

'Yeah, mate. OK, see you.' He got in his ute, made a U-turn, and disappeared down the road, dogs barking.

In a situation like that, there is only one thing to do: wait for someone to come and ask questions. I could have driven off, but whoever was flying the plane would have spotted me.

12

Four little specks

If I found alluvial gold by panning in one of the creeks, I knew it had to come from somewhere nearby and higher up. To trace it back to its source, I needed to follow the creek upstream until it intersected with another creek, then pan at the intersection on both sides of the creek, and also upstream and downstream. It is a process of elimination. You can be sure that if you find specks of gold in a creek, they come from a source at a higher elevation upstream. Erosion takes a hell of a long time, maybe a million years or more until the gold falls into the creek. A huge amount of gold may be sitting at a hundred metres above the creek. I was confident that if I had enough time to search, I would find indications of the presence of gold in the area. I was not about to be influenced by any of the Rennes-le-Château fairy tales. Most importantly, I knew that Salsigne was not far away.

I made myself a baguette of Camembert and slices of apple – delicious. Then I left my gear by a tree and walked for about a half-hour thinking about 2003, the red earth, the quartz and the ironstones. Salsigne and Rennes-le-Château are both in a location that was known to be gold-bearing; geologically speaking, they were close. Gold was discovered in crosscutting quartz veins at Salsigne; the mineralisation was the same as the gold fields of Hill End near Bathurst. There must be gold here, there had to be. I kept on walking, scanning the land, always on the lookout, checking any unusual-looking rocks. There was quartz around, but not a lot.

I came back to where I had left my gear and smoked another

cigarette. I looked along the side of the river. Up ahead, I could see that it took a sharp bend towards the left. If there was gold at this spot, it would be on the inner side of the bend. Why? Simply because the current is faster on the outer side of the bend and gold, being heavy, will deposit itself on the inner side.

One hour later, I had nothing. I changed location. Four hours later, still nothing. I had another walk – nothing interesting. It was close to four o'clock and my hands were turning blue from the cold river water, so I picked up my gear and finished for the day. Time to head back to Taty, our evening meal and a warm bed.

The next day, I was ready for action. My holidays could not have been better; I was in my element, doing something I love. This day, I picked up pieces of quartz, some kind of slate-like compressed mud, three pieces of ironstone and one intriguing piece of rock, which I thought was pyrite or perhaps chalcopyrite, which was a good sign – but no gold. Still, with every find, my heart pumped faster and adrenalin kept me warm.

For three days, I panned until lunchtime at different spots with no results – nothing at all. The only positive thing was that unusual piece of rock and the ironstone. I am not the sort of person who gives up easily – I knew I was on the right track. I only had six days left in France – realistically only five, because I had to return the hire car on the last day. I kept thinking of the old prospector's saying: 'There's gold in them hills.' It was like an inner voice telling me that I was on the right path. I made up my mind that the next day would be my lucky day.

The next day, I chose a different location. I walked along the creek until something told me to stop and begin panning. I knew from experience that a small lead can twist and turn in a matter of feet, so I panned as much as I could, following my instinct. On the sixth pan, I dug deeper into the gravel on the bank, remembering what Peter had told me back at Brisbane Valley Creek: the deeper, the better. Washing and watching the pan, the water swirled as I rotated it with a steady action, just firm enough so that the light stuff went out with the flow of water. Then I saw something shimmer in the top left of the pan. It was bloody small, less than a millimetre in size, but it was definitely a small speck of gold. Even that small, in full daylight, there was no way I could mistake it for anything else – wow. Gold is gold; to see it once is enough for a lifetime. My heart was pounding like mad – I was trembling from head to toe. I lay the pan on the ground, sat down and lit up a cigarette. If there was one speck, there had to be more. I headed upstream for about twenty metres, continued panning and found three more specks. That made four specks in one day. Thank you, God – whoever, whatever and wherever you are. I went back to the car and drove back to Mazamet, but not before stopping in Carcassonne for a stiff drink.

The specks were small – microscopic, in fact – but they were gold, alluvial gold from the weathering of a vein or a reef. Four specks might not sound like much – but the gold had to come from somewhere upstream; maybe a small deposit in the bank, but everything eventually leads back to the source, the mother lode or any gold for that matter, which had to be upstream from where I found the specks. All I had to do was to continue upstream and keep panning. I knew there had to be more.

Over the next four days, I travelled from Mazamet to Carcassonne, Limoux and Couiza, with the final destination somewhere after that – refer to the third rule of treasure hunting. Looking back, I feel a bit guilty for having trespassed, but I could not help it. The rules change when the fever of the treasure hunt takes hold. Anyhow, I did not cause any damage; but if there is a need to apologise, I am certainly doing it now.

13

Thirty-eight specks

In eight days, I found an interesting piece of rock, which I needed to check on the net; pieces of quartz; some ironstones; some kind of compressed mud; schist; and believe it or not, thirty-eight specks of gold, with an average size between half and one and a half millimetres. Edward Hargraves's find in New South Wales in 1851 was small enough to fit on a threepenny piece, but it was enough for the authorities to accept his claim, making him a rich man and beginning one of the world's greatest gold rushes.

In the last week of November, I was on the road again, or rather in the air, on a flight out of Paris to London, then the long-haul Qantas flight from London to Sydney via Singapore. The thirty-eight specks were safely secured in a small container tucked into the top pocket of my coat. I was looking forward to Christmas in Sydney, the sunny 35º days, the big blue skies and even the heavy traffic. I thought how lucky and lovely Taty must feel to be a hundred years old with all her faculties. I hoped to see her again full of life. I wondered what my legacy would be if I made it to a hundred.

It had been nearly a hundred years since Bérenger Saunière's death in 1917 and over thirty years since the mystery of Rennes-le-Château exploded onto the international scene with the publication of *The Holy Blood and the Holy Grail* in 1982. Hundreds of books had been written about the mystery, each one contributing a new angle, introducing new 'evidence', or debunking the old 'evidence'. The story of the 'millionaire priest' had taken on all the elements of an international conspiracy and caught the public's imagination like a flame to spinifex grass; but still no one had solved the mystery. No new theory had succeeded in entirely replacing any of the previous ones, but plenty of people had made plenty of money from perpetuating the old stories.

Twenty-four hours in the air gave me a lot of time to contemplate the future. How was I going to proceed and with whom could I discuss my story? It seemed extraordinary to me that no one had given serious consideration to the geology as a possible solution, or part of the solution, to the mystery of Rennes-le-Château – all the indicators were there. What surprised me most was that in all my reading, little or no attention was given to the possibility that Saunière found native gold; perhaps stumbling on it by sheer luck around the same time gold was discovered at or near Salsigne in 1892. To me, it seemed logical. I was confident that I had a theory that was verifiable and independent of any of the previous theories. I was prepared for the naysayers who would be ready to point the finger. After all, I was a retired French chef and part-time prospector, one of the little guys. However, lone individuals with a dream, following their intuition, believing they were on the right track, have made some of the world's most amazing mineral discoveries. After the prospectors have worked the surface, the big mobs move in, providing the capital needed for costly underground mines.

In 2009, entrepreneur Paul Fudge sold his coal-seam gas exploration permit in Queensland to the giant Origin Energy for $660 million. Formerly a trader in expensive fabrics, Fudge was seen as something of an outsider in the mining world. The gossip has it that people in the mining world told him to 'stick to his day job'. In 2004, I gave Paul's secretary some of my diamond indicators and my proposal, but at that time, he must have been busy with all the dealings with Origin, as nothing eventuated.

Chuck Fipke and Stewart Blusson discovered the first indicators of diamonds in the Northwest Territories of Canada as early as 1985. Initially, mining companies and people in the mining industry rejected Chuck's theory. However, Chuck knew he was right and the multimillion dollar Ekati mine officially opened in 1998. Lang Hancock, a grazier and amateur prospector, discovered the biggest reserve of iron ore in the world in Western Australia in 1952. He waited eight years to stake his claim, being careful not to arouse interest in the meantime. I worked in Port Hedland in the 1970s; people drive and walk on iron ore – it is everywhere. You would think that someone would have found it earlier, but they didn't. Gina Reinhart, Lang's daughter, is now one of the richest women in the world.

De Beers might dominate the world's diamond mining industry, but the world's greatest diamond fields in South Africa, for example, were discovered mainly by small prospectors, in much the same way as the gold fields were opened up in Australia.

Old prospectors did well for their nation; their discoveries created jobs and brought wealth and happiness.

Minerals exploration is always a risk, but one that the big players are prepared to make. Two of the biggest players in the industry had interests in the area that would eventually become the Argyle diamond mine in Western Australia. BRGM had an exploration licence for a hundred thousand square kilometres, De Beers about the same, spending around $350 million over thirty years, without finding a cent. Big companies and large organisations are not exempt from failure.

I imagined all the questions from the sceptics and cynics: had I really found the specks of gold from around Rennes-le-Château; was it real gold; why didn't I search for the reef, the lode or the vein myself? The truth is I could – the problem does not reside in the will to search, but what is involved. I am not equipped for the task; I do not possess the equipment; nor do I have the financial means. To stumble upon a treasure costs nothing, to search for one costs a fortune. How likely was it that I could stake a claim in France? Remote, if not impossible. A mining company would need to assess the potential for payable gold. Applications for exploration licences would need to be lodged with the French government, which I anticipated would probably create significant disturbances within the farming community.

The old Seekers song kept buzzing around in my head: 'Leaving on a jet plane, don't know when I'll be back again…' Truly, I did not know when I would be back again. Then halfway through the flight the answer materialised itself. This was a story that was worth telling; my only realistic option was to write it. In some ways, it was scarier thinking about writing than driving like a maniac through the streets of Paris, or across some of the most remote and barren land in outback Australia in my trusty old Toyota ute. The problem was that even though I had been in Australia for over forty years and was fluent in English, it was my second language – I still counted in French. I had to find a writer to help me, ideally someone who knew about the mystery of Rennes-le-Château, who was open to new ideas and prepared to think outside the square.

In 2011, six years after Lesley and I broke up, I met Rebecca. Several weeks later, I had quit my job at Doyles, put my flat up for sale, loaded my ute with some of my belongings and I was on the road to the Canberra to be with Rebecca, happy as Larry. Work was no longer in the way. Beauty. Rebecca and I married on 3 December 2011 at her brother's waterfront house at Pelican Water, on the Sunshine Coast in Queensland. With Rebecca working and me not, I had plenty of time on my hands to do some thinking. I had not given up on my diamond project. My friend Barry and I and a mob from Melbourne planned to register a company – Auzdiamond Resources Group – and lodge three licences of a hundred units each. We were very excited about it. However, we could not raise the necessary funds and once more it was back to the drawing board.

It was over a year since my trip to Rennes-le-Château. I wondered how a simple story of hidden treasure had become so complicated. I emailed several authors, including Dan Brown, author of *The da Vinci Code*. All I said was that I had an interesting new theory about the source of Bérenger Saunière's money, but needed help to write the story. No one replied – no one seemed to be at all curious about my proposal.

Rebecca regularly bought the New Age magazine *New Dawn*. It was not something I usually bothered reading, but for some reason I picked this one up and flicked through the pages. An article caught my attention: 'Jesus Christ: from Jerusalem to Rennes-le-Château' by Adelaide author Enzo Fardone. Enzo presented Andrews and Shellenberger's theory that Jesus did not die on the cross but travelled to the south of France and was buried in a hidden tomb on the side of Mount Cardou. At the end of the article was an advertisement for Enzo's book *The Poussin Enigma*, a fictional account of one man's spiritual quest through the south of France, including revelations about the secrets of the treasure of Rennes-le-Château.

Like so many of the other authors, it seemed that Enzo was a man steeped in the religious and mystical aspects of the Rennes-le-Château mystery. However, I had a good feeling about him; he sounded like the man for the job and I hoped that my story would interest him. Adelaide was a long way from Canberra, but at least we were in the same country and I figured that he must be knowledgeable about the history of Rennes-le-Château.

Lucky for me, his publisher sent me his contact address. The next day I wrote to Enzo telling him that I had a new theory about Rennes-le-Château and asking him if he was interested. I received his reply; a meeting was of the utmost necessity – it was worth a shot.

In the meantime, I needed to do more research.

14

Gold dust or bulldust

The first reference I found to Bérenger Saunière, the 'treasure hunting' priest, was in a travel article written in 1936 by Dr Jean Girou (1889–1972). Girou described how the villas and towers in Saunière's estate were 'new and modern' and formed a strange contrast with the ruins of the old castle. 'This is the house of a priest who built these sumptuous living-quarters with the money from a discovered treasure – or so the locals say anyway!'[6] Was there a touch of cynicism in Girou's comment?

The earliest known press article that suggested something other than treasure hunting was going on appeared in 1948 in the Belgian magazine *Le Soir illustré*.[7] Journalist Roger Crouquet reported that Saunière had placed advertisements in foreign newspapers, especially in the United States, seeking donations to restore the church, as it was archaeologically significant. Crouquet did not name his sources.

In 1956, the treasure story reached the ears of Albert Salamon, a journalist working with the regional newspaper *La Dépêche de Midi*. Salamon interviewed writer Noël Corbu, the owner of the Hotel de la Tour in Rennes-le-Château. Corbu had been entertaining his customers with the story, presumably in an attempt to drum up business. Corbu and his family moved into the Villa Bethanie in 1946 at the invitation of Marie Dénarnaud, Saunière's housekeeper. Marie bequeathed the estate to Corbu, who in return agreed to take care of her for the rest of her life.[8] Saunière had put the estate in her name and now she had someone to look after her into her old age; she was on to a good thing.

Marie and some of the villagers told Corbu stories about Saunière, which Corbu used in his marketing strategy. His daughter Claire said that when she was a child, Marie told her that she was 'walking on gold' and that there was 'more money that she could ever spend'.[9] Marie hinted to Corbu that Saunière's wealth was not exhausted, and promised to reveal its source before she died. She died in 1953 without, it seems, keeping that promise.

In 1955, Corbu converted the Villa Bethanie into the Hotel de la Tour and established a restaurant in the belvedere. Times were tough and business was slow; the story of the 'millionaire priest' and a 'fabulous hidden treasure' was the perfect drawcard. He even named the source of the treasure – Queen Blanche de Castille (1188–1242).[10] Corbu claimed that due to the Révolte des Pastoureaux in 1251, the queen had sought refuge with the Count of Voisin, her powerful ally, and the Lord of Rennes, taking with her what remained of the royal treasure to keep it out of the hands of the barons, who were revolting against royal authority. The fortune was allegedly buried somewhere in or around Rennes-le-Château, possibly in an underground passage below the château. The Voisin family held Rennes-le-Château from 1209 at the time of the Albigensian Crusade to 1442. When Blanche de Marquefave, a descendant of the Voisins, married Pierre Raymond d'Hautpoul, Rennes-le-Château passed to the Hautpoul de Blanchefort family, who held it until the French Revolution.[11] Pierre Raymond moved from his chateau near Mazamet to the Château Blanchefort, which then became the Château Hautpoul. The Hautpouls were one of the most distinguished houses among the high nobility of the Languedoc; some researchers say they were descended from the Visigoth King Ataulphe.

According to Corbu, in 1892 workers restoring the church's original high altar found wooden rolls containing scrolls in one of the stone pillars supporting altar. The pillar is believed to date from Visigoth times and now stands in the church garden topped with a statue of Notre Dame de Lourdes. Allegedly, the diocese of Carcassonne paid Saunière to travel to the church of Saint-Sulpice in Paris, where the documents were decoded and explained. When Saunière returned, he restarted work to restore the whole church. He also started working on his own in the churchyard, and allegedly erased the inscriptions on the tomb of the last Countess Hautpoul-Blanchefort, Marie de Nègre d'Ables. There is however, no verifiable evidence that Saunière found any parchments, went to Paris with parchments, or cracked any codes.

Corbu claimed that whatever he discovered eventually led Saunière to the hiding place of part of the treasure of Blanche de Castille, a staggering '18 million and a half golden coins' (about a hundred and eighty tonnes), plus jewels and cult objects. According to Corbu, a golden coin of that time was worth 472,000 francs, which makes the value of the treasure the equivalent of four thousand billion francs in Corbu's time (1956).[12] The old French franc was revalued in 1960, with each new franc being worth a hundred old francs. Corbu's estimate of four thousand billion francs in 1956 becomes forty million new francs today, which converts to approximately US$6.7 million dollars.* In reality, it is practically impossible to estimate the value of a golden coin from the Middle Ages in order to establish the value of a treasure, the provenance of which is uncertain and which itself is the subject of a legend.

Corbu also claimed that there were 'files' in Carcassonne that listed the treasure, explaining its origin. If these files exist, as far as I could find they have not seen the light of day. I wondered who would make a list of the content of such a huge a treasure. It sounded more like the *X-Files* to me. But Salamon's story 'The fabulous discovery of the millionaire priest of Rennes-le-Château', which featured over three issues, caught the public's attention and the 'treasure seekers' began to trickle into the village to try their luck.

In 1958, a group called the Treasure Seekers' Club, formed in 1951 by author Robert Charroux, began scanning the village using a metal detector. Known for his writings on ancient astronaut theories, Charroux included Corbu's treasure story in his 1962 publication *Trésors du monde: enterrés, emmurés, engloutis*, Treasures of the world: buried, walled, swallowed up.

* The French franc was replaced by the Euro in 1999.

In April 1961, the French television channel RTF made a documentary entitled *The Wheel Turns*, with Noël Corbu cast as Father Saunière.

I could see why the treasure story had gained momentum. The existence of buried treasure is part of the history and the mythology of the south of France. There is a wealth of hiding places in the region, including deep limestone caves, natural and man-made tunnels and old abandoned mines. There were any number of possible sources of treasure, including Visigoth treasure from the sack of Rome in AD 410 or the mysterious Cathar treasure allegedly taken out of Montsegur before it fell in 1244 during the Albigensian Crusade. Treasure allegedly secreted away in the fourteenth century by the Knights Templar, who were active in that region, and various treasure caches hidden by nobles escaping the guillotine during the French Revolution. There are records of many treasure finds in Europe, often involving the Church and the nobility. One of the most famous is the tomb of the Merovingian King Childeric I, who died in AD 481. His tomb was discovered in 1653 not far from the twelfth-century church of Saint-Brice in Tournai, now in Belgium. It contained various items of gold jewellery and three hundred golden bees. People still find caches of coins and other valuables. In 2015, the grave of a Celtic prince or princess was found in Lavau in north-central France, with a golden torque still in place.

From the sixteenth century, numerous archaeological discoveries around Rennes les Bains began to attract collectors, including archaeologists, numismatists, antique dealers, researchers, geologists and members of scientific societies. Paul Urban Villecardet, the Count of Fleury (1778–1836) had a small museum to show off his collection of coins and medals. Among the amateur archaeologists and collectors was Abbé Henri Boudet (1837–1915), Saunière's colleague and the priest of Rennes les Bains from 1872–1914. He often gave artefacts that he found around his parish to Henri Rouzaud, the president of the Archaeological Commission of Narbonne. Saunière's brother Alfred was also a member. Nevertheless, apart from some eyewitness reports of his housekeeper wearing antique jewellery and an alleged witness account of Saunière finding a pot filled with gold coins or medallions when he was renovating the church, there was no verifiable evidence that Saunière found treasure in Rennes-le-Château. Still, Rennes-le-Château became a Mecca for treasure seekers and all sorts of colorful characters with other agendas. The story was ripe for mischief-makers and pranksters, much to the dismay of the mayor. The interest in Rennes-le-Château became so intense that on 28 July 1965 the local municipal council introduced a local by-law prohibiting excavations in the village – hence the sign I saw at the entrance to the village. Among the colourful characters was the author Gerard de Sède and his friends and fellow writers, Pillipe de Chérisey, and Pierre Plantard. With the assistance of de Chérisey and Plantard, de Sède wrote a book about the mystery: *Le Trésor Maudit de Rennes-le-Château*, The Accursed Treasure of Rennes-le-Château, published in 1968.

In spite of all the interest generated by the publicity, the story was still pretty much contained within France – but that was about to change.

15

Just because of a little book

In 1969, Henry Lincoln, actor and scriptwriter for the BBC, was on holiday with his family and friends in the south of France. One day, looking for some light holiday reading, Lincoln chanced upon de Sède's book. He describes the story as an entertaining blend of historical fact, mystery and conjecture. Reproduced in the book were two parchments, allegedly found by Saunière in 1891 when he was renovating the church.* They comprised Latin texts taken from the New Testament and are commonly referred to as 'Parchment 1: the Dagobert text', which describes Jesus and his disciples walking in the cornfields on the Sabbath, and 'Parchment 2: the Shepherdess text', an account from John's Gospel in which Mary of Bethany (believed by many to be Mary Magdalene) anoints Jesus. There was no explanation as to what they meant.

Lincoln noticed that the Dagobert text contained strange markings, which seemed to indicate a cipher or code. To his surprise, he found that he could decode the cipher, revealing the following text: '*A Dagobert II roi et a Sion est ce tresor et il est la mort*. This treasure belongs to Dagobert II king and to Sion and he is there dead'.[13] According to official French history, Dagobert II, the last of the Merovingian kings, was assassinated in AD 679. His son Sigisbert IV predeceased him in AD 678.[14] Was the reference to a Merovingian treasure a clue to the source of Saunière's wealth? Lincoln realised that the mystery had all the elements required for the BBC's popular *Chronicle* program – a great hid-

---

* See a detailed analysis of the parchments here: https://archive.org/stream/Indagini_su_Rennes-le-Chateau2#page/n435/mode/1up

den treasure, possibly linked to the history of the Merovingian bloodline and the presence of an important dead body or tomb. The BBC agreed – but just how reliable was de Sède's information?

Lincoln met with de Sède in Paris in 1970 and a cat and mouse game ensued. He told Lincoln that his colleagues, Philippe de Chérisey and Pierre de Plantard, had directed him to the *Dossiers Secret* in the Bibliothèque Nationale de Paris. The work was a collection of twenty-seven pages deposited anonymously in the French National Library between 1964 and 1967. It included a genealogy of the Merovingians and their descendants, a list of the grand masters of the Priory of Sion from AD 1188 and an image of the epitaph on the tombstone of Marie de Nègre d'Ables recorded by local history enthusiast Elie Tisseyre in 1906.[15][16] Plantard presented himself as a descendant of the Merovingian bloodline and the 'Grandmaster' of the Prieure de Sion, Priory of Sion. The priory is said to be a secret order that created the Knights Templars as its military and administrative arm with the objective of restoring the Merovingian bloodline and dynasty to the thrones of France and other European nations.[17]

Right from the outset, Lincoln considered that the provenance of the information was questionable; nevertheless, it was intriguing – pure mystery gold.

Lincoln had easily decoded the Dagobert parchment but the code in the Shepherdess parchment was much more complex. De Sède sent Lincoln this decipherment of part of the text:

> *Bergère pas de tentation. Que Poussin Teniers gardent la clef. Pax DCLXXXI (681). Par la croix et ce cheval de dieu. J'achève ce daemon de gardien à midi. Pommes bleues.* Shepherdess no temptation. That Poussin Teniers hold the key. Peace 681. By the cross and this horse of God. I complete [or destroy] this guardian daemon at midday. Blue apples.[18]

He told Lincoln that the code referred to two paintings: *The shepherds of Arcadia* by Nicholas Poussin (1592–1666), and *The temptation of St Anthony and Saint Paul* by David Teniers (1610–1690). He also told Lincoln that Saunière had returned from Paris with copies of these paintings, implying that they were both clues to 'the secret', although this has never been verified.

Poussin's painting features three shepherds and a woman gathered around a large stone tomb. One of the shepherds is pointing to an inscription on the side of the tomb that reads *'Et in arcadia ego'*, usually translated as 'And I am in Arcadia' or 'Even in Arcadia I exist'. Many Rennies interpret the 'key' referred to in the Shepherdess parchment as the location of an important tomb. De Sède sent Lincoln photographs of a tomb at Arques, with instructions that it was located some four miles to the east of Rennes-le-Château to the right of the road between the villages of Serres and Arques.[19]

When Lincoln located the tomb in 1971, it was clear to him that this was in fact the setting for Poussin's painting.[20] Intrigued, Lincoln asked Christopher Cornford of the Royal College of Art to analyse Poussin's painting. Cornford concluded that the painting's underlying geometry was based 'with precision upon the pentagon, the five sided figure whose chords form the five-pointed star – the pentagram'.[21] He suggested that Lincoln look for this geometry in the landscape. Coincidentally, Lincoln had already discovered a pentacle coded into the Dagobert parchment.

A tomb located somewhere within a pentagram formed naturally in the landscape around Rennes-le-Château – in other words, 'Paradise' or 'Arcadia' – was the genesis for what would become an intense focus by many researchers over the years on the significance of specific geometric forms to uncovering the 'secret'. Lincoln went on to discover what he describes as an 'awe-inspiring' pentagon formed by the natural mountain peaks at Blanchefort, La Soulane, Bezu, Serre de Lauzet and Rennes-le-Château, with La Pique marking the centre.[22]

One of the documents in the *Dossiers Secret* claims that on her deathbed on 17 January 1781, Marie de Nègre d'Ables confided a Hautpoul family secret to the priest of Rennes-le-Château, Abbé Antoine Bigou, and entrusted him with the entire family archive.[23] The

Hautpoul-Blanchefort family owned most of the territory of Rennes-le Château and Rennes les Bains. This archive may have included the family wills, testaments and genealogies. Marie's husband, François-Henri d'Hautpoul, the last Lord of Rennes, had died in 1753. The problem came in 1789 when the French Revolution broke out. Along with many other priests, Bigou was forced to flee to Spain. Some researchers claim that the Hautpoul family 'secret' was of such importance that Bigou chose to leave the documents behind in the seigneurial crypt beneath the church. He then left clues in and around the church for someone in the future to find. These clues may have been encoded into the parchments featured in de Sède's book and the inscription on Marie de Nègre's tombstone and headstone. According to the story, after he found the parchments, Saunière defaced the headstone, removing all the inscriptions. According to Jean Luc Robin, Bigou's clues led Saunière to the tomb of the seigneurs, the lords, under the church altar, where he discovered more documents and a small amount of treasure. There is an entry in Saunière's journal dated 21 September 1891 that reads, '*découverte d'un tombeau*, discovery of a tomb', which may confirm this. A few days later, he recorded seeing and visiting several colleagues.[24]

Most of the treasure theories are based on the existence of the various coded messages revealed through de Sède's book and the *Dossiers Secret*. The documents in the *Dossiers Secret* certainly exist, but the question is who wrote them, who deposited them in the library and for what purpose. Their authenticity was questionable; they included authors using pseudonyms and references to publishing houses and organisations that did not exist. Right from the outset, Henry Lincoln was sceptical: 'It seems clear that we can take none of de Sède's account at face value… If it's not verifiable then…it must be treated with extreme caution.'[25]

Lincoln was not the only one who considered the possibility that the treasure story was a mystification, a hoax or even a practical joke on an enormous scale. In a review of de Sède's book in 1967, journalist

Jean Dunyach planted the first seeds of doubt that perhaps the story was indeed an elaborate hoax; describing it as being full of 'pseudo-historical comments'. He noted that de Sède himself stated that, given that he had only ever seen copies of the documents in question, one should remain sceptical about their authenticity.[26]

As he began to delve deeper into the mystery, Lincoln discovered many variations of the 'facts'. There were different versions of how and where the documents were found. De Sède's story of the parchments in the Visigoth stone pillar proved impossible. When Lincoln examined the pillar, he found that it was not hollow, and could therefore not have contained parchments. Jean luc Robin writes that during the church renovations, Saunière's bell-ringer found a small glass phial in a cavity in the seventeenth-century wooden pillar that had supported the old pulpit. Inside was a little rolled-up parchment, which he gave to Saunière, who spent the whole night deciphering it.[27] There were also different eyewitness accounts of Saunière finding a cache of gold coins – none of these accounts has been verified.

Despite the lack of hard evidence, or maybe because of it, Lincoln was hooked. Someone had gone to a lot of trouble to create the ciphered messages. The story was intriguing and, over the next seven years, the BBC produced three Chronicle programs about the mystery: *The Lost Treasure of Jerusalem* in 1972; *The Priest, the Painter and the Devil* in 1974; and *The Shadow of the Templars* in 1979. The programs struck a chord with viewers. People began contacting Lincoln with all sorts of information. A retired Anglican minister told Lincoln that he had 'incontrovertible proof' that the crucifixion was a fraud and Jesus was alive as late as AD 45. However, when Lincoln met with him, he failed to produce the alleged proof.[28]

Lincoln joined forces with Richard Leigh and Michael Baigent. Leigh was a novelist and short story writer with a deep interest in history, philosophy, psychology and esoterica. He had done a considerable amount of research into the history of the Knights Templar. His friend Baigent was a psychology graduate who also had a great interest in the

Templars. Their collaboration ultimately resulted in the publication of the controversial bestseller *The Holy Blood and the Holy Grail*, one of the primary source books for Dan Brown's novel *The da Vinci Code*, published in 2003, which again captured the world's attention. The success of these two books took the Rennes-le-Château enigma to a completely new level internationally. Seekers of a different kind began to pour into the village. Tour groups of New Agers interested in the theory of a sacred bloodline from the union of Jesus and Mary Magdalene – or mystical happenings; alien landings; sacred geometry; earth energies and the like – were beginning to overtake the treasure hunters and in their own way cash in on the mystery.

What Lincoln could not have guessed at the time was that his chance discovery of de Sède's book was the turning point that would take the story from a local mystery and simple treasure hunt to a conspiracy of monumental proportions. The more I read, the more it seemed to me that what the authors of *The Holy Blood and the Holy Grail* had clearly put forward as theories were frequently interpreted as facts by subsequent authors. Some of the 'evidence' was based on oral traditions passed down in families – eyewitnesses were long gone. Criminologists have found that people can have false memories going back a week, let alone twenty or thirty years. Like a game of Chinese whispers, myths and legends evolve over time as fact and fiction intermingle; but they cannot be dismissed as they often have a basis in fact. Even hoaxes can have some grounding in fact and actual events. Nevertheless, without observable events and verifiable information, it was hard to tell fact from fiction. When searching for gold or treasure, it is paramount that fiction does not interfere with facts.

I had enough experience in the world of minerals exploration to know that people will sometimes do anything to protect their interests. It is not uncommon for myths and legends, and even hoaxes, to be used as smokescreens. Like the Australian legend of Lasseter's reef: a vast gold reef, rumoured to be somewhere on the western edge of the MacDonnell Ranges in central Australia, allegedly discovered by Harold Lasseter around the turn of the nineteenth century. As with the mystery of Rennes-le-Château, Lasseter's story is full of old documents, 'treasure maps', witness reports and hoaxes. Lasseter allegedly died in a remote part of the Australian outback. People have been searching for the reef ever since. Some claim to know its location, but so far, no one has come up with the gold.

One of the first things Lincoln asked de Sède in 1970 was why he had not revealed the message coded into the parchments in his book. De Sède's cryptic response – 'We thought it might interest someone like you to find it for yourself' – added to the intrigue.[29] De Sède had made the curious comment that 'they' had been waiting for someone like him to come along. Who were 'they' and why did they need someone like Lincoln? A so-called secret organisation would only release information if there was an advantage in doing so. Was it Lincoln's media connections, or were they looking for someone who would buy the idea of the hoax? Then again, why would 'they' go to all the trouble to perpetrate a simple hoax, unless whoever fabricated the story had a reason for constructing a cover story, a diversion, in order to deflect attention away from what was really going on?

Some researchers suggest that Saunière's support for the monarchists led him to become part of a bigger plan. During his short exile from Rennes-le-Château for giving anti-republican sermons, his younger brother Alfred introduced him to important and powerful people who may have known of the existence of something in Rennes-le-Château or surrounds that would legitimise their monarchist claims, or perhaps delegitimise somebody else's. Maybe finding the 'treasure' was simply a by-product of this search.

Saunière certainly found or accessed 'something'. The problem is that if the finder needs to convert a treasure into cash, it must be sold. Eventually, items from the find make their way onto the open market, the finder is usually found out, and the find is confiscated. Unlike Michel the Corsican's father, the finders keepers rule did apply to Saunière. His wealth was obvious to the villagers, most of whom were quite happy to benefit from his spending. Whatever Saunière found, he did not advertise it, and he resisted all attempts by the church hierarchy to uncover its source, to the extent of providing misleading information when he was accused of trafficking in masses. Eventually, he was suspended from his priest's duties, a right that was only lifted at the moment of his death in 1917.

According to most theories, the noble families who owned Rennes-le-Château over the centuries knew of an important secret, a secret they shared with certain priests in the Languedoc. Was this secret revealed in the documents Saunière allegedly found, was it interwoven within the myths and legends passed down through the centuries, or was it possible that the 'secret' was in plain sight?

16

A story to tell: Adelaide, 2014

Within two weeks, I was on the road heading twelve hundred kilometres west to Adelaide. The long drive was not a deterrent. I feel free when I am driving, stopping anywhere I like, sleeping under the stars – it is relaxing, almost like a meditation. I take everything I need with me, including water, camping gear and gas to cook with. I carry my favourite Aussie camping food: coffee, tea, sugar, bread, fruit, biscuits and beef sausages. Not forgetting cigarettes, my digital camera, maps and, most important, a swag – plus at least two very warm blankets in case of a breakdown. Temperatures in the Australian bush can drop dramatically overnight – no blankets and you freeze. I also carry at least three spare wheels. Travelling in Australia is an adventure and sometimes it is a real expedition.

Leaving Canberra around noon, sleeping overnight in the back of the ute, I arrived in Adelaide around noon the next day. A quick text, then Enzo and I were sitting in a café on The Parade, the main street of Norwood, not far from his house. Enzo wore an elegant black suit with a white shirt unbuttoned at the collar. He was Italian by birth but there was a touch of French nobility about him. I gave him a copy of the summary of my story then ordered two coffees.

It did not take long for Enzo to finish reading. After a moment's silence, he looked up at me with a broad smile. 'Amazing. I don't believe it, unbelievable – I'm in. Let's go to my place. It's just around the corner.'

Enzo's house was a quiet oasis from the commercial precinct. A classic stone-fronted, return-veranda villa on a corner block in an old tree-lined street. I figured it would be worth a mint. A ramble of bushes obscured any evidence of the formal layout of the small front garden. We headed down the long central corridor to the back of the house; a faint scent of incense lingered in the air. Bookshelves lined the walls, each shelf crammed with books, sometimes two deep. At the entrance to the kitchen, a copy of the Koran sat open on a low table next to an elegant ceremonial dagger. A collection of crisply ironed shirts of every colour, some plain, some with swirling bohemian patterns, black silk, ruffled cuffs hung on coat-hangers from the door handle. The kitchen sink was piled with dishes and a row of ripening persimmons decorated the windowsill like bright orange ornaments.

Gargoyles and other Gothic oddities dotted around the room seemed to fix me in their stony stare. Even in the kitchen, tottering piles of books and magazines jostled for space on every available surface, including the floor. We settled at the kitchen table, which was covered by a tapestry wall hanging featuring a medieval scene of ladies and their knights – there was just enough space for our coffee cups.

I asked Enzo how he became interested in the Rennes-le-Château mystery.

'I read *The Holy Blood and the Holy Grail* as soon as it was published and since then every book written by the three authors, singly or together. It was the first time that the theory that Jesus did not die on the cross, and that there was a bloodline from the union of Jesus and Mary Magdalene, reached such a large mainstream audience. The theory was not new of course. Students of the ancient wisdom like myself were very familiar with the sangreal – sacred or holy bloodline – and it was well known throughout Europe, especially in the south of France. However, this was the first time this knowledge became so widely disseminated across the world, much to the concern of the Catholic Church of course. The Vatican labelled the book heresy. It was even banned in some Roman Catholic-dominated countries. When the Church reacts violently against something, you know that there is something to it, so I had to go to Rennes-le-Château. In 1988, I spent several months in

Macchia d'Isernia, the village in Italy where I was born. Then I hired a little car and travelled through France. I guess I was among the first wave of international treasure seekers inspired by the book,' he said with a faint smile. 'But the treasure I was after was not physical gold, but spiritual gold.'

'And what do you call spiritual gold?' I said.

'That elusive sacred object called the Holy Grail, Gerard, the Holy Grail. All initiates of the sacred orders undertake the Grail quest.'

Enzo explained that the Grail has been described as many things, including a cup, the philosopher's stone, a secret doctrine, the kingdom of heaven, the pearl of great price, the sangreal, and even a spiritual experience. However, to him they were all synonyms for the same thing: the physical representation of the divine, and the link between the two. He had bought hundreds of books on the subject and related subjects, including the Templars; the Rosicrucians; Arthurian legends; Gnosticism; esoteric Christianity; chivalry; alchemy; and comparative religions – the list went on. One of his favourite pastimes was to rummage through bookstands at second-hand bookshops and antiquarian dealers. What one author overlooked or dismissed another would highlight. The small clues, the insights of brilliance, it was all there like some gigantic puzzle waiting for someone to make the right connections. Enzo's collection must have been pushing at least ten thousand; but in all this literature, he agreed that he had not found anyone who gave serious consideration to the possibility that Saunière discovered native gold.

'When I returned from France, I started writing a novel about a character called John Sinclair and his quest for the Holy Grail, which took him to Rome and the South of France. It had all the elements of a great thriller – foul play by P2, the Priory of Sion, the Templars, various secret plots by certain Catholic bishops, a love interest of course, and the mystery of Rennes-le-Château.'

'What is P2?'

'P2, Propaganda Due, was a clandestine Masonic lodge heavily involved with certain elements of the Vatican and the Vatican Bank. It had links with all the usual suspects – elements in the French government, the CIA, the Mafia and ex-Nazis – and it was involved in money laundering, murder, cover-ups: a conspiracy theorist's dream. The book that inspired me most was *The Tomb of God*. Andrews and Schellenberger's theory that there is a hidden tomb in an inaccessible part of the Pyrenees somewhere near Rennes-le-Château, possibly Mount Cardou, fascinated me. In 1998, Transworld Publishers in the United Kingdom put out a call for manuscripts – that was the break I needed. I submitted my story, at that time titled *Vision of the Holy Grail: The mystery and treasure of Rennes-le-Château*. I was bitterly disappointed when I received a rejection letter saying that they doubted that the story would be a commercial success. I put it to one side along with all my other manuscripts. Then in 2004 I bought a copy of *The da Vinci Code* along with everyone else. In 2006, two of the authors of *The Holy Blood and the Holy Grail* took Dan Brown to court for plagiarism. Doomed to failure of course: one book is non-fiction and the other is fiction. You can only copyright the way ideas are expressed, not the ideas themselves. Henry Lincoln didn't want a bar of that court case, but ironically he ended up benefitting from it because the case significantly boosted sales of *The Holy Blood and the Holy Grail* – it's never been out of print.'

'So what happened next?' I said.

'Do you know how many copies of *The da Vinci Code* were sold?' said Enzo.

'No idea.'

'About eighty million. Add to that the film, the merchandising, the game and on it goes. If Transworld had published my manuscript, I have no doubt that it would have appealed to the same readers as *The da Vinci Code* and attracted worldwide sales. I decided to have another go at getting my book published. I made some revisions to the original plot and just by chance met a South Australian publisher who agreed to publish it, and so *The Poussin Enigma* was born.'

I looked at the copy of *The Poussin Enigma* on the kitchen table. The front cover featured the face of Jesus as it appears on the Shroud of

Turin, overwritten with the words 'Where is the body of Christ buried?' Below this was an image of Poussin's famous *Shepherdess* painting with the enigmatic phrase *Et in Arcadia Ego*.

'So what do you think about the theory that the so-called secret of Rennes-le-Château is revealed in Poussin's painting?' I said, pointing to the cover.

'Poussin was an initiate,' said Enzo. 'The phrase *Et in Arcadia Ego* was used as a sort of code by an underground stream of initiates. You could say they were kindred souls, who shared their esoteric knowledge with one another via a network of secret societies and mystery schools. People like Rene d'Anjou, Giordano Bruno, Leonardo da Vinci, Nicholas Poussin and many others used it in their work. Lincoln proposed that it could refer to a hidden bloodline. Poussin painted the phrase on the tomb in his *Shepherdess* painting. There is a suggestion that around 1678, Jean Baptiste Colbert, the finance minister, had a tomb on the road to Pontils destroyed on the orders of the king for unknown reasons. It was rebuilt in more recent times, but unfortunately, the landowner destroyed it in 1988 because of all the attention it received after *The Holy Blood and the Holy Grail* was published. Andrews and Schellenberger suggest that the actual tomb that Poussin was alluding to in his painting is located between the twin peaks of nearby Mt. Cardou.'

'The tomb of Jesus Christ,' I said.

'Exactly. Some researchers believe that Jesus survived the crucifixion assisted by the Essenes.' Enzo picked up a copy of *New Dawn* and read from his article:

> ...they administered a mixture of herbal and other medicines to the severely wounded Jesus. Following his recovery, Jesus travelled to Scetis in Egypt where he stayed for a while with members of a branch of the Essenes. From there it is proposed that he travelled to the town of Rennes-le-Château situated in the Languedoc region of the south-west of France. It is asserted that this is the true resting place of Christ's body.[30]

He closed the magazine and placed it on top of a pile of books. 'Think about it, Gerard. If Jesus did not die on the cross, then there was no resurrection, which would mean that the entire basis of the Church of Rome is false. Even if he did die on the cross, proof of the existence of an actual body would show that the bodily resurrection did not happen and we reach the same conclusion. The implications of that are sensational. I believe that Poussin was trying to tell us something very important about that part of France.'

'And the Shroud of Turin – real or a hoax?' I said.

'It's hard to say. I am inclined to think that it is real. In my novel, John Sinclair's DNA is compared with that from the blood on the shroud to prove that he is a direct descendent of the sangreal bloodline. Imagine if we had Jesus's bones for that testing,' said Enzo shaking his head. 'When *The Holy Blood and the Holy Grail* was published, the mystery of Rennes-le-Château became much more than a simple treasure story. It challenged the basis of Christianity and introduced one of the world's most compelling and potentially damaging conspiracy theories involving the Church. If the bloodline theory could be verified by authentic documentation, the impact on the Vatican, let alone the entire Christian world, would be nuclear in its intensity. It doesn't take a genius to see that there's a lot riding on the sangreal theory being wrong.'

'Ok,' I said. 'I can see that if Jesus's mummified body was discovered in a hidden tomb, buried under a pile of rubble, that would be sensational, especially if there was actual verifiable evidence. But how would that explain Saunière's wealth?'

17

The documents

'According to de Sède, Saunière discovered the coded parchments when he was renovating the church…'

'*Allegedly* discovered parchments – originals have never been sighted,' I said. 'If there are any originals.'

'Right, but just because originals haven't been sighted doesn't automatically mean that they don't exist,' said Enzo.

'Absence of evidence isn't evidence of absence,' I said.

'Indeed. Speculation runs wild, but let's do a hypothetical,' said Enzo. 'Let's assume that Saunière did find coded parchments which led him to the crypt and the Hautpoul archive. From a legal perspective, it is reasonable to assume that a family archive of that time would include documents that had been handed down for generations – wills and testaments, details of fiefs, genealogies and titles the family held.'

'Well, the documents I'm most interested in are the wills. I assume they would have contained information about the estates, wouldn't they?'

'Of course,' said Enzo. 'It seems that Saunière accessed the wills of two key figures – François-Pierre d'Hautpoul, dated 23 November 1644, and his grandson Henri d'Hautpoul, dated 24 April 1695.[31] Five saints are invoked in Henri's will – coincidentally the same five that Saunière later put statues of in his church. De Sede wrote that in 1644 François-Pierre deposited his will and some important papers about the family's origins with a notary in Espereza by the name of Captier. It seems that there was secrecy surrounding the documents because they mysteriously disappeared. In the meantime, Rennes-le-Château passed to François-Pierre's son Blaise d'Hautpoul, then to his grandson Henri, and finally to his great-grandson François d'Hautpoul, the husband of Marie de Nègre d'Ables and the last male in the line. François dies suddenly in 1753. Naturally, Marie attempts to retrieve the family papers but another lawyer, Maitre Jean Baptiste Ciau, refuses her request.

'That's unusual, isn't it? Can a lawyer do that?'

A faint smile crossed Enzo's face. 'Lawyers can do anything, Gerard. Apparently, the reason was that it would not be prudent of him to divest himself of a will of such great consequence. He also refused a distant cousin's attempt to retrieve the papers in order to lay claim to the estate. Marie eventually retrieved the documents before she died in 1781 and entrusted them to Antoine Bigou, the village priest. Bigou had been François's assistant in many private and business matters, so we can assume that he would have been well aware of the Hautpoul holdings, land, titles and the like.'

'And mines,' I said.

'Good point, and presumably the genealogy and any "big secrets" the family held. The problem for Antoine Bigou came several years later in 1789 during the French Revolution. The country was in chaos and the Church under attack. Priests and bishops who refused to swear the oath of fidelity to the new order faced dismissal, deportation or even death along with members of the nobility. Mass drowning was a favoured execution method reserved for priests. Many of them fled to Spain, including Abbé Bigou and Abbé François-Pierre Caneuille, the priest of Rennes les Bains. Bigou didn't know if he could ever return. According to the story, he couldn't risk taking the documents with him, so he hid them in the church, hoping that in the future someone with the necessary knowledge would find them – most likely a priest. There is also a theory that Bigou told the "great secret" to Abbé Caneuille, who passed it on to the Abbé Jean Vié, the parish priest of Rennes-les-Bains from 1840 to 1870, and the Abbé Emile François Cayron, the parish priest of St Laurent de la Cabrerisse in the Aude, at the same period. Abbé Henri Boudet succeeded Jean Vié, so it is highly likely that Abbé Jean Vié would have passed the secret on to Boudet.'

'So you are saying that there may have been a network of priests who knew about the "secret" and handed the information down by word of mouth.'

'Yes, it's highly possible. Transmission of important information by word of mouth was widely practised.'

'There were over ten priests at Rennes-le-Château between the time Bigou left and Saunière took over,' I said. 'Why weren't the documents discovered sooner?'

'France was in turmoil during and after the revolution. It seems that they weren't discovered until the church renovations started. However, it is also possible that Saunière was one of a select group of priests who were told the secret and he knew what to look for.'

'And the genealogies?' I said.

'One was dated from 1244 and bore the seal of Blanche de Castille and the other was a genealogy for François-Pierre d'Hautpoul dated 23 November 1644 and was signed by Captier. Apparently, they establish a link to the Merovingian bloodline and prove that Dagobert II's son Sigisbert IV survived his father in 681 and was taken to safety in his mother's hometown of Rennes-le-Château, or Rhedae as it was known then. If that is true, then it is possible that he went on to become lord of the region and father his own dynasty, thus continuing the Merovingian bloodline amongst the nobles of the region. The Merovingians were known as "priest kings" or "sorcerer kings" with a divine right to rule. It is possible they were descended from King David, even from Jesus and Mary Magdalene through intermarriage.'

'The sangreal theory,' I said.

'Exactly. This is widely disputed by professional archaeologists and historians of course. However, if it could be proven that he did survive, his tomb may even be in the vicinity. According to the theory, the Knights Templar discovered the original sangreal genealogy inscribed on the walls of an underground room beneath the Temple of Solomon.

They brought this information back to the south of France, where the bloodline already existed and continued through intermarriage. The Knights Templar and members of the sangreal families were responsible for keeping the information safe and hidden – not revealing it even in the face of death.'

'But without the actual documents, it is impossible to prove,' I said.

'True, but remember that in Saunière's time there was a strong movement attempting to reinstate the monarchy. The last heir to the throne, the Count de Chambord, died in 1884 – if a bloodline from Dagobert was alive and kicking in the south of France, it would have changed the course of French history. It would have equally been sensational news in 1791, when Saunière's predecessors fled the Revolution to Spain.'

'So you really believe this is part of the big secret?' I said. 'Doesn't that mean that the Merovingian bloodline may have survived to this day with a legitimate claim to the French throne?'

'Yes, Gerard.' Enzo nearly jumped out of his chair. 'Yes, the royal bloodline, the Merovingian line had a legitimate claim to the French throne, then and now.'

'Surely someone must have had access to these documents from 1644 to 1781,' I said. 'If they were that important, copies would have been made. What lawyer could resist keeping secret such information that could potentially change the course of history?'

18

The information

'Let's assume that Saunière found hidden information with significant religious and political implications,' said Enzo. 'He was a local – he knew the history of the region, the stories about the Merovingian bloodline, the history of the Cathar persecution, the Knights Templar and all the various treasures. After all, his church was dedicated to Mary Magdalene. Given the politics of the day, a Catholic priest holding that information in his hands would have been sensational. It is information that was deliberately and violently suppressed for hundreds of years by the Church. Saunière would know that there are people who would do and give anything to get their hands on it and he knows that his life is now in danger.'

'He can sell the information, for a good price of course.' I said. 'However, there's a dilemma: now two people know about it. Can the buyer trust him to keep the secret? It's hard to say, so his life is in danger. Theoretically, he could sell the information again, to a second buyer, as long as the two buyers don't know each other. However, that becomes an even riskier business. Saunière had a reasonably regular source of revenue. Will the buyer pay again for something he has already bought?'

'Unlikely, unless he decides to blackmail the buyer,' said Enzo.

'You mean, like the Vatican, as some researchers have suggested. If the information was that explosive, do you honestly think that Saunière would have lived as long as he did? If anyone wanted things kept quiet, they would have silenced him far more cheaply, efficiently and permanently. The Church has been silencing inconvenient truths for centuries.'

'Of course there's always the "nuclear stand-off" concept,' said Enzo. 'Andrews and Schellenberger say that the possession of weapons of guaranteed mutual annihilation ensures a rather nervous insecure peace only when both sides are aware of each other's capabilities.'

'In my view, Saunière having access to cash over a long period of time shows that the source of his money had nothing to do with the sale of secret information,' I said. 'So if we rule out that theory, what else do we have to account for his money? The case for treasure and the body of Christ is full of holes. Surely, as a lawyer, you would find it hard to prove. The only verifiable evidence we have to account for his income over and above his priest's stipend and his own savings is that he claims to have received some money from the Countess of Chambord, gifts from donors who preferred to stay anonymous, and money that was paid into his housekeeper's account by Abbé Boudet. He even said he won a lottery. We know there was money from trafficking in masses, but some researchers agree that none of it comes anywhere near to accounting for his actual expenditure.'

'Donations to the church from the nobility were very common,' said Enzo. 'France has always been a strong Catholic country and still is today – it was called the "eldest daughter of the Roman Church".'

'The question is still how he makes money from his lucky find,' I said. 'Perhaps the powers that be knew that the land contained something of great importance, and wars, crusades against heresy and a revolution were all used as convenient vehicles to gain control over specific parcels of land in the Languedoc. We need to check the French archives and find out what was happening with the Hautpoul estate through the seventeenth and eighteenth centuries.'

Enzo stood up, picked up the coffee cups and placed them alongside the mountain of dishes in the sink. 'You're right, Gerard. Your evidence throws a new light on the mystery. I need to review everything. We don't have to disprove the other theories in order to prove ours, but if we analyse them through the lens of geology, then maybe we will see them in a different light. Given Saunière's penchant for the good things in life, we know that he was no pious ascetic. I expect as a boy he would have dreamed of finding some Visigoth treasure or a gold nugget.'

'I know I did,' I said.'

Enzo gave me a copy of his book. 'By the way, when she was in Rennes-le-Château, a friend of mine who worked with me on my manuscript gave a copy to Henry Lincoln in 2007. He told her that he wished a better book than *The da Vinci Code* had been written.'

'Did you hear from him?' I said.

'Unfortunately, no.'

'I guess he receives a lot of mail from all sorts of nutters,' I said with a grin.

The following day back in Canberra, I received an email from Enzo saying he had spoken to Jennifer, the friend who had given his manuscript to Henry Lincoln. She was very interested in helping with our project; was I interested? You bet! I shot back a positive response and a commitment to return to South Australia in a couple of months. Enzo's enthusiasm for the project spurred me on. I was re-energised and looking forward to meeting Jennifer.

19

Anticlines and synclines: Adelaide, 2014

After a lot more research and communication via email with Enzo, I was back on the road to Adelaide, this time bearing gifts. For some reason, Rebecca and I had accumulated four cappuccino makers. I brought one for Enzo, complete with several weeks supply of coffee pods. Enzo's eyes lit up when he saw the machine and he set to work making the first of many coffees we would enjoy over the next few days.

Working well into the early hours of the morning, we pored over maps, geological surveys and diagrams. I spread the Department of Mineral Resources Geological Survey map of New South Wales across the table.

'This map spans a hundred-kilometre radius and shows the occurrence of gold in the Bathurst Regional Council. Geologically speaking, all these locations are in close proximity to each other. I've had a bit to do with Hill End Gold Limited – they're still mining gold in the old goldfields around Hill End, Sofala, Hargraves and Maitland Bar, over a hundred and fifty years after the initial gold rush.' I spread a map showing the geological survey of the Big Nugget Hill Project on top of the other map.

'Certain geological environments favour the formation of certain minerals. To put it simply, anticlines and synclines are the places to look for gold. An anticline is a fold of stratified rock in which the strata slopes downwards from the crest. A syncline is a fold of stratified rock in which the strata slopes upwards from the axis. Usually, precipitation of the gold ore happens following the axis of the anticline or the axis of the syncline.'

I pointed to a string of red dots on the map that clearly marked the gold deposits along the anticlines and synclines at Hill End. 'See how the gold is found in relation to quartz reefs on the anticlines. Within a radius of more than a hundred kilometres, the most productive areas are the anticlines and the synclines.' I placed a geological map of the Languedoc on the table.

'OK, now let's compare Hill End with this geological survey from BRGM-Quillan of the Pyrenees. See how the gold deposits coincide with the anticlines and the synclines in the area around Rennes-le-Château and Salsigne. Rennes-le-Château and Rennes les Bains are perfectly situated with the anticlines and synclines axis.[32] Rennes les Bains is located in a synclinal depression squashed between the two anticlines of the Mouthoumet. Rennes-le-Château is miles away from Australia, but the geological situation is remarkably similar. *Voilà* – it's all there,' I said waving my hand across the maps.

Enzo studied the two maps for a moment, glancing from one to the other. 'So you're saying that the geology in both locations favours the formation of gold.'

'Yes, the mineralisation at Hill End is the same as Salsigne: pyrite, quartz, chalcopyrite, pyrrhotite, arsenopyrite, silver and gold. The gold in the Hill End district occurs in quartz veins generally about ten to twenty centimetres wide, but they can range up to thirty to forty centimetres. Some of the veins were followed for more than six hundred metres horizontally. The Star of Peace and Mica veins at Hawkins Hill were followed down for over two hundred metres, but the richest values came from the top hundred and twenty metres. In fact, the largest single piece of reef gold ever discovered in the world, the Beyers and Holtermann nugget, was found in the Star of Hope mine on Hawkins Hill in 1872. It weighed about 286 kilos. Can you believe it? It was one of the largest nuggets ever found, with an estimated gold content of three thousand troy ounces. That's ninety-three kilos. It was worth at least £12,000 at the time. At today's gold price, it would be worth a stunning US$3.6 million. There are also alluvial deposits along the Turon and Macquarie Rivers and other major streams.' I pushed the Hill End map to one side and focused on the French map.

'Salsigne is located in the Languedoc-Rousillon region on the southern edge of the Montagne Noire, the Black Mountain Range, which stretches over seventy kilometres from east to west in central southern France, at the south-western end of the Massif Central. The highest point is the Pic de Nore. Here is Mazamet, where I lived with Taty. Salsigne was the biggest opencast mine in Western Europe. In geological terms it is just a stone's throw from Rennes-le-Château. The geology of Rennes-le-Château is the same as Salsigne. People knew there was gold in the Black Mountains for centuries. It was one of the most important gold regions in France. Analysis over time of hematites, limonites and *terres rouges* or red earth from different locations in that area shows a high content of gold. Carcassonne is here, about fifteen kilometres to the south of the range,' I said, pointing to the famous city on the map. 'There were gold mines around Carcassonne.'

'That's interesting,' said Enzo. 'In 1975, Pierre de Plantard told Henry Lincoln that the secret of Rennes-le-Château was not only at Rennes-le-Château but also around Rennes-le-Château. Plantard bought parcels of land in the area between Blanchefort and Black Rock. He said that the 'so-called' secret lay beneath the Black Rock in a huge underground temple – a former Celtic sanctuary that he called the Temple Rond. That is hotly disputed, but he also mentions an old Roman gold mine around that area. He even published a map of the area in *Vaincre* magazine with the numbers of the various parcels and the access points to the gold and copper mines.[33] Could Plantard's motive have been less esoteric and more, shall I say, down to earth?'

'I think that's more than possible,' I said. 'The gold industry at Salsigne began in 1898 with the exploitation of the deposit in arsenopyrite veins located in the Cambrian shale near Villanière. The other key areas for gold were at La Belliere and La Lucette in the north-west of France, and Le Bourneix, Le Chatelet and Cheni in the centre. Nearly ten and a half tonnes of gold were extracted from La Belliere gold mine between

1905 and 1953. A gold-bearing vein was even discovered in the backyard of the castle of La Belliere by its owner who happened to be an ingenieur des mines. Gold mining at Le Bourneix dates back to Roman times. From 1988 to 2002, gold was produced from several open pit and underground operations. In 1992, they produced more than two thousand kilos of gold. The operations closed when gold prices declined in the early 2000s. Around eleven tonnes of gold were extracted from Le Chatelet between 1905 and 1955, when it closed.'

'It's obvious when you think about it, Gerard,' said Enzo. 'The Celts were in Gaul from about the fifth century BC. They were immensely rich. I've read that there were over four hundred gold mines dating from Celtic times in Gaul alone.'

'Exactly,' I said. 'That's the main reason the Romans invaded Gaul, starting in around 121 BC. They took over the extensive gold mining industry, which the Lemovici people had developed in La Tène, the second Iron Age. They minted gold coins at Lugdunum and at Calagurris in northern Spain from gold mined in those regions. The amount of gold that came into Roman hands actually brought down the value of gold at one stage. Don't forget that the Romans had thousands of slaves at their disposal to exploit the alluvial deposits and mines. The Greek geographer and historian Strabo gives an account of the Tarbelli, who occupied the seacoast from the Pyrenees to the Lake of Arcachon and possessed rich gold mines, finding "masses of gold as big as the fist can contain" often close to the surface and requiring hardly any purifying.[34] People in France in Saunière's day knew of the similarity in geology in the auriferous regions of the world. In 1897, M. Nauric, an engineer working on a plan by the French government to build a railway line through the Black Mountains, noted that the location had the same geological characteristics as gold-producing countries like America, Australia and the Transvaal: quartzsic and cristalic ground.[35] It's no accident that the two main rivers in the Black Mountains are called *l'Orbiel*, which means old gold, and *L'Argent Double*, meaning double silver, which by the way can also mean double money.'

'That's around the same time that gold was discovered at Salsigne,' said Enzo.

'Yes,' I said. I told Enzo the story of the gold deposits in the slag underneath the village of St Martys.

'You're joking,' said Enzo, eyes widening. 'Is it still there?'

'Yes, but impossible to access.'

'Why is that?' said Enzo.

'Simple: the little village of Les Martys is built on top of it.'

Enzo shook his head. 'The Romans would have loved to find the gold. This might be a stupid question, Gerard, but if you were a mining company and knew nothing about the Rennes-le-Château mystery, looking at this map of the Aude, would you think it was worth investing in exploration around Rennes-le-Château?'

'Without question,' I said. 'That and knowing that it's a location where gold has been found in the past. The Aude is riddled with ancient and more recent mines including silver, iron, copper and gold. Today the only evidence of some of these mines is a small entrance, often obscured by rockfalls or scrub. Some of them are so hidden that without modern technology it would be impossible to find them again. You could walk right past one and not even notice. Look, what people don't realise is that just because a mine is abandoned doesn't mean that the gold deposits have been exhausted. Mines close for any number of reasons. The cost of production may have outpaced the price of gold and it becomes uneconomical to mine, the company goes broke, or there may be political upheaval in the country. This has happened many times in France's history. The mines at La Lucette in the north-west of the country were abandoned in 1934 and La Belliere gold mine closed in 1953 because the company went bankrupt. The curious thing is that even though people were taking notice of the geology and the distribution of gold in France in the seventeenth, eighteenth and nineteenth centuries, for a long time it was believed that gold was not exploitable. In 1805, the statistician Jacques Peuchet said that there were no useful gold mines in France and claimed that the gold vein at La Gardette, which was discovered in 1770 and worked up to 1841, was probably the only vein of gold in the country.[36] Then you have the French sceptics who didn't believe there was much gold to be found in the Aude, or geologists and other experts who made all sorts of claims. At one point, the gold at Salsigne was better known overseas than in France. In 1935, a geologist predicted that there was an enormous amount of untapped gold at Salsigne. Do you know what department Rennes-le-Château, Rennes les Bains and Salsigne are in?'

'No.'

'The Aude. Au is the symbol for gold. It comes from the Latin *aurum* and *de* means "of" – it is the department of gold. Is that a coincidence? I don't think so. I wouldn't be surprised if people are exploring the area around Rennes-le-Château right now, assessing the potential to mine payable gold, waiting for the price of gold to go up. With the application of modern advances in exploration techniques, some people in the industry believe that a world-class deposit is still there to be uncovered. Large parts of the main mineral provinces of France are essentially unexplored, just like in Australia.'

'That's sensational, Gerard.'

'I know.'

20

'One day I will make you very rich'

Enzo jumped up and left the room, returning with an armful of books, which he placed on the only spare space left on the table. Each book had sticky notes protruding from the top. He picked up *The Tomb of God*. 'I've been going over everything again looking for clues. This is what Marie Dénarnaud is alleged to have told Noël Corbu: "...with that which the Monsieur has left we could feed Rennes for a hundred years and there would still be enough left over".'

'If you heard that statement from a prospector, you could be sure that they have hit the mother lode or something close to it,' I said. 'At today's value of about US$1,200 per ounce, the takings from Salsigne alone would be worth close to US$5 billion.'

'Five billion – that's hard to visualise,' said Enzo.

'Now Saunière wasn't accessing an opencast mine, but think about it. Gold can be traded for money anywhere at a very good price. Good nuggets on average fetch two and a half times the price of gold on the stock exchange. Usually, the buyer doesn't ask questions, unless it's a large quantity. One ounce in your pocket is really nothing at all, but if you have ten ounces, it makes a big difference. We're speaking about three hundred grams in your pocket and a tenfold value. Collected incognito in the morning or the afternoon, knowing there is plenty more. All Saunière needed was a little pick, something to carry the rocks in, eyes in the back of his head, and a safe place to store what he found.'

'And a willing helper sworn to secrecy,' said Enzo, flipping to another page. '"...one day I will tell you a secret which will make of you a rich man – very, very rich".'

'Let's go back to de Sède's account of what Marie Dénarnaud is alleged to have said,' I said. 'I think she was being quite literal when she said ,"*Les gens du coin marchent sur de l'or, mais ne le savent pas.* People are walking on the gold but they don't know it." Now if she had said *sur l'or*, I would understand that to be a more general comment meaning people are lucky but don't know how fortunate they are. *"Avec celui qu' a laisse le monsieur*, with the one that has been left monsieur" – meaning that there is some left, there is the possibility to go back and get more. *"Nous aurions de quoi nourrir Rennes pendant cent ans et il en resterait.* We could feed Rennes for a hundred years and there would still be some left." It could also explain why the money supply started to run out, and why after Saunière's death in 1917 she was poor, because she couldn't collect the gold. Movement was restricted when World War I started in 1914. Accessing money from foreign accounts was impossible.'

'That would explain his many absences,' said Enzo. 'He had to go somewhere he wasn't known. Imagine going to a dealer in Carcassonne. The word would have spread and Rennes-le-Château would have eventually become another Salsigne. Why did Salsigne close in 2004?'

'All I've been able to find out is that it closed for cleaning. I've emailed one of the Australian geologists who was working at the mine to see if I can find out more.'

The room fell silent.

'How sure are you, Gerard?'

'When I saw the red earth on the way to Rennes-le-Château in 2003, something in my brain just clicked. For some reason, the old goldfields around Bathurst flashed into my mind. Then when I saw the gold mine at Salsigne in 2006, I had this incredible sensation. Just for a second, I imagined Edward Hargraves in 1851, stepping down from his horse at Yorkey's Corner where the Lewis Pond Creek joins the Summer Hill Creek, looking at the scenery before him and having an overwhelming feeling that gold was under his feet. I know that feeling. It is as if somehow you can smell the gold. He had just returned from the Californian goldfields, not with a fortune, but with an insight. In the first few days of digging in California, he was struck by the similarity of the Californian countryside to the countryside he knew so well in New South Wales. The same class of rocks – slates, quartz, granite and the red soil. He was convinced that there was gold in the hills where he had farmed years before in Australia and I've been convinced since 2003 that there is still gold to be found in the land around Rennes-le-Château. Do you know how many specks of gold Hargraves took to the authorities to convince them that there was payable gold on that land?'

'No.'

'They fitted onto a threepenny piece, but it was enough evidence for the authorities to accept his claim and grant him the £10,000 reward offered by the New South Wales government for anyone who found payable gold and claimed it. The colonial secretary was amazed at Hargraves's find, given that the government geologist had not found any native deposits in that area. That was the beginning of the Great Australian gold rush, and the rest, as they say, is history. It went on to be one of the biggest gold rushes in the history of mining. Prospectors came from all over the world to join the rush. Even the French flag flew over the diggings. Coincidentally that's around the time that Bérenger Saunière purchased several plots of land around his church in Marie Dénarnaud's name. We know that Saunière did a lot of digging in and around the church, the cemetery and his estates in Rennes-le-Château. These are on a fault line. In fact, his building work was carried out along the length of the fault line. A recent study of the St Ives goldfields in Western Australia has confirmed that small-scale fault systems in the Earth's crust have a strong correlation with the location of gold and are often the source of rich bonanzas. Apparently, all major gold deposits are controlled by faults, but small fault systems are more likely to lead to gold than larger ones.[37] The configuration of the opencast mine at Salsigne is similar to that at Hill End. The ore in both locations occurs in veins that cross-cut faults. Mining at Hawkins Hill resulted in the discovery of a number of east–west trending faults.'

We sat for a moment looking at the maps and taking in the significance of our theory.

'What I don't get,' said Enzo, 'is how a gold vein could be lost for centuries, then found, then lost again?'

'Easy,' I said. 'Landscapes change, rocks fall naturally and cover an entrance or are deliberately hidden. Floods or earthquakes change the landscape. Old prospectors pass on their secrets on their deathbeds but leave out one vital piece of information, or the listener gets the directions mixed up, they go north instead of south. Landowners blow up old mines because they are too dangerous and costly to preserve. Then there are the decoys – clues that are deliberately planted to lead people down the garden path. I'll give you an example. In 1991, I decided to take a trip to the old gold mine at Burraga in New South Wales, where gold was found in 1901, so close to the surface that people were literally *marchant sur de l'or*. Getting there was a bit tricky. The mine had closed around 1989 and didn't show on my map. I had to rely on my memory and the clues that people had given me. I knew that the mine was on the right-hand side of a straight stretch of dirt road after a bend. The straight stretch goes for about three kilometres before you reach the township of Burraga. Coming out of the bend, I stopped many times and checked my bearings, but couldn't see anything. Eventually, I ended up in Burraga. I turned around and headed back towards the bend, but again I saw nothing and ended up back at the bend. I remembered that someone had told me to look out for an old power line. I turned around and headed back toward Burraga and then I spotted the line on the right. I stopped the car, got out, jumped a low fence and started walking over the scrubby flat land in the direction of the power line. It was hard to imagine that gold had been found there. After about a kilometre, I reached the old pit, half filled with water. Last year, I went back to take photos of the mine. I remembered the dirt road, the bend and the straight stretch of road, but it took a while to find the spot where I had jumped the fence. In ten years, trees had grown and small bushes dotted the landscape. The power line was gone – dismantled. Eventually, I found the mine but it took me ages. Time changes everything: maps become outdated, buildings are gone, witnesses are truly gone, vegetation takes over, memories fade and no one knows the history of the place. This was only ten years on, the mystery of Rennes-le-Château covers centuries of change. In 2012, a mining company was undertaking gold exploration to examine the possibility of a large, high-grade gold resource in Burraga in a geological setting similar to that of the McPhillamy's gold deposit about fifty kilometres to the north. Have you heard the story of Lasseter's lost gold reef?'

'Of course,' said Enzo. 'It's probably the most famous legend, or some would say hoax, in Australia's mining history.'

'Right, well, in 1930 Harold Bell Lasseter told the president of the Australian Workers' Union in Sydney that in 1897, when he was just seventeen years old, he stumbled on a gold reef which he estimated was seven miles long, four to seven feet high and twelve feet wide. He said that he was fossicking for rubies in the western MacDonnell Ranges on his way from Queensland to the Western Australian goldfield. A seven-mile reef of gold – think about it for a moment, Enzo.'

'I am.'

'What comes into your mind first – gold, money or both? If you had the necessary funds, would you be tempted to search for it, or would you keep on dreaming? Nineteen-thirty was the middle of the Great Depression in Australia and only about eighty years after the gold rush in New South Wales. Stories of fabulous nugget finds were still alive in people's minds – a reef of that size would contain unheard of wealth. Lasseter's story seemed to stack up. Private funding was secured for an expedition and the group set out into the harsh country of the Northern Territory. There were all sorts of logistical difficulties, extreme physical hardship and many disagreements. Days dragged on, they found nothing and at one point Lasseter disagreed with the direction the leader wanted to head. Finally, they declared that Lasseter was a charlatan and the group ended the expedition, leaving Lasseter with a dingo-shooter and his team of camels to continue the search. According to the story, one afternoon Lasseter returned to their camp with some concealed rock samples announcing that he had found the gold reef but he refused to reveal the location. There was a fight and Lasseter was left to his own devices. The poor bloke died of malnutrition and exhaustion. There have been many explorations searching for the reef, but it has never been found.'

'If it does exist, where do you think it is, Gerard?'

'If I knew, do you think I would be alive now?'

Enzo thought for a moment. He drained the last drop of coffee from his mug. 'So how much gold do you think could be left in the Aude, in the ground untouched?'

'Who knows, Enzo, who knows? But remember, don't tell anyone, hey.'

21

Secrets and lies

In 1995, gold prospector George Dimitrovski pulled a 6.6-kilogram gold nugget from the red dirt around Marble Bar in the Iron Ore Triangle in Western Australia. Grant and his wife packed the nugget in a plastic crate and headed towards civilisation.[38]

George said that at that time he didn't want to cash it in, because he did not feel like he needed the money. Forgetting the most important rule of prospecting, the couple showed the nugget to a publican mate in Carnarvon, who displayed it to his customers. Not surprisingly, fellow prospectors were keen to discover the location of the find. Some even contacted police, believing that George may have illegally poached the nugget from one of their leases. George said he didn't want to reveal the spot because he believed it would spark a gold rush on his lease and instead said that it was found on vacant Crown land. A court case that went all the way to the Supreme Court followed. In May 2000, after a costly legal battle, the finders were declared the nugget's rightful owners.

At today's gold price, the Millennium Nugget, as it is known, is worth about US$254,400. However, big nuggets have a special value, so the nugget could fetch between two and three times that amount because of beauty and rarity. This could have been Saunière's fate, fighting the state and the Church. He was definitely smarter, observing the secrecy rule to the end.

Since I last talked with Michel the Corsican, I had found out that the French police were continuing to investigate the case of the Treasure of

Lava. According to official information, the state had traced and identified less than a hundred of the coins, which had been sold illegally in Europe and the US. More than four thousand coins found, but only a hundred or so in state hands. Where are those beautiful coins? The reality is that most of them would be impossible to trace. Identifying the location of one or ten is a casse tête, a nightmare for the cops. Would you tell if you had some in your drawer? The authorities hadn't given up trying to find the rest of the haul. Details of the missing coins were added to Interpol's database. Specialist dealers and collectors were warned about the illegal sale of the ancient Roman gold coins and plates, after a number of items were recovered from the open market. More people were arrested in Paris. Police suspected that there had been a secret sale involving a buyer in Belgium. Authorities launched an investigation and arrested the intermediary in the sale at the train station at Charles de Gaulle airport. One of the three divers died in a shooting in 2004. I imagined the new lifestyle of the finders and sellers – the ones who got away with it, that is.

If anyone had found a significant treasure cache around Rennes-le-Château, it is very unlikely he or she would advertise it. The problem for the finder is to sell it without losing any, if not all, of its value . The French authorities are dogged in their pursuit of lost treasure. Better to keep their mouths shut in order to bypass any state rules; once it has been reported, it is too late. As we say in French, '*Faites vos jeux, rien ne va plus*. All bets down, the wheel is now turning.'

As in treasure hunting, secrecy is of the utmost importance in minerals exploration. The right word in the wrong ear can result in disaster, or even worse. Some people will go to great lengths – even kill. Then again, the wrong word in the right ear is commonly used to divert attention away from what is really going on.

Geologist Grant Boxer tells the story of the Argyle diamond find in 1979.* Grant was working for CRA Exploration (CRAE) in Western

---

* Retold here with permission from Grant Boxer.

Australia at the time of the find. He was there when Ashton Joint Venture* pulled out all the stops to ensure secrecy.

Grant was involved with reconnaissance stream sediment sampling in the East Kimberley and testing magnetic targets in the West Kimberley. He was relocated to the exploration camp in the East Kimberley before the pegging of the Argyle diamond pipe. Sampling involved collecting about forty kilos of gravel less than four millimetres in size from heavy mineral trap sites, where heavy minerals like gold, garnet, ilmenite, chromite and diamond accumulate. The area was very remote in a steep mountain range with almost no roads and tracks. Initially, access was only by helicopter – Bell JetRangers were the most widely used, followed by Squirrels and Hughes 500 aircraft.

In August 1979, the company discovered diamonds in two reconnaissance stream samples collected in Smoke Creek, one ten kilometres and the other twenty kilometres downstream from what we now know as the Argyle pipe, the motherlode. This was a very unexpected result. It was more common to find indicators than diamonds. Mineral observer Lyn Tagliaferri found the first diamonds. To find a number of diamonds in these initial samples was very exciting. She actually thought that they were test diamonds put in by the mineralogist; a common practice designed to check the efficiency of the mineral observers. You can imagine what happened when she said to the mineralogist, 'I found those test diamonds.' Management scrambled to locate the source. Secrecy was critical so that no one else heard about the diamonds and pegged the area.

Uranerz, another exploration company, held a mining tenement for uranium in part of the area that CRAE wanted to peg for diamonds exploration. CRAE knew that the Uranerz tenement was about to expire. They had a person at the Mines Department in Perth waiting for the notification that the tenement had expired. As soon as this occurred,

---

* Ashton Joint Venture was an exploration project managed by CRA Exploration (CRAE now Rio Tinto Exploration) and including Ashton Mining (purchased by Rio Tinto in 2000) and Northern Mining Corporation.

CRAE jumped into action and pegged the area around the Argyle pipe. The exploration tenements were pegged over the area in late October. Pegging involved erecting corner posts at the four corners of the rectangular mineral claims and intermediate pegs every three hundred metres along the boundaries between the corner pegs. Daily temperatures were around 40°C, with energy-sapping high humidity. Any metallic item placed on the ground for more than ten seconds became extremely hot and difficult to pick up again. Occasional thunderstorms could dump anything up to fifty millimetres of rain in a short time. The base camp was well stocked with equipment, vehicles and helicopters, which were accumulated while waiting for the all clear to pegging.

The operations manager purchased all the available topographic maps of the area and hired all the available four-wheel drive vehicles and most of the helicopters from the region. This was designed to slow down any other exploration company from competing with the pegging. A large area of tenements was pegged in the West Kimberley area, some thousand kilometres to the south-west of Argyle, to throw other companies off the scent of the Argyle discovery. The only forms of communication between the camp and Perth, about three thousand kilometres to the south, were by HF radio or by party-line telephone. Both of these were open communication lines and anyone could listen in on phone or radio calls. All communication that dealt with the pegging of the new find was in code, or from a more secure phone line in Kununurra about forty-five minutes away.

Argyle went on to become the largest diamond producer in the world by volume. More than ninety per cent of the world's rare pink diamonds and all of its hydrogen-rich violet diamonds come from the mine.[39]

The incredible story of the race to secure the site, the decoy created a thousand kilometres away from the centre of the action, the number of people involved and the cost, is an example of the lengths that some people will go to when the stakes are high.

22

Lunch at number 18

The next day, we travelled to the other side of the city to visit Enzo's friends, Jennifer and her husband Mario. The house was a Mount Gambier stone-fronted 1920s 'gentleman's bungalow'. It was clear that Jennifer and Mario were keen gardeners. The back garden was equally as impressive as the front. The branches of a huge walnut tree hung over a wisteria-covered gazebo; persimmon, avocado and mango trees jostled for space.

Jennifer flung open the French doors and greeted us with hugs and kisses. She wore a vintage- style frock, which she later told me she made from one of her grandmother's original 1960s dress patterns. The doors opened onto a large family room and kitchen.

There is an old saying that the only jewel for a lady is a naked diamond, but for now the chocolates and wine I bought on the way would have to do.

The table looked like it was set for a banquet.

'*Mon dieu* – how many are we expecting?' I said.

'Just us,' she laughed. 'This is a special occasion.'

She insisted that we all sit down as she brought plates of food from the kitchen and placed them at the end of the table: rustic spinach pie, eggplant lasagne and salad accompanied by crusty bread and red wine. It was a real feast.

'I hope you like vegetarian food. Enzo's a vegetarian,' she said, smiling at Enzo.

She had texted me a couple of days previously and asked me if there was any food that I did not eat; tripe and shellfish was my response.

We talked about the old days. Like me, Mario and Enzo had immigrated to Australia from Europe, Mario from the province of Campania on the Sorriento in 1956 when he was nine years old and Enzo from Abruzzi when he was just three.

'It wasn't all smooth sailing for me,' I said. 'In fact, at one point I was so desperate to leave I ended up being a stowaway.'

Enzo scooped another serving of the eggplant lasagne onto his plate, and mine.

'So you stowed away on a ship from Paris,' said Jennifer, eyes widening.

'Well, actually it was the other way round: it was from Sydney hoping to get to England trouble-free. I came to Australia as an immigrant in 1967 for the cost of ten English pounds. I flew from Paris to London, stayed overnight in a really nice hotel paid for by the Australian government and left the next day flying to Bombay, then on to Darwin, eventually landing in Melbourne. From there, I went by bus to the Bonegilla migrant camp. It was Australia's first post-war immigration camp opened in 1947.'

'What was it like?' said Jennifer.

'We were well looked after. The people were very understanding, especially given that a lot of us couldn't speak English. I had made a friend on the plane out, a French guy. After about a week, we decided to go to Sydney to find a job. We were told to go to the Villawood Camp as a base. It wasn't like Bonegilla, it was depressing and miles away from the centre of Sydney. Some days we hitchhiked to Sydney, wandering around, spending time in coffee shops and looking for any opportunities to earn money. After two weeks of the same routine, we finally got a job in a factory putting chemicals into twenty-kilo bags.'

Mario shook his head. 'The last job I had like that was coating the inside of containers with epoxy resin.'

'Well, we lasted two weeks. I thought, I've left a city like Paris to end up in a place like Villawood.'

'Oh, my god, that's insane,' said Jennifer, passing me the salad.

'Anyway, one weekend we were walking the streets out of boredom and some guys in their big cars started throwing raw eggs at us, most probably because we were dressed differently.'

'I know how that feels,' said Mario. 'I used to hang out with the surf lifesavers down at Semaphore beach. That was the time of the bodgies and widgies. I was always being picked on. Lucky I had the Arctic Wolf Pack protecting my back.'

'So that's when my friend Jean Paul and I decided to head back to France. Of course, I had no money for the fare so I called my grandmother asking for a loan of $400, which I would pay back, hoping to get my old job back at Moto Presse. I received a letter saying that the money was on its way and should be in the Banque Nationale de Paris within three weeks. I booked my fare with an old Jewish guy who had a dingy little office in the back of George Street. I told him that the money for the fare would be in my bank account very soon. The deal was done and he gave me two visitor passes for the ship.'

'Which ship?' said Mario.

'The *Castel Felice*.'

'I know the *Castel Felice*. It's in the Italian fleet,' said Mario. 'I think it used to come to Port Adelaide.'

'The only problem was that on the day of departure from Sydney the money was not in my account. However, we had the two visitor passes, so Jean Paul and I decided to go aboard anyway. The atmosphere was incredibly exciting, a mix of joy and sadness. The funny thing was that we were part of it. Unbelievably, when the towboat started towing the ship out into the harbour, we just stayed on board. After about five minutes, we could feel the towboat slowing down. Then the ship stopped in the middle of the harbour. We looked over the rails and saw a police boat heading towards us – that's when we started to panic. We weren't sure if we had been noticed.'

'What did you do?' said Jennifer frowning.

'Hey, we had no tickets. We were stowaways, illegals. When the police boat got to the ship, we saw crew members lowering a guy down onto the boat with ropes. We weren't the only ones without a ticket. He must have been hiding in the lower part of the ship. He was unlucky. We felt sorry for him. The police boat left and we sailed out onto the high sea. After a couple of hours, our problems began. The crowd from the open decks started to disappear. It was getting dark – we were sitting on the deck with very little money in our pockets, no drinks, no food and knowing we had no access to the bar, the dining room or anywhere else for that matter. We didn't know what to do, but youth was in our favour. Then I heard a French accent. Three girls sitting behind us were speaking English, but we could tell from the accent of one that she was French. We were kind of waiting for that opportunity. We didn't take long to engage in conversation. After all, we were young, good-looking guys. They were young and pretty – just what we needed: a contact, someone who could help. Our main thoughts were drinks, food and a place to sleep, in that order.'

'Are you sure that was all?' said Jennifer.

'*Mais oui*, of course, we really didn't want to get them into trouble. The girls threw question at us like "Where are you going?" "Wherever" was our answer. We were very cagey. Eventually we told them we didn't have tickets. Well, they thought that was very exciting "Wow, wow, wow" came their reply. Well, it wasn't really exciting for us, we said. Then in the middle of the conversation, the French girl disappeared, only to reappear few minutes later with sandwiches and coffee. Then as a chorus they shouted, "But where are you sleeping?" "Don't know," we said. "Well, you can sleep in our cabin." It was a tempting solution but we couldn't accept. I can tell you that they were disappointed, but we told them that if we were found sleeping in their cabin they would be an accessory for helping two stowaways, which could put them in big trouble. For two nights, we walked the ship. In the mornings, the girls brought us coffee and food. At lunchtime, we went to their cabin to shower and shave. We only had the clothes that we were wearing, but we looked clean. By the third night, we were getting apprehensive, feeling that the Italian crew was suspicious of us, so around midnight we decided to give ourselves up. We knocked on the door of the ship's bridge. The duty officer opened the door and told us to come back the next day as it was the wrong time for a tour of the ship. "No," we said. "We have no tickets." He went silent then got on the phone. A few minutes later, another officer took us to an empty cabin which could accommodate six people. He told us to have a good night then locked us up. It was a fantastic night, warm beds, clean sheets and a bathroom – we slept like babies.'

I continued, 'Around nine the next morning, the door opened and a big Italian guy walked in carrying a large tray. "*Alors*, little French clandestines, had a good sleep?" I think he took pity on us. "Yes" we replied. "Here you are," he said, putting the tray on the table. Wow, we thought, the tray had everything a five-star hotel would have: coffee, hot chocolate, croissants, brioches, jam, buttered bread, fried eggs and bacon – what a feast. At eleven a.m., we had to face the ship's captain. After presenting our papers, including our passports, French IDs and French driving licences, I told him that my fare was booked on his ship and that I was waiting for the money but it hadn't come through in time for my tickets and all we had were visitor passes. He was very kind and told us that he had no other option than to put us in the ship's hospital, which was going to be our cabin for the next two days until we reached Auckland in New Zealand. The voyage from Sydney to Auckland took five days in total. A crew member escorted us to our "cabin". There were six beds, a table, shelves and a handbasin – in other words, very comfortable. Within about half an hour, two crew members came in with two English stowaways, guys about our age. They must have been found after the ship's departure from Sydney and the unloading of the guy on the police boat. They had been in the ship's gaol but I think the captain had a soft heart and felt that putting us together meant we would have company. An hour later, a crew member brought us playing cards, a chess board, books, magazines, toothpaste and brushes, soft drinks, coffee, tea, sugar, milk and cigarettes. Most of the day consisted of reading, playing cards and chess, drinking coffee and smoking cigarettes. We were well looked after. The holiday had started, thanks to our captain. Before we got off the ship, the captain and one of the crew came to say goodbye. To our great surprise, they gave us each a large paper bag with all necessary things like coffee, sugar, toothpaste, biscuit, fruit and cigarettes. Leaving the ship and this captain was very emotional. I will never forget it.'

'Don't you love the Italians,' said Jennifer, leaning over to Mario and resting her hand on his arm.

'Our holiday ended when we got to Auckland. A police car was waiting for us like in the movies, where the cop car is waiting next to plane for the gangsters. Our "taxi" was ready to take us to the main police station. At the station, they separated us into two groups, putting one English and one French speaker together. Obviously, it was a little trick to make communication difficult for us. However, we went to town in the police car with two officers who kindly bought us burgers and chips for lunch, then took us on a little tour of the city. At four p.m., they took Jean Paul and me to the airport, destination Sydney. When we landed, two officers came onto the plane, handcuffed us and told us to stay on the plane until all passengers had disembarked. We got off the plane with everybody looking at us, as if we were criminals. They took us to the police station at Circular Quay in the harbour and because it was a Friday we ended up in a cell for the weekend. Each day, we were fed with different burgers, but the same chips. However, we didn't complain. Everyone was kind to us, the weather was beautiful and we were in high spirits. On the Monday, we went to court in the same building. The judge asked us if we had the money to pay for the trip to Auckland and the return flight from Auckland to Sydney. Someone rang the French bank and it was confirmed that the money was in my account so I paid for both of us and that was it, we were free to go. The funny thing was that when we gave ourselves up Jean Paul told me that if I ever met his parents not to tell them about our adventure because his father was high up in the police force in the town of Tours. What we didn't know then was that the captain had already contacted Jean Paul's father informing him of our adventure, saying that it was regrettable, and although we had been irresponsible, we were nice polite boys and most of all very respectable.'

'What a fantastic story, Gerard,' said Jennifer. 'It seems you were destined to come to Australia.'

'Oh, I have many more of them, Jennifer, but now we do the dishes.'

23

The coded parchments – fake or real?

Jennifer, Enzo and I moved to the elegant formal dining room at the front of the house. Deep maroon curtains framed the window seat that looked out onto the rose garden. A print of Leonardo's *Annunciation* hung above a 1930s sideboard topped with antique books. I half expected a clue to a hidden meaning to jump out at me from the painting. Jennifer had reapplied her red lipstick, which perfectly matched the colour of the roses on her dress; she took centre stage.

'Any investigation needs to examine three things – motive, opportunity and means,' she said with a theatrical flourish. 'Bérenger Saunière was a small town priest in a big black cassock…'

'It's called a soutane in French,' I said.

'…a soutane, who presumably has taken a vow of chastity and poverty…'

'I think you mean celibacy not chastity,' said Enzo. 'There's a very practical reason that priests were celibate – no offspring to inherit their wealth if they had any. Everything went to the Church.'

Jennifer smiled and gave him a quick glance, '…tall, well built with dark eyes, handsome – the sort of man that a woman could swoon over. Handy around the church and in the cemetery. An artist and an author – well read. He fished, hunted, and went for long walks in the countryside to collect rocks. Protector of the faith or heretic? A man caught between a rock and hard place, or a pope and a holy place. Who was Bérenger Saunière and how did he go from poverty to fabulously wealthy almost overnight?' Jennifer looked at both of us in turn as if expecting applause then burst into laughter.

'Sounds like we're writing a detective novel,' I said.

'Well, all the elements are there,' said Jennifer, resuming her seat. 'Corbu, de Sède, Plantard and de Chérisey were all writers. Noël Corbu did write detective novels before he wrote about the millionaire priest.'

'Remember,' I said, 'that much of Corbu's and de Sède's information came from oral sources, family memories, and legends and we all know how unreliable they can be. I'm not saying that people lied, but there's a certain glamour in being a part of the mystery.'

'OK, so let's consider the parchments,' said Enzo straight-faced, looking up from his smartphone. 'The treasure and bloodline theories rely heavily on the existence of the coded parchments in de Sède's book.'

Jennifer leaned forward, resting her elbows on the table. 'The provenance of the parchments is highly doubtful, don't you think? The story changes depending on who is telling it and at what time in history it is being told. Corbu didn't mention parchments – it's possible they are a huge red herring, an elaborate hoax cooked up by de Chérisey, de Sède and Plantard in the 1960s. De Sède admitted that he had never seen originals.'

'There is a story that original parchments do exist and are with the Knights of Malta,' said Enzo. 'Patrice Chaplin believes that parchments existed but that the ones in de Sède's book are not the originals. She was connected to a secret society in Spain in the 1950s and believes that the original versions were coded instructions indicating the location of certain mysterious material and would have been copied and changed many time since 1891.'

'However,' said Jennifer, 'there was a view at the time that they were crude attempts at imitating certain literary manuscripts of the early Middle Ages. According to Henry Lincoln, Plantard eventually told him that de Sède had engaged de Chérisey to fake the parchments to add authenticity to the story. De Chérisey described how he fabricated them, how the ciphers were set and how to decode them – he even called himself the prankster.'

'Indeed,' said Enzo. 'But Plantard later said that the real parchments were in London.'

'I know,' said Jennifer. 'However, seven years before his death in 2000, Plantard admitted under oath that he had invented the whole thing and the documents were forgeries – *voilà*.'

'No one has ever seen the originals,' I said, 'because in my view they don't exist. De Chérisey even admitted to faking them in a letter to the writer Pierre Jarnac.'

'What if that letter was a fake?' said Jennifer.

'This is starting to sound like a plot from the Marx Brothers,' said Enzo frowning.

'Look, there's more recent evidence that the parchments were faked,' said Jennifer. 'In 2008, Italian researcher Mariano Tomatis presented a detailed intertextual analysis of the Shepherdess parchment – the one with the reference to Poussin and Teniers. It shows that the text is the result of the fusion of two elements: a long Latin text taken from the Gospel of Saint John (12:1–11) in the Vulgate translation and at least three shorter messages from Wordsworth and White's *Nouum Testamentum Latine* published in Oxford in 1889, which have been inserted in the text.[40] Tomatis suggests that perhaps de Sède and his colleagues wanted to attract the same level of publicity for their parchments that the discovery of the Dead Sea Scrolls had resulted in. He suggests that their aim was to prove Plantard's claims that the Priory of Sion was a medieval society – the source of the underground stream of esotericism in Europe. You know they were into surrealism.'

'Who?' said Enzo.

'Who's on first?' said Jennifer smiling. 'De Sède and Chérisey were surrealist writers. Chérisey was a member of the surrealist movement called Oulipo – one of the Marx brothers was also a member. They did all sorts of weird things – mixing fact and fiction, using quirky writing techniques, creating complex codes and cryptograms, hidden symbolism in paintings and literature and ingenious wordplay – sound familiar? Their stated aim was to liberate the imagination by creating alternative realities in their art and literature. If the mystery is a hoax, then it's pure surrealist gold.'

'So the aim was to suck people in,' I said.

'Well, I guess you could interpret it that way,' said Jennifer. 'The chief archivist of the Aude suggested that de Sède might have been trying to create a humorous pastiche, a joke, more than a counterfeit document. Jean Luc Robin says playing jokes and creating hoaxes is part of Rennie culture, but to a surrealist, the hoax is elaborate performance art – there's no tag line, it's an end in itself. Oulipo was a subcommittee of the College of Pataphysics. Their aim was to subvert reality by building alternative worlds with imaginary solutions. Part of the technique is to see how the public reacts, and the hoax is never revealed. According to Tomatis, it's like a game with no rules that doesn't have an end point and new players keep on entering the game – just like us.'

'So why did they eventually spill the beans?' I said.

'I don't think they imagined how successful they would be,' said Jennifer. 'Eventually, they fell out over money and book royalties, and all sorts of accusations started flying back and forth.'

'So Dr Jean Girou makes the first reference to treasure in his 1936 article,' said Enzo. 'Corbu picks up the theme in 1956 as part of his marketing strategy to drum up custom for his hotel. Then when de Chérisey, Plantard and de Sède come onto the scene, one or all of them cook up a plan to add authenticity to the plot by creating the coded parchments. De Chérisey does the job, and captures the public's attention for decades. It's brilliant.'

'Or it's a cover story to divert attention away from what was really going on,' I said.

'If it was revealed so early in the piece that the parchments were faked, why would people keep pushing the parchments story?' said Jennifer.

'Because they make the story sell,' I said. 'People love the idea of old parchments that reveal hidden truths that change our view of the world. Treasure hunting 101: "the mysterious coded parchment". De Sède even tried to trick Lincoln into believing they had access to Saunière's treasure. He sent him a photo of what he purported to be the treasure. Turns out it was a photo of the treasure of Petroassa that had been reversed.'[41]

'If the whole thing is a hoax, or a cover story, then who can we believe?' said Jennifer, raising both hands and shrugging.

'We're assuming that if it's a hoax, it's a modern-day hoax,' I said. 'In my view, whoever created those documents went to a lot of trouble, too much trouble for a simple hoax. What if the hoaxer was much closer to the scene of the crime, so to speak?'

Jennifer and Enzo both looked at me.

'Yes, Saunière,' I said. 'Think about it

'Oh, very Agatha Christie,' said Jennifer, picking up her copy of Jean Luc Robin's book and flicking to a page with a yellow sticky note protruding from the top. 'You could be right. Architect Paul Saussez is certain that Saunière found the tomb of the Lords of Rennes in 1891. Its existence is confirmed in the parish register kept by the priests of Rennes between 1694 and 1726, which Claire Corbu and Antoine Captier found amongst Saunière's papers.[42] He also includes a copy of writing by Jean Bigou, Antoine Bigou's uncle. He was the priest of Rennes-le-Château from 1736 to 1774: "Beneath the altar in the church at Rennes-le-Château there is a chamber in which are tombs dating from the time of the ancient kings [sic] as well as documents, which must not fall into unintended hands. For this reason I have had the access to this crypt sealed."[43] He also includes a copy of an extract written by the priest of Saint Just Le Bezu stating that the "tomb of the seigneurs" is beside the baluster.[44] Why would Antoine Bigou need to hide a message in a phial in a column if his uncle Jean had written a note in the parish register stating that there were amazing documents in the crypt under the church that must not fall into certain hands? Oh, and also the crypt is beside the baluster.' Jennifer closed the book and placed it gently on the oak dining table, brushing her hand lightly across the cover.

'He didn't,' I said. 'Because in my view Saunière did.'

24

What would you do?

'What would you do if you stumbled on a gold vein?' I said. 'Think about it.'

The room fell quiet.

'Saunière is an intelligent man,' I said. 'He knows about the treasure legends, but he also knows something about the history of gold in these parts. Let's assume that during one of his walks in the countryside, for whatever reason, he stumbles upon a gold vein.'

'As one does,' said Jennifer with a smile.

'Believe me, it does happen,' I said. 'What is the most important rule of prospecting?'

'Secrecy.' said Enzo.

'Exactly. His next steps require serious consideration. Should he share the secret with someone close or keep it to himself?'

'It would depend on whether he needed any help,' said Enzo.

'Yes, that's certainly part of it. Let's try to understand his way of thinking. He's a priest, living in a village where everybody is spying on everybody, as if there is nothing else to do, and believe me, there is nothing else to do.'

'Well, his housekeeper Marie Dénarnaud was in on the secret,' said Jennifer. 'And as far as we know she maintained it to her deathbed.'

'I can understand that,' said Enzo. 'She was dedicated to him for years and used to help him on his jaunts into the countryside. The question is whether he told anyone else, or whether in fact anyone else already knew.'

'Collecting gold requires some physical strength,' I said. 'Bérenger was well suited to the task – he loved walking and could carry heavy loads. We know that he and Marie would pack a picnic then set off, he with a grape picker's basket on his back. The story we assume that he told the villagers was that he was collecting rocks for the grotto he built by the *calvaire* in front of the church, a common practice at that time. Apparently, he and Marie would arrive back in the evening looking dishevelled and with the basket full of rocks, wood – anything as part of the cover. When I am prospecting, all I carry is a small pick and a backpack. All he needed was a little pick. He could have easily carried gold in his pockets. You would be astonished at the value of two pockets full of gold. Then not long afterwards he starts to spend lots of money.'

'Guy Patton writes that according to the villagers he also took rocks into a secret part of the sacristy after he returned from his walks in the surrounding hills,' said Jennifer. 'Even Jean Luc Robin says that collecting the rocks was probably some sort of cover. Some say that he was going to a place above the Couleurs Stream. It's near a cave called the Grotte du Fournet, which was also called Cave de la Madelaine – you can see it from the top of the Tour Magdala. If you line up the corner opposite the turret with the little window, there is an alignment that falls exactly onto this grotto. They also say that he walked towards Rennes les Bains, through the forest of l'Homme Mort, the Dead Man, then jumped across the small stream of La Blanque and climbed up the hillside of Serbaïrou towards la Pierre du Pain, the Stone of Bread on which it was said the Devil had left his fingerprints. There is an entry in his diary on 29 December 1891 that says, "*Vais au Bal, douleur des reins*" and that's where he went on his rock collecting jaunts. What does that mean, Gerard?'

'Going to the ball, pain in my back, or pain in the back,' I said. 'Of course he has pain in the back with all that rock collecting. Now I don't think for one minute he was going to the ball. Perhaps it's a reference to the Valley of the Bals, south of the village, where the Ruisseau de Couleurs flows. The rock face there is studded with grottoes, and natural faults go back into the rock, forming galleries and chambers. He later bought a piece of land on this spot. Let's assume he found the gold vein. He's excited, he knows it will bring him cash, but he must keep his cool and wait. The mining and prospecting laws of the day state that minerals are the property of the government, not the finder or the landowner unless they hold a licence. He has a huge problem – what he is doing is illegal. He cannot sell it for money yet, because going from poor to rich without a reason doesn't happen instantly. If he suddenly starts spending as if he's the local nobility, it becomes a questionable affair. People will be suspicious, assuming he's done something dishonest. I know what it's like in those small villages: gossiping is the main occupation. Everybody is hiding behind their curtains or shutters, watching who is coming in and who is going out, what they are doing, who they are talking to.'

'I know what that feels like,' said Jennifer. 'When Mario and I visited family in a little village in Calabria, people went inside and peeped through their lace curtains.'

'Holders of secrets are constantly aware of the need to keep certain audiences from learning a specific version of events,' I said. 'He must elaborate a believable scenario to account for the wealth he is about to come into – something full of mystery that correlates with all the legends about hidden treasure. When he is satisfied with the amount of ore he has collected, he hides it until it is time to sell. But first he must establish the ruse.'

'He's an educated man,' said Enzo. 'He knows Latin, Greek and a little Hebrew. This tale has to relate to the history of the region, the Church, the religious wars, Solomon's treasure, the Visigoths, Blanche de Castille, the Knights Templar, the Cathars, the crusades, or anything else as long as it's linked with treasure.'

'*Exactement*. His religious background and knowledge certainly help,' I said. 'What could be better than creating an imaginary treasure? The only thing missing in the story is a treasure map.'

Jennifer and Enzo looked at each other then looked at me.

'Are you saying that Saunière may have created parchments and planted them in the church as a cover story for what was really going on?' said Jennifer.

'Yes, it's possible,' I said. 'Every child knows that the hero finds a treasure map that leads him to the spot. X marks the spot, so they say. What better way than to be seen to find some old parchments hidden somewhere in the church that lead him to a treasure. They only need to be placed where someone can easily find them. Bérenger creates a fictitious and misleading story about an elusive treasure but he knows that someone must actually see the documents for the story to work.'

'Go on,' said Enzo.

'Bérenger was *une grosse tête*, one of the village bigwigs. He knows that the people of these small towns are gullible. According to one version of the story, Saunière's bellringer Captier found parchments in a wooden pillar. They look old and mysterious. After all, someone has gone to the trouble of hiding them in the pillar in the church, the house of God. He goes directly to the priest, thinking it must be important, but to his surprise, Saunière's answer is that it is not important. Captier may have accepted the answer. However, several months later, the priest suddenly starts spending money. Hey, the answer received some months earlier now becomes suspicious, the parchments now become important. Suddenly, the priest's unusual activities start to add up, digging in the cemetery, taking over the renovations of the church himself, the piles of rubble in the church hidden by screens, buying land. The priest must have found a treasure. What else could it be? His decoy is a success, leaving him free to pursue the gold vein. Think about it: a wooden pillar can easily be knocked, damaged, displaced or replaced. Wood breaks, burns or rots, it's definitely not a good hiding place, unless you want someone to find what you're hiding – I smell a rat.'

'There is another possibility,' said Enzo. 'Maybe Saunière was telling the truth when he said the documents in the pillar weren't important. There is a Catholic tradition that when a church is consecrated, a document recording the ceremony is placed inside the *capsa* along with a few relics. Before everything is finally sealed up, the masons add a few coins for good luck.'

'Yes, I suppose that is possible,' I said. 'Nevertheless, it still means the coded parchments are irrelevant. Paul Smith is convinced that Saunière's actual accounts show that he received a huge income from trafficking in masses. It is possible that the 'evidence' of trafficking in masses was part of Saunière's scheme to hide the real source of his income. There are records showing that he made several trips to Lyon and corresponded with a goldsmith and a jeweller. The Fanthorpes write that Saunière made trips abroad taking heavy suitcases with him. Patrice Chaplin has evidence that he was a frequent visitor to a mysterious woman in Girona. There is even a report that after investigating Saunière's death in 1917, the gendarmerie of Couiza spoke of trafficking gold with Spain.[45] If it was me, I would have contacts with several gold dealers – I would not put all my eggs into one basket. It makes sense that he would have several dealers in different cities. Selling ten ounces each time would be a nice amount. Even twenty ounces would be easy to fit in his pocket. Any less than that would require more trips to the point of sale – meaning more risk. The timing between sales would need to be carefully planned. When the going is good, he could collect more ore, resulting in more cash in hand, but it would also be critical to save some and hide it against any unpredictable events.'

On the way from Tibooburra to Innamincka with Fred in the Suzuki, circa 1995.

Towards Birdsville. Dog fence on the left.

Jenolan Caves House, 2006.

Worlds End near Mudgee, where nuggets were dug from the ground like potatoes during the Australian gold rush in the 1850s.

Bob Fraser, Underground Manager for Northern Gold, standing inside a cave showing rich veins, 1986. Located in an area of old workings which had been closed since 1917. (Courtesy Bob Fraser)

Col Ribaux's house in the Garden of Stone National Park, 2015.

Kanangra Walls in the magnificent Blue Mountains National Park.

Burraga mine old pit, 2014.

Old battery near Hill End.

White Lady Rock that I was taken to in 2016.

The old 'Go Devil' bogged near Brisbane Valley Creek, circa 1989.

Monique & Jean Claude (1947–2017) Villeneuve on a camping trip in the Blue Mountains National Park, circa 2005.

My old mate Col Ribaux (1937–2018) from Lithgow, a legend in the prospecting world.

My A team at Watsons Bay Hotel, 2010.

Feeding the locals at Worlds End.

Jennifer signing a copy of her poetry book Heavenly Seduction and other poems at the book launch, September 2019.

Wearing my lucky 2,000-year-old Roman coin, Sydney, 2010.

Taty, Madame Eliane Nicolas (1910–2012).

Enzo takes delivery of his book The Poussin Enigma, 2007.

Lesley & Nathalie, Rennes-le-Château, 2003.

Across the valley towards Mount Cardou, the White Mountain, Rennes-le-Château, 2003.

The Magdala Tower taken from the car park, Rennes-le-Château, 2003.

Hotel Le Grand Balcon in Mazamet, where I trained as a chef (now a bank), 2003.

Rare gold coins from the treasure of Lava with comparison to French coins.

Gold coins from the treasure of Lava.

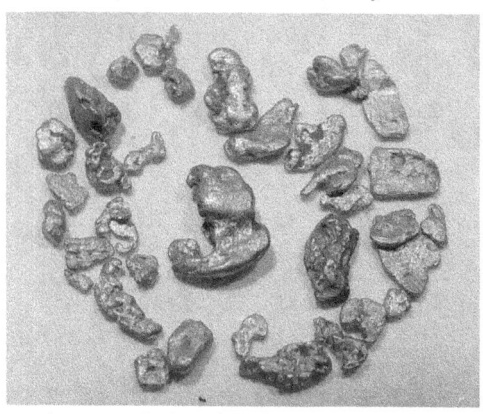

The 38 specks found while prospecting around Rennes-le-Château in 2010.

Pierre Jezequel in his BRGM lab in Orléans, 2003.

A narrow street in Carcassonne, 2006.

La Taverne du Chateau, Carcassonne, 2010.

Area around Carcassonne in the Languedoc-Rousillon region of the South of France.

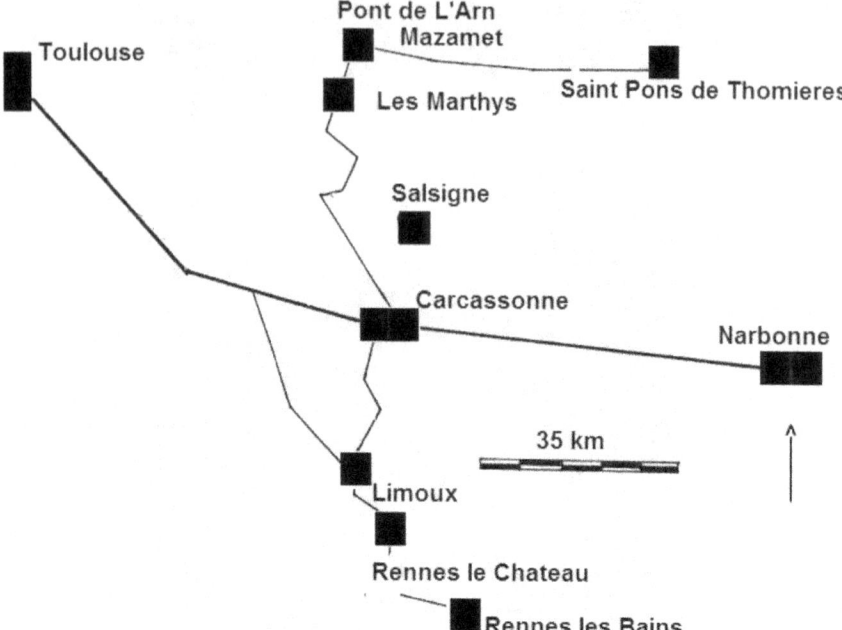

Australian distances.

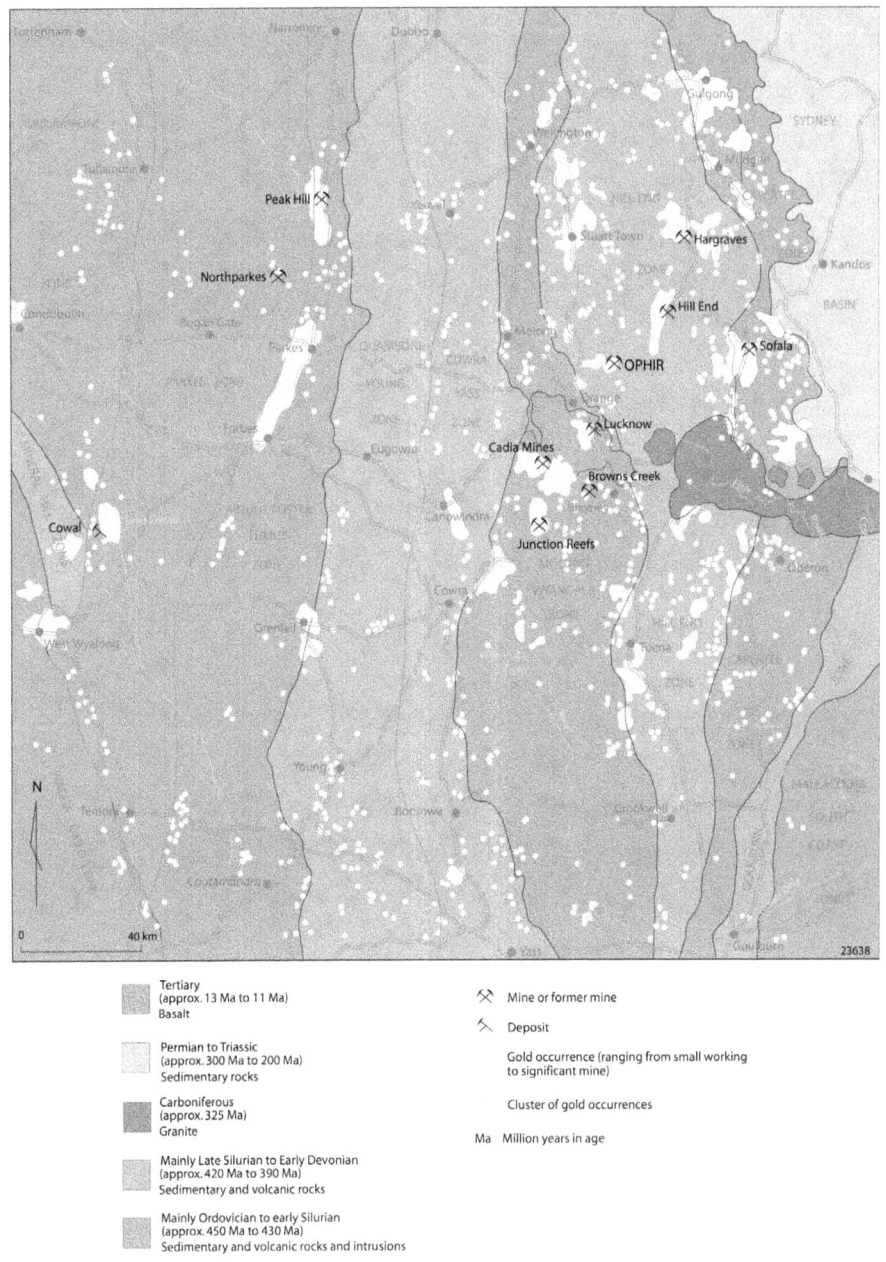

Geological Survey of New South Wales, showing clusters of gold that have been found within a radius of approximately 200 kilometres of Bathurst, where the Australian gold rush began in 1851. (Courtesy The Geological Survey of NSW, Australia.)

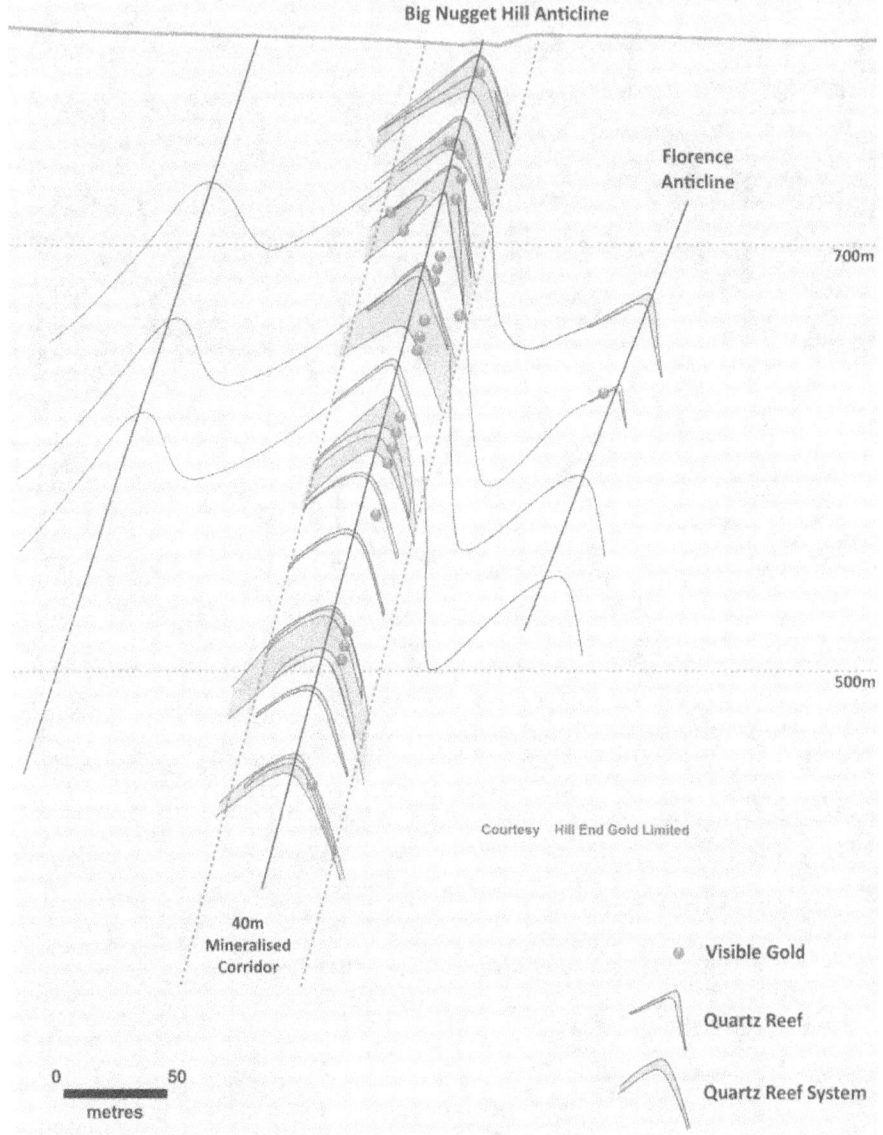

Big Nugget Hill Project: Hargraves Cross Section. (Courtesy Hill End Gold Limited)

Gold deposits along the Hill End Anticline. (Courtesy Hill End Gold Limited)

Types of gold deposits in the Milparinka-Tibooburra area

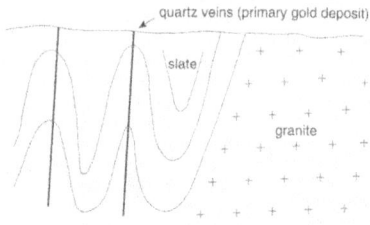

Types of gold deposits in the Milparinka–Tibooburra area. (Courtesy Professor Ian Plimer, Adelaide University)

From the book "Minerals and Rocks of the Broken Hill, White Cliffs and tibooburra districts by Professor Ian Plimer

finds at Mt. Browne, Four Mile Diggings, Nuggetty Gully, Good Friday, Easter Monday, Two Mile Diggings and the Warratta field.

A number of types of gold deposits have been worked in the area. These are reef gold (e.g. Warratta field), gold in ancient gravels (e.g. Nuggetty Hill), alluvial gold (e.g. Warratta Creek) and eluvial gold (e.g. the Granite Diggings).

The oldest rocks in the area are a sequence of schists and slates. The gold deposits within this sequence (e.g. Warratta field) are known as slate belt-type gold deposits

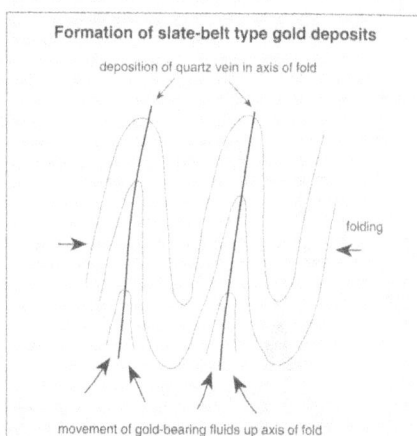

Formation of slate-belt type gold deposits. (Courtesy Professor Ian Plimer, Adelaide University)

From the book Minerals and Rocks of the Broken Hill, White Cliffs and tibooburra districts by Professor Ian Plimer

25

'I have no more money…'

Enzo had been listening intently and flicking through Jean Luc's book. 'We know that Saunière was cunning and capable of being devious in his dealings. He used to leave undated handwritten letters with Marie stating that he was visiting a sick parishioner in another town in order to explain his frequent absences to his superiors. Marie could just pop the date in, so clearly she was a partner in the subterfuge. If we can believe de Sède, Elie Bot, Saunière's builder, is reported as saying that sometimes Saunière would say in his dialect, *"Je n'ai plus le sou, il faut que j'aille en chercher.* I have no more money, I need to get some more." In those day, there were no banks or ATM machines where Saunière could just easily pop in and get some cash, so where did he go to get some more? Could it be that he needed to get more gold?'

'Elie must have been confident that Saunière had the cash to cover the extensive building works,' said Jennifer. 'According to Jean Luc Robin, Saunière kept money in the Banque Fritz d'Orge in Budapest away from the scrutiny of his supervisors.'

'I don't think we should underestimate his capacity for subterfuge,' said Enzo. 'Then again, maybe the subterfuge was a form of self-protection. Don't forget it was only a hundred years earlier during the revolution that priests and bishops had to swear an oath of fidelity to the new order or face dismissal, deportation or death along with members of the nobility.'

'Surely someone would have followed him to the secret location,' said Jennifer. 'There's a story that some of the villagers followed him one day to find out where he went and what he was up to. So how does he keep the secret?'

'You would be surprised how canny prospectors can be Jennifer,' I said. 'My friend Michel Laroche knew a farmer who owned land near Tarana in New South Wales. The story goes that during the Depression the grandfather used to disappear on horseback for weeks at a time. When he returned, he bought lots of land. Nobody knows where the money came from. It was around the same area that the first official report of gold discovery was made in 1823, when James O'Brien found gold in the hills adjacent to the Fish River near Tarana. Then there's the old Aussie legend about an Aboriginal man by the name of Billy Blue who lived with his wife, possibly in a cave, somewhere in the Shoalhaven Gorge, on the Shoalhaven River in south-east New South Wales.[46] Apparently, he knew the location of a native gold vein or reef. Whenever he needed some money, he would go and hack off pieces of gold with an axe then come into Marulan with small quantities of gold, which he exchanged for supplies. He rotated between towns, just like Saunière. He had quite a number of routes through the scrub and was so expert at bushcraft that no one could track him. It is said he would swim across the Shoalhaven River to throw people off his track. His wife acted as lookout, alerting him to any intruders and Billy would quickly take another trail through the bush. The story goes that on his deathbed he was asked to reveal the location of his gold. He said if they got his brother he would tell him, but by the time they returned with his brother, Billy had passed on.'

'Did his wife know the location of the gold vein?' said Jennifer.

'I doubt it. Apparently there was no more gold after his death. Billy took his secret with him – shades of Saunière and Lasseter, hey. Some older prospectors and locals believe that the gold is still there somewhere down in the Shoalhaven gorges, but you would have to be an experienced prospector and expert bushwalker to have any hope of finding the lost reef, if it exists. The location borders on the Morton National Park. It's rugged terrain, with thick vegetation, cliffs and river crossings. Prospectors and geologists have tried to find the reef without success.'

A large part of keeping a secret is making sure that the other people who know it do not reveal it. As soon as a secret is revealed, it becomes a risky business for the holder of the secret. So the next question was, who knew about the gold and how did Saunière keep them quiet.

26

The ecclesiastics

The murder of priests in the South of France was nothing new. From the Albigensian Crusade in the thirteenth century, when Cathar parfaits were tortured and executed by the Roman Catholic Church for their heretical beliefs, to the execution of Roman Catholic priests during the French Revolution.

A small group of Saunière's colleagues, connected by their profession as priests of villages in close proximity to Rennes-le-Château, and by the curious fact that several had received unexplained windfalls, have held the public's interest over decades. In 1975, the *Midi Libre* published three articles about the murder in 1897 of Antoine Gelis, the priest of Coustassa. The articles suggested that there was 'no link' between Gelis's murder and the 'mysterious treasure of Rennes-le-Château'. I was intrigued that there was still a link in the public's mind between Saunière, the murder and the mystery of Rennes-le-Château seventy-eight years after the event.[47]

Some researchers have been scathing in their criticism that the murder conspiracies are overhyped. However, many Rennies continue to link the priests' deaths to the 'secret', and conspiracy theories abound. A disagreement between the ecclesiastics, the assassination of priests who knew too much, a deterrent to others who knew the 'secret', or just coincidence?

'Let's assume that there was a network of priests who knew about the gold vein,' I said, and I ran through the list. 'Antoine Gelis, priest of Coustaussa and Saunière's mentor, brutally murdered in his presbytery on the night of 31 October 1897. Monsignor Billard, Bishop of Carcassonne at the time when Saunière became a priest at Rennes-le-Château, struck down with paralysis in 1898. Like Saunière, he had also been suspended from his post at one time for administering the assets of his diocese in an irregular fashion and for having contracted large debts. Abbé Gaudissard, priest of Antugnac, died unexpectedly on 9 January 1901 at the age of forty-nine. Saunière had been looking after the village of Antugnac on Sundays since 4 May 1890. Gaudissard took over as priest on 12 June 1891. Henri Boudet, priest of Rennes les Bains, died in 1915 after a sudden illness. The official cause of death was intestinal cancer. However, Jean Luc Robin writes that, based on the manner in which his body decomposed, Boudet may have been poisoned. Boudet had given money to Marie Dénarnaud – the source of which remains unknown. Curiously, Joseph Rescanières, the young priest who replaced Boudet, died unexpectedly on 13 February 1915. Saunière died on 22 January 1917. Marie found him collapsed on the Belvedere five days earlier, apparently having suffered a stroke. Gerard De Sède and researcher Graeme Simmans both speculated that Saunière was poisoned, but there is no evidence for that.'

'Gelis is the only one we know for a fact was murdered,' said Jennifer.

'A poker wound to the head would seem to confirm that,' I said. 'The report of his death is intriguing. There was no forced entry or struggle. Apparently, he was a recluse, almost a hermit, so he must have opened the door to someone he knew, unless he was taken by surprise. The first suspects were two drunk vagabonds who were singing and behaving badly in the street of Coustaussa. However, they were quickly ruled out because they slept in Montazel on the night of the crime. The next suspect was the priest's nephew, who was to be a beneficiary of his will. Apparently, the testament was in a bag, which was clearly visible, however not found by the assassin. There were gold coins stashed everywhere, with a value equivalent to more than twenty years of his income, which was only nine hundred francs per annum.'

'Odd that the money wasn't taken,' said Jennifer. 'Where did that money come from and why wasn't it touched? Clearly, whoever murdered him had another motive.'

'Exactly,' I said. 'De Sède linked the murder to the Rennes-le-Château treasure story. The article in the *Midi Libre* mentions an argument between de Sède and Rene Descadeillas, the former chief librarian of Carcassonne, about the murder weapon of all things.'

'Descadeillas had his own agenda, though,' said Enzo. 'He debunked the treasure theories, but according to Lincoln, at one time he was actually searching for treasure. Many of the researchers have played things very close to their chest.'

'The police found two words written on a Czar cigarette paper left at the scene: *Viva Angelina*. None of the villagers were familiar with the brand of tobacco or the name,' I said. 'The police thought they had tracked down the mysterious Angelina to a *lupanar*, a brothel in Chanzy Street, Narbonne. But it turned out that, fortunately for her, she was known as Henri IV not Angelina.'

'So was the case ever solved?' said Jennifer.

'No. The main lead was that it was a crime of passion,' I said. 'According to the villagers, a handsome young Spanish shepherd was in love with a beautiful young woman of the village and wanted to marry her. The woman's family sought advice from Abbé Gelis, who apparently was totally opposed to the marriage. There was another rumour that the girl was the best singer in the choir and Gelis did not want to lose her. The heartbroken young Spaniard swore to seek revenge. Of course, the fact that the murder was never solved benefits Saunière.'

'How do you reach that conclusion?' said Enzo.

'Gelis was murdered at the time that Saunière was making trips to gather rocks in the countryside. At one stage, Saunière was a suspect. If the murder was connected with the secret, what better decoy than a crime of passion committed by a heartbroken lover? The only loser was Gelis. He didn't see it coming.'

People might think that members of the clergy have no interest in money and anything attached to it. However, the Church has always been involved in the search for gold. The lure of gold has attracted priests and missionaries for centuries. Many have been involved in precious metals trade, even staking claims during gold rushes. Jesuits were involved in gold mining in the Spanish colonies in the new world. Priests were even among those who staked claims in the area of the diamond mines discovered by Fipke and Blousson. The Vatican keeps gold reserves worth over $20 million with the US Federal Reserve.[48] In 2014, Australian bishop Cardinal Pell, at the time the Prefect of the Vatican Secretariat for the Economy, announced with typical dry Aussie humour that the Vatican was 'not broke'.[49]

27

A pain in the derrière

The earthy aroma of freshly brewed Italian coffee permeated the room. Mario popped his head around the door. 'Anyone for coffee and biscuits?'

The diversion was a welcome relief. We stood up and stretched. Enzo walked over to the sideboard and began examining the *Annunciation*.

Mario returned with a tray of cups, the sugar jar, a jug of warm frothy milk and a plate of homemade biscuits. 'Well, have you solved it yet?' he said, pouring the coffee.

'They all knew,' said Enzo, returning to the table, selecting one of the golden biscuits and taking a bite.

'Who knew?' said Mario. 'What did they know?'

'All the great painters: da Vinci, Poussin, Teniers. Their paintings are full of esoteric meanings that can only be read by the initiated. Truths are concealed in the symbolism.'

I took one of the biscuits. It was crunchy, not too sweet and deliciously tangy.

'Did you make these, Jennifer?' I said.

'Of course. It's an Italian recipe: *biscotti di limone*, I always add twice as much lemon peel to get that really tangy flavour.'

'Yes, delicious,' said Enzo, examining the biscuit. 'They knew about alchemy. It works on several levels from the physical to the spiritual. Physical gold, the most perfect of precious metals, is the physical representation of spiritual gold, the perfected human spirit. Alchemists consider the natural man to be equivalent to lead and the transformed spiritual being to be gold. We know that Saunière owned books on alchemy. Some researchers suggest that he may have known the secret that allows the transmutation of the base metals into gold. In ancient times, the knowledge of metals and their properties, such as creating steel for weapons and the process of refining gold and other precious metals, was considered the ultimate secret or divine right of a royal house.'

'Truths can be revealed on many levels,' said Jennifer. 'Physical gold is the most fractally recursive element on earth. In a way, you could say that it is the perfect representation of the Grail in the precious metals kingdom.'

'Did you know that da Vinci made a prophecy about gold?' said Enzo, reaching for another biscuit. 'He said it would make men torment each other with many kinds of subterfuge, deceits and treacheries.'

'Look, why spend time slaving over a hot stove trying to make gold when you can just go out and collect some?' I said. 'To me, the answer is simple, maybe too simple for all the mystery buffs and conspiracy theorists.'

Mario smiled at me – I gave him a wink.

'So you really think that Saunière just stumbled on a gold vein,' said Jennifer. 'And that's the answer to the whole mystery.'

'Yes,' I said. 'Stumbled on a gold vein, or knew of its existence.'

'No wonder Dan Brown didn't reply to your email,' said Jennifer, reaching for her copy of *The Holy Blood and the Holy Grail*. 'Have a look at this.' She flicked to the title page and held it up. 'Henry Lincoln signed my copy.' A handwritten dedication in thick black pen almost jumped off the page: 'Vive Sinclair HL Rennes-le-Château.2:VIII 2007'.

'Roman numerals, nice touch,' said Enzo. 'It would be worth a lot to a Rennie with that inscription.'

'Well, it's worth a lot to this Rennie. Look closer – what else do you notice?'

'Oh, I see,' said Enzo. 'He's blacked his name out as author. That's unusual.'

'Yes, he told us that they got some things wrong. But they never said everything was true – just theories. Lincoln said that he's only interested in new information if it can be verified and if it moves the investigation along. He's not interested in treasure with a monetary value. When he discovered that he could map the mountains and the location of various churches against pentagonal geometry, it became his major focus – it was demonstrable and provable, everything else paled by comparison. He has pretty much disassociated himself from the rest of the story. I have a feeling we will find a connection between Lincoln's pentagonal geometry and native gold.'

'When Lincoln asked Plantard about the significance of the pentacle, Plantard replied, "I can't answer that",' said Enzo. 'That could mean either that he genuinely didn't know, or that he knew but could not reveal the information.'

What the pentagonal geometry meant and whether it had any connection with Saunière's wealth I did not yet know. As far as I knew, the pentagram, contained within a circle for protection, was a symbol of black magic used for conjuring, but that was about it. I wasn't sure if it had anything to do with geology.

'There's a lot of speculation, but very little evidence that can be verified,' I said. 'Lincoln's advice not to believe anything in the story just because someone said it and because it is repeated by others is definitely worth taking.'

Enzo stood up, walked over to the fireplace and picked up a sword that was leaning against the hearth and began examining it. 'Saunière's rapidly becoming a pain in the derrière.'

'We need to find out who found the gold at Salsigne,' said Jennifer, placing the empty cups on the tray. 'If they are connected with Saunière, maybe that's how he found the vein or the reef or whatever it is, and we can't rule out the aliens.'

Enzo tucked the sword under his arm, promising to mend the leather scabbard, which had cracked in two. We bade our farewells. I chuckled to myself, thinking that we must have looked like a squire and his knight as we made our way down the driveway to the car.

'What do you think Jennifer meant about the aliens?' I said.

28

Elizabeth Van Buren

Back at Norwood, Enzo began searching through the pile of books on the kitchen table. 'Here,' he said, handing me two books: *The sign of the dove* and *Refuge of the Apocalypse: Doorway to other dimensions*, both written by Elizabeth van Buren, the former in 1983 and the latter in 1986.

Enzo started making cappuccinos. He brought two mugs of coffee over to the table and sat down next to me. 'Elizabeth van Buren was one of the original Rennies. She moved to Rennes-le-Château during the 1980s and settled at the bottom of the hill – I saw her when I was there. She bought land because she believed that the area around Rennes-le-Château was a place of safety.'

'Safety from what?'

'The Apocalypse – the great cataclysm, the end of the world as we know it. The first one was the flood that destroyed Atlantis. Next time, it will be destruction by fire. Van Buren believed that the whole area was criss-crossed with a vast network of underground tunnels that connect chambers which would provide a place of safety when the cataclysm comes. Apparently, there are a number of portals into this underground network and she believed that Rennes-le-Château was one of them.'

'Maybe she knew about the gold,' I said.

'Maybe, but I don't think she was interested in physical gold,' said Enzo, dunking a biscuit in his coffee and retracting it just before it became a lump of mush. 'Actually, she was a millionaire.'

'What's so special about Rennes-le-Château for it to be a place of safety at the so called end-times?' I said. 'If any place was going to be a haven of safety, I would have thought it was Australia, a relatively peaceful isolated continent.'

'Van Buren, like many others, believed that space people colonised the Earth thousands of years ago and created humans by genetic engineering. They implanted a fertilised egg created from the sperm of one of the space males and the egg from a local female into the womb of a space female, a birth mother. She believed that before the space people left Earth, they appointed certain human priest-kings who would represent them until they returned sometime in the future. This was the beginning of the so called royal bloodline.'

'The sangreal.'

'Exactly. They were the so-called elect, the beginning of the Merovingian bloodline. There is a legend that Merovee, the first king of this bloodline, was born of two fathers, and had the blood of both running in his veins, which gave him longevity. Julius Evola, the Italian philosopher and esotericist, says there was a special quality in their blood that gave them paranormal capacities and abilities like hands on healing, which would have been considered magical.'

'Just like…'

'Jesus, yes. According to the legend, Merovee's mother was already pregnant when she went for a swim in the ocean one day and was either seduced or raped by a strange sea creature. Van Buren suggests that the space people emerged from their craft, which had come down in the water. The locals would have seen them as strange sea creatures which some described as griffouls. The implication is that Merovee was created by the DNA from three beings: two human and some sort of space person.'

'Well, it all sounds pretty far-fetched to me,' I said.

'Which bit – the DNA from three sources, or the space person?' said Enzo, finishing his coffee. 'Scientists recently implanted three different sets of DNA in animals to create an embryo that's clear of any abnormal mitochondrial DNA and they are seeking approval for human trials. As far as I'm concerned, this is the same principle.'[50]

'So when are these space people supposed to be coming back?'

'Elizabeth believed that they would return at the end of the millennium, around 2000, after the cataclysm.'

'Well, the so called end of the millennium cataclysm was a fizzer, just like the end of the Mayan calendar in 2012,' I said. 'I saw some media reports about people travelling to Mount Bugarach believing it would be a place of safety at the end of the Mayan calendar. Apparently, the mayor was very upset. I don't blame him. Maybe the whole apocalypse thing is yet another red herring. But I do know about the geology of the area, and there is a network of limestone caves around Mount Bugarach – the Cathars used them. The Romans mined for gold there. The geology is interesting. There are reports of sightings of strange lights around the mountain.'

Enzo waved his hand as if swatting a fly. 'We don't need to worry about the alien theory, Gerard. It complicates the story. We must dig down to the esoteric roots of the region with reference to the influence of the Cathars, Templars, Rosicrucians. The Grail, Gerard, the Holy Grail, for Christ's sake.'

Enzo stood up, walked over to the mantle mirror and examined his reflection for a moment. He smoothed back his hair, then turned and looked down his aquiline nose at me, holding my gaze. 'There are certain things that I cannot reveal at this time, Gerard. All you need to know is that after the apocalypse, in the last days, a grand monarch will emerge from the chaos.' His lips curled into a smile. 'Now let me make you some crêpes for supper.'

I could not tell if this was for dramatic effect, or if Enzo actually believed what he was saying. I was still full from lunch so declined his offer of crêpes.

I had maintained a degree of scepticism about the more way-out Rennes-le-Château theories involving UFOs, aliens and various paranormal happenings, but I had to admit that several unusual experiences over the years had taught me that strange things do happen. Later that night, Jennifer sent me a text and we arranged to meet at a café in the city the next day.

That night, I had trouble sleeping.

Back in the 1960s, I read Eric Von Daniken's book *Chariots of the Gods*. It was an incredible wake-up call. It was the first time that the theory that beings from space had visited the planet reached such a large international audience. Von Daniken proposed that the stories of the gods coming to earth as recorded by the ancient Sumerians on stone tablets were not myths but actual events that occurred thousands of years ago. The tablets were discovered in stages beginning around 1850, and subsequent researchers had made various interpretations. Some researchers believe that the Bible is a reinterpretation of the original Sumerian stories.

I knew that indigenous cultures all around the world had creation stories that involved advanced beings from the stars coming to earth. Were these myths or was there some element of truth in them? Perhaps Enzo was right – maybe the paranormal activities and alien theories did complicate the story. However, I was not immune to the idea that they might play a role in the mystery. I had read many reports of strange experiences and sightings in the area around Rennes-le-Château and I had to admit that some things seem beyond logical explanation.

I have had enough strange experiences over the years, maybe not of the third kind (as far as I know), but definitely of the first and possibly the second kind, to know that there is more to this world that we can see and understand.

29

Close encounters: Sydney, 1972

Suzie and I were living in Neutral Bay on Sydney's lower north shore, a hot spot for UFO sightings.

One night, we had both worked late shifts, Suzie at the Mediterranean Motel at Chatswood and me at the Hindquarter Restaurant in Crows Nest. Suzie picked me up at about midnight. Usually, we went for a drink with friends, but on that night, we went straight home. I was looking forward to relaxing on the balcony with a coffee and a cigarette after a busy night of cooking, sweating and yelling – in commercial kitchens, you don't shout, you scream and yell.

It was one of those typical balmy Sydney summer nights – still and hot. The sky was so clear that I decided to get the binoculars to watch the stars. Lying comfortably on the balcony tiles, making it easier to hold the binoculars, I started to scan the sky – it was magnificent. Suddenly I picked up a red flashing light right at the zenith. Its brightness was about the same as a star – but this was moving. At first, I thought it was a satellite, but satellites do not have flashing lights. It took about forty-five seconds to go from the zenith to the horizon, where it disappeared. Its trajectory was south towards the airport. Helicopter, airplane, rocket, weather balloon – nothing fitted the bill. My mind jumped to a possible solution – could it be my first UFO sighting?

I found the number for the UFO Research Bureau of Australasia in the phonebook and dialled it, expecting a recorded message, as by then it was one-thirty a.m.

'UFO Research Bureau of Australasia. Can I help you?' Wow, someone answered. I described what I saw. The reply was brief: 'Thank you very much for your call', nothing more, and nothing less. Don't call us, we will call you – you know the drill, end of story. Or so I thought. I made another coffee, lit up another cigarette and went back to the balcony floor, binoculars in hands, scanning the sky, hoping that – and yes, there it was again, red flashing light, same direction, and same speed.

I poured myself a glass of white wine, and then dialled the number again. Someone answered, 'Night duty officer, Richmond Base. Can I help you?' Now it seemed I was dealing with the Royal Australian Air Force. For a minute, I thought I heard wrong. All I could answer was 'Sorry, I must have the wrong number' and hang up. I dialled several more times; each time, the person gave me the same calm response. I was dealing with a very well trained individual, a member of the military. Secrecy was involved and who knows what else. I was flabbergasted – this was happening in the middle of a beautiful summer night, in a city of three million people.

I rang the phone company to check the number. Within five seconds of putting down the phone, it rang. 'Good morning, night duty officer Richmond Base. Can I help you?' I hung up without saying a word. The red flashing light was real, the UFO Research Bureau of Australasia was real, but then it became the Department of Defence. It was the same telephone number, same office, and same person. The only difference was the answer given by the person behind the desk. I was left with one thought: see no evil, hear no evil.

Rex Gilroy has been investigating UFO and paranormal activity in the Blue Mountains for years. He is convinced that there is a secret Australian-US underground space technology base there, somehow connected with a plan to colonise Mars. I wrote to him once but he did not reply.

Like the Blue Mountains, Mount Bugarach, the highest summit in the Corbières Mountains, has a reputation for unexplained light phenomena, UFO sightings, mysterious events and anomalies. According to reports, the locals frequently spot strange moving objects over the summit. Magnetic fields are said to knock out mobile phones and laptops permanently. Both locations have been subject to speculation that perhaps the sightings are connected to secret weapons testing in underground bases and even the possibility of alien involvement. There were stories of alien visitors moving in and out of 'windows in time' to reach earth, and cover-ups by the CIA and ASIO.

Then there was Mount Canigou, located in the Pyrenees of southern France, just over the border from Spain. It is full of iron and regarded as sacred by the Catalans. Strange lights that flash on then vanish are said to appear around the mountain. There are stories of spirits and alien landings.

Reports of UFOs over France have been documented for centuries. A French *jeton* minted around 1680, during the reign of Louis XIV, depicts what appears to be a UFO hovering over the landscape. *Jetons* were coin-like educational tools used as money substitutes for playing games and counting. Some researchers believe that it represents the biblical account of Ezekiel's encounter with a flying 'wheel' in the sky. The Latin inscription on the *jeton* reads, '*Opportunus Adest*. It is here at an opportune time'.

I had read modern accounts of UFO encounters in France, experienced by people who were driving at the time. They reported electromagnetic effects and interference to their vehicle's electrical circuits: car engines ceased functioning temporarily; radios cut out or buzzed with static interference; car headlights dimmed, or were extinguished; or car batteries overheated and deteriorated rapidly. Some events were associated with orange clouds or 'discs' in the sky, sometimes stationary, sometimes hanging like a low orange moon. The appearance of an orange/red cloud or disc is a feature of many close encounters and other paranormal phenomena.

Back in the 1990s, geologist Harry Mason was investigating earthquake risk in an isolated area of the eastern goldfields of Western Australia.⁵¹ He discovered that earthquakes in that area were often preceded by the appearance of strange light events, sometimes moving, sometimes stationary. Some of the people he interviewed reported seeing large moon-sized orange/red 'fireballs', and some events were accompanied by power generation overvoltage outages and other electrical events. Mason put forward a theory that the light events, which he called plasmoids, were possibly part of a secret military weapons program or even the work of UFOs. In the movie *Close Encounters of the Third Kind*, the mothership is concealed in a red cloud. UFO author Jenny Randles describes cases of mysterious clouds that create distortions in the flow of time and space. Villagers in Chernobyl, Russia, reported seeing a stationary orange cloud in the sky hours before the disaster at the nuclear plant there.

I had seen the words '*Terribilis est locus iste*' above the front doors of the church at Rennes-le-Château. The phrase is inscribed below a statue of Mary Magdelene, who is depicted holding a cross and grail cup. It is frequently translated as 'This location is terrible', but the word *terribilis* can also mean 'awesome'; this is a place of awe. The mass for the dedication of a church begins with this phrase. It is taken from the Book of Genesis 28:xvii, and refers to the place where Jacob dreamt of a ladder that reached to heaven, where angels ascended and descended. I wondered if this dedication was the only reason for this inscription, or whether Saunière knew something more about the physical location that caused him to describe Rennes-le-Château as 'awesome'.

30

Gremlins in the Go-Devil: Good Forest, New South Wales, 1989

In 1989, driving on the Victoria Pass road through the Good Forest, I had an encounter I still cannot explain. I was working at Jenolan Caves House. Every Tuesday on my day off, I made the four-hour trip to Balgowlah Heights to see Suzie and the kids. On Wednesday night, always around ten-thirty p.m., I was on the road again heading back to Jenolan. People along the way came to recognise me in the open-top army jeep.

On this particular night, I left at the usual time and reached Katoomba between midnight and one a.m. Another hour and a half and I would reach Jenolan. The road from Katoomba to Jenolan passes through Medlow Bath with the Hydro Majestic on the left, a beautiful old building steeped in history, then further on is Blackheath. Another seven kilometres and you arrive at Mt Victoria, the highest point of the Great Dividing Range for the area. Not long after is the truck checking station, and then the steep descent of Victoria Pass for about six kilometres.

It was freezing in the open-top but at the same time exhilarating, a real adventure. The cold heightened my senses. Maybe it was the thrill of the drive – my adrenalin was pumping. I could smell everything: trees, flowers, fumes from the trucks, all the country smells. The engine was purring and the jeep was going like a bomb – it is practically indestructible and can handle any sort of terrain. As the advertising slogan says, 'The sun never sets on the mighty jeep'.

I passed Little Hartley with the old buildings on my left, then left the busy main road and took the Jenolan Caves turn-off, drove for another two hundred metres and stopped by the side of the road for a coffee and a cigarette. Back behind the wheel, I switched off the car lights just for the thrill and drove in the dark with only the moon and the stars lighting the way – but only for a minute, even though I knew the road by heart. On clear nights, you can see lots of rabbits. Kangaroos appear later, bounding across the road; luckily, I was not in the danger zone.

I crossed the bridge over the Cox River and the road started to wind its way towards Good Forest. It was about twenty minutes since I had the coffee. The road follows a U-shape from the bridge, the longest left bend for the whole trip. I reached the Good Forest sign, five hundred metres more, and it is a straight road just before some houses on top of the ridge. I imagined that if I was a bird, I could fly over the deep ravine to my left for five or six kilometres and reach Victoria Pass on the other side of the ridge.

That is when I saw the disc. I stopped the jeep.

Hanging halfway between the top of the ridge and the bottom of the valley was a disc of orange light. My skin began to crawl. At first, I thought it must be the moon, but this was bigger and much lower in the sky, and it was orange. It was just hanging there – motionless – no shine, and no twinkle. I watched for a good thirty minutes and then I had to drive on.

That same morning at work, I mentioned the orange disc to friends – no one had seen or heard anything. The day was busy, the week went fast; Tuesday came round again and I was back behind the wheel going to Balgowlah. Wednesday came like a flash – I bade my farewells, then I was back behind the wheel returning to Jenolan. I left Balgowlah around ten-thirty p.m., the same time as the previous week. Everything was great. I had fuel, water, coffee and cigarettes. The weather was fine, life was wonderful, another trip, another adventure.

I was relieved when I reached the Jenolan turn-off as it was freezing. A cup of coffee and a cigarette boosted my spirits. Back at the wheel, over the Cox River, then the winding road followed by the long left bend. The jeep took the bend well in third gear, the top gear. I saw the

Good Forest sign, then without warning the jeep lost power. I could not hold top gear or second, only first. I could not get the speed above two miles per hour. Was she running on three cylinders or two? I could have jumped out and walked alongside without any trouble. It was nearly two a.m., Jenolan was at least thirty kilometres away and there was no chance of someone to help me. It was the exact same spot where I had seen the orange disc the week earlier.

I could not feel the cold any more, all I was thinking was I must keep the motor running at all cost. It took two and a half hours to reach Jenolan. Was I glad to see the carport of cottage 13. I could not believe my luck when I stopped and pulled the handbrake – she was still running. I turned the ignition off, and then on, crank, crank – nothing. She would not fire. I felt very lucky, went to bed and slept like a log.

On the same morning, I walked to work past the man-made Blue Lake, its surface still and peaceful like an expanse of shimmering glass. I did a short working day, as I could not wait to find out what was wrong with the jeep – the problem had to be solved. Walking back to cottage 13 after work, my mind was already doing a 'heart transplant' on the old Go Devil. Within minutes, my tools were on the ground. Up went the bonnet. One jump behind the wheel, ignition on, cranking, cranking – nothing. She would not fire.

The engine has four cylinders and four spark plugs in line on top of the engine block. A high-tension lead goes from each spark plug to the distributor. The distributor distributes the high voltage to the plugs and the plugs give the electrical sparks needed to explode the fuel in the cylinders. In each cylinder, there is a piston, which goes up and down. These four pistons do not move randomly – things are organised in there. There is a firing order: 1-3-4-2 meaning that the fuel explodes in cylinder 1, then 3, then 4, then 2 and the cycle starts again. The distributor organises all this. It is like an old-fashioned clock: everyone knows where three o'clock, six o'clock, nine o'clock and twelve o'clock are on the clock face. I checked the jeep manual. It said that when the hand of the clock is at three o'clock the lead goes from the distributor to the plug of cylinder 1, at six o'clock to cylinder 3, at nine o'clock to cylinder 4 and at twelve o'clock to cylinder 2. The only way the high-tension leads can be moved to a different position is by hand.

I took the distributor cap off, got the crank from the back of the jeep, and turned the engine slowly to position the hand of the 'clock' to the desired position so that I could check the firing order. To my amazement, the firing order was wrong. It was not 1-3-4-2 but 2-3-4-1; the first and last leads were in the wrong position. Can you imagine the chaos in there?

I took each lead and placed it into the right position, going from the distributor to the plugs. I replaced the distributor cap, jumped in the jeep, turned on the ignition and off she went firing like a rocket aiming for the moon. Everything was back to normal.

Everything had been going well until I got to Good Forest. The engine was running perfectly; but at Good Forest, something went wrong. Something happened to the jeep at that location, exactly at the same spot where I saw the orange disc the week before.

When the jeep fired, instantly a memory of an old *Twilight Zone* program flashed into my mind. A man was on a commercial flight flying through a violent storm at night. He looked out of the window and saw what appeared to be little demons ripping bits off the wing and the engine, creating a spectacle of flames and sparks. He tried to tell the air hostess but she ignored him and finally the plane went down – he was the only survivor. It was as if he was operating in some parallel universe and could see things others could not.

When I look back even now, it is hard to understand what happened to the jeep and why it happened where it did. One minute the leads were in the right position and the jeep was running perfectly, the next minute everything was back to front. Was I imagining it? Were there little demons under the bonnet playing with the high-tension leads?

If you ever go to Jenolan Caves, stop at Good Forest. On the straight stretch of road just before the houses, look to the left, at the valley with only a few hills on the lower side – it is an awesome sight.

31

Geometry and the goddess

I arrived early and sat outside under the front veranda to smoke a cigarette and gather my thoughts. The café was tucked away on a quiet corner of Halifax Street on the eastern edge of the city amongst rows of single-fronted cottages and small businesses. A street planting of pink bush roses was the perfect foil to the yellow climbing rose in full bloom on the veranda wall.

I had lived in Adelaide for a short time with my first wife Suzie and our kids. We bought our first house in Manly, a one-bedroom free-standing property, a real doll's house, and sold it fourteen months later when the market was booming. In 1982, we moved to South Australia on a business venture; unfortunately, it turned out to be the biggest quicksand operation ever and eighteen months later, we moved back to Sydney. Still, I liked Adelaide; it had an old world charm and the streets were easy to navigate.

Jennifer arrived right on time. '*Bonjour*, Gerard,' she said, offering me her cheeks and two kisses. She dumped her bags on the spare chair, sat down, pulled her laptop from her carry bag and placed it carefully on the table, followed by several books.

'So tell me, Jennifer,' I said. 'How did you get interested in the south of France?'

'My family has always been interested in all things French. *Je parle un peu de Français.* Just schoolgirl French, I'm afraid. A friend of mine told me about American inventor Dan Winter, who lives in the south of France. He's one of the foremost authorities on sacred geometry and the scientific nature of consciousness. My friend's husband is a building designer and into biological architecture. They studied with Dan in Machu Picchu and suggested that, if he ever did a course in France, I should go, so when the opportunity came up in 2006, I didn't hesitate. Well, that's not quite true, I did hesitate – a lot. I had never travelled overseas alone before. Anyway, I had a Tarot reading done. It was very positive, so I decided to go. It wasn't long after *The da Vinci Code* was published, when the media stories about the sacred bloodline were going viral and Rennes-le-Château was the place everyone was dying to visit, so to speak. The course was described as an opportunity to find out what the Holy Grail, Mary Magdalene, the da Vinci code, the Cathars, Templars, Rennes-le-Château, the golden ratio, alchemy, pharaohs, Freemasons, science and modern physics all had in common.'

'Sounds intense.'

'It was, and fascinating. At the time, I was interested in Gnostic Christianity, especially the Cathars, and once I started helping Enzo with the research for his book, I was hooked. In the past, many things that couldn't be explained by science were explained as divine intervention or magic. We have been conditioned to think that science and spirituality are mutually exclusive, but they're not at all. Both languages can speak about the same reality. The other attraction of course was the French food and countryside.'

'So you became a Rennie.'

'Exactly. Our group stayed in the Domaine de Fraisse, a chateau about half an hour's drive north of Rennes-le-Château. The countryside reminded me very much of South Australia, especially the vineyards. In between lectures, we visited key places, including Rennes-le-Château, Rennes les Bains, Montsegur and Mount Bugarach. We even swam naked in a sacred rock pool in a gorge in Mount Canigou.'

'I've never heard of biological architecture,' I said, trying not to think of the sacred rock pool.

'It's architecture based on the geometry in nature and the principle that all biological organisms – that includes us – require a fractal electric environment in order to thrive. It's also called sustainable architecture. Dan would say the ultimate goal is to create fractal charge fields that are implosive and therefore support life.'

'Can you explain that in English?'

'OK, think of nesting Russian dolls. Each doll is an exact replica of all the others, but at a different scale so that they all fit neatly into each other. That's what fractal means. It's a geometric form where each part is an exact replica of the others but at different scales: fraction of the all or as above, so below.'

'Oh, OK, I get it. Now that you say that, I've noticed that when I take a photo of a very small speck of gold under the microscope, even as small as a quarter of a millimetre, whatever size I enlarge or decrease the image to, it becomes like the Russian dolls.'

'How do you mean?' said Jennifer.

'Well, if I enlarge the photo, say tenfold, to fit in a nice frame, it looks exactly like a nugget. The more you enlarge the photograph, the bigger the nugget gets. Looking at it, you would think it really was a huge nugget, not a tiny speck. I have been taking photos of different mineral grains, but this only happens with gold. As you said, each part is an exact replica of the others but at different scales.'

'When biology arranges molecules in a fractal, it accomplishes what Dan calls perfect non-destructive distribution of charge – in other words, life,' said Jennifer. 'Think of the earth as a giant capacitor with charge in the environment all around us. Everything, from trees to us, is made out of compressed charge – the denser the matter, the more compressed it is. Creation is simply the process by which charge is compressed to create matter.'

Jennifer leaned forward – her face lit up. 'Here's the best bit. The golden ratio spiral is the best way to compress charge waves. It's the only angle at which a wave can enter itself without hurting itself. You can easily see the spiral in a pine cone and of course a rose. The charge can never cancel itself out – it's infinitely expandable, non-destructible, you could even say immortal. The designs in biological architecture are based on the golden ratio in order to maintain charge and sustain life. I tried to explain the principles to my work colleagues when we were investing a lot of money in a major building project. They just looked at me as if I was nuts. It went straight over their heads.'

'I can understand that,' I said, smiling.

Jennifer laughed, opened her laptop and clicked on a YouTube video.[52] It showed how the golden ratio of 1:1.618 is found throughout nature, the human body and even the solar system – it was awesome. Phi, 1.618, known as the golden number, is the original definition of beauty and perfection in nature as well as art and architecture. The ancient temple builders used the golden ratio as did painters like da Vinci and Poussin. Photographers use it today. It attracts the viewer because it is perfectly balanced in accordance with nature.

'As a pine cone or rose unpacks, it begins gathering charge from its environment inwards towards the centre, causing implosion, which is the electrical principle of life,' said Jennifer. 'Next time you are in one of the great Gothic cathedrals built by the Templars, have a look for the pine cone sculptures – they are everywhere. Have you ever wondered, why pine cones? What I find truly awesome is that the human heart is also arranged in the same geometry, and our DNA is based on the golden mean spiral. It has the geometry of a dodecahedron formed by twelve pentagons – it gets fractal to suck in charge from our environment. The simplicity is perfect.'

'So the Pythagoreans were right,' I said. 'They believed the pentagram was a symbol of life, good health, and eternity, in other words the Grail – God geometrises.'

'Exactly, you've got it. Phil Gruber, another sacred geometry expert, told our group that the word Grail originally meant pattern. In fact, in October 2003, a team including French cosmologists analysed NASA data to come up with a theory that the universe is a dodecahedron based on Phi.[53] According to Dan, our solar system is at the centre of a very big fractal in the universe. He also explained how the planet is crisscrossed with telluric currents – channels of subtle natural energy. They are invisible to our eyes, but sensitive people like dowsers and many Indigenous peoples can feel them. The Australian Aborigines call them song lines. They walked the lines over thousands of years and sang melodies along them to recharge them. Some can even see the song lines. The Chinese call them dragon lines and the Celts called them fairy paths. They are the dragons and serpents in folk tales from many cultures. Some researchers believe that the ancients knew how to focus and distribute the dragon's power, by positioning piezoelectric and paramagnetic standing stones, dolmens and menhirs in the right fractal geometry at points of strong telluric energy. Stones like granite and limestone act like giant acupuncture needles in the earth. France is literally bristling with sacred sites located at the intersection of the powerful earth energy lines. Carnac is probably the most famous example: there are over three thousand stones, including dolmens, burial mounds and single menhirs. Did you know there are menhirs around Mazamet?'

'No, I've never noticed them. But now I can see why they were considered to be sacred and venerated.'

'Dan introduced us to the work of geobiologist Stephan Cardinaux.[54] He's a trainer and researcher and a highly skilled dowser. Stephan explains how placing a menhir on telluric line crossings makes it a transmitter, pushing the telluric lines a few metres and creating a sacred space. He has worked alongside archaeologists and believes that the majority of ancient sacred sites are aligned on telluric lines. Ancient cultures knew about the increased magnetic wave energy where multiple telluric lines meet. Machu Picchu, the pyramids of Egypt, the Gothic cathedrals in France and ancient known indigenous resting places, are all examples. That is why these sites are called sacred – it's not magic, just simple science. The ancient Irish constructed round towers up to thirty-four metres high from paramagnetic stone. They were designed to collect energy from the earth and the cosmos. Apparently, the soils around the towers are very fertile.[55] There are geobiology schools that teach the ways that the ancient shamans and Druids used to switch magnetic towers on and off for specific purposes. The interesting thing is that the geographical arrangement of the towers mirrors the positions of the stars in the northern sky during the winter solstice. According to Stephan, the stars influence the telluric networks. He has even measured the variations in the grid lines during an eclipse of the moon. It seems that the ancients understood that there was an energetic resonance between specific terrestrial locations and different celestial bodies.'

'Could that explain the esoteric meaning of the Camino?' I said. 'The famous pilgrim walk that begins in Provence and heads west across the Pyrenees and northern Spain until it reaches Santiago de Compostela.'

'I believe it could,' said Jennifer. 'Apparently, the route lies directly under the Milky Way and follows the ley lines on earth that reflect the energy from those star systems above.'

'As above, so below,' I said. 'The Templars used to police Il Camino to protect the pilgrims.'

'Actually, it goes past Rennes-le-Château. Scallop shells mark the route,' said Jennifer. 'There's one in front of the fireplace in the Tour Magdala.'

'Ah, perhaps that explains the shape of those delicious little shell-shaped cakes called madeleines – I've made thousands when I was working.'

'Rob Gourlay is an environmental scientist based in New South Wales. He identified a magnetic grid of ley lines over Braidwood on the south coast, using advanced aerial geophysical technology. He told me that there are powerful electromagnetic waves that travel between vortexes where multiple ley lines meet.[56] Rob also discovered that the ley lines coincide with the song line Dreaming tracks walked by the Wandandia people, the Indigenous owners of the region between the Shoalhaven River and Ulladulla. Apparently, two ley lines meet at a spot which just happens to be the original resting place of the Wandandian people. Unfortunately, there is a high incident of accidents in that location because of the chaotic urban planning and built environment design.'

'Have you heard about the book Henri Boudet wrote in 1886: *La vrais langue Celtique et le cromlech de Rennes les Bains?*' I said. 'The true Celtic language and the cromlech at Rennes les Bains?'

'Yes, I've heard of it.'

'Boudet spent a lot of time walking the hills surrounding the village of Rennes les Bains and believed that he had discovered a megalithic structure, a Celtic cromlech with a circumference of about sixteen to eighteen kilometres, spread over the countryside.[57] Menhirs and strange stones like the Trembling Rocks delineate it.'

'The circumference of the inner circle of Sarsen stones at Stonehenge is ninety-two metres,' said Jennifer. 'A cromlech of approximately sixteen to eighteen kilometres would definitely be considered awesome.'

'He sent a hundred copies to libraries and royal courts all over the Europe and Britain,' I said. 'So he must have believed that he had discovered something of great importance and wanted to ensure its survival.'

'According to Dan, the characteristics of an area of high telluric activity include underground water, radioactivity and the odd appearance of rocking stones. Most of these are present in the physical characteristics of the area around Rennes-le-Château and Rennes les Bains. I wonder if Boudet knew that the churches that encircle the area around Rennes-le-Château and the unusual features of the landscape are located at points of strong telluric energy.'

'Perhaps he did,' I said. 'He knew about archaeology, geology and the ancient history of the area. His brother Edmund drew a map of the cromlech – it covered the areas of Blanchefort and Cardou and included the menhirs and the Trembling Rocks. I read in the *Tomb of God* that there are some surprising inaccuracies on the map – details that contradict the officially surveyed and recorded results.'

'Maybe he was trying to emphasise the importance of those locations,' said Jennifer.

'Or was it a deliberate mistake to conceal something?' I said. 'Edmond's job as a notary would have given him access to documents and manuscripts related to the location of mines and various land transactions in the area. One of Henri's predecessors, Antoine Delmas, the priest of Rennes les Bains and Montferrand, had written about the mines and minerals in the Black Rock in 1709. Maybe Edmond and Henri knew about a dormant source of native gold. I imagine that Henri's reaction would have been nearly instantaneous. The search was on and Saunière was the perfect man for the job: fit, strong and intelligent and he was a priest, the perfect cover.'

I imagined Boudet descending into a bat-infested cave or an old mine on his ladder, which he apparently took with him on his many excursions into the countryside. Perhaps the old mine on the mountain slope between the Château Blanchefort and Black Rock, or the ancient mine close to the bank of the river Blanque where it runs parallel to the narrow winding D14 road connecting Rennes les Bains with Bugarach. Experienced cavers warn people to be cautious about exploring the caves and old mines around Rennes-le-Château, as many of them are extremely dangerous.

Jason, the owner of the café, appeared at the doorway. We ordered coffees.

'I've been going back over my notes from the study tour and I've found something interesting about gold,' said Jennifer. 'Gold, by its atomic geometry, is the most fractally recursive element. Dan says that gold forms in veins in the places where the Earth's magnetic lines cross in a fractal. Salsigne and Rennes-le-Château are located in one of those places.'

'If we used that as the criterion for finding gold, I don't think we would be very successful,' I said with a smile.

'Perhaps, but Henry Lincoln was captivated by the pentagonal geometry he found in the Dagobert parchment, then in Poussin's painting and ultimately in the pattern of mountains and man-made structures in the Languedoc around Rennes-le-Château. He concluded that it was the key to the mystery. According to Dan, native gold is associated with pentagonal geometry in the landscape. So the secret, as Lincoln suggests, could in fact be the pentagonal geometry, the code nature uses to create life – finding native gold is a lucky by-product. The real gold is the life enhancing qualities of living in such a sacred environment, and that's the Holy Grail.' Jennifer's eyes widened. '*Voilà*. People have been watching Henry's website for years waiting for further information, which he has promised to reveal. However, unless you understand the geophysics behind sacred geometry you won't get the connection. Perhaps the rest is, as Henry says, "all a bloody fantasy".'

32

A rose for a lady

Jason returned with two large mugs of coffee, extra hot for Jennifer and not too hot for me. Jennifer wrapped her hands around the red mug and gazed at the heart patterned into the froth on the top of the milky liquid.

'They say that once you become a Rennie, your life becomes full of synchronicity. Now I meet you and find out that in the same year that you're having your big revelation at Salsigne in 2006, I'm in the south of France visiting Rennes-le-Château, and learning about sacred geometry. Then in 2010, I'm in Provence staying in a château on the property once owned by Nostradamus's brother and attending the annual festival at Saint Marie de la Mere celebrating the arrival of Mary Magdalene in France, and you are finding gold somewhere in the Languedoc near Rennes-le-Château with the famous church dedicated to Mary Magdalene.'

Jennifer blew across the froth on her coffee and took a small sip. 'There's a saying that the land actually calls to those who were there before in a past life. To me, that's synchronicity, don't you think, Gerard?'

'You don't think it's just a coincidence?'

'No, I don't. It's more than just coincidence. It's when there's a meaningful connection between what happens but without any recognisable cause. Something unexpected happens that has a special meaning for the person it happens to.'

At that point, I'm not kidding, a man carrying a basket full of long-stemmed roses walked past the veranda and spotted us tête-à-tête, as it were.

'Buy a rose for the lady?'

Jennifer and I looked at each other, raised our eyebrows, and smiled. A rose had to be bought. We both gave the guy some coins and he handed Jennifer a long-stemmed orange rose.

'Aha, Rat Scabies and the red minis,' she said, smelling the rose. 'What do you say now about synchronicity?'

She must have seen the puzzled look on my face.

'Ratty was the drummer in the Damned, one of the major punk rock bands in the UK. He was infamous for setting his drums on fire.'

I was not any clearer on the connection.

Jennifer held up one of her paperbacks titled *Rat Scabies and the Holy Grail*. It featured a garish blue cover with, among other things, an illustration of the devil statue from the church at Rennes-le-Château complete with beams of red light streaming from his eyes.

'Everyone wants to get in on the Rennes-le-Château act,' I said, chuckling. 'Now it's punk rockers.'

'This must be the only English language book on the Holy Grail that Enzo doesn't have,' said Jennifer. 'Ratty and his mate Christopher go in search of the Grail and try and solve the mystery of Rennes-le-Château. Ratty is a total Rennie and believes that there's a magic about the mystery that people get drawn into once they start on their grail quest. Anyway, at first Christopher is a sceptic about synchronicity. He tells Scabies that as soon as you start focusing on something – like, for example, a red Mini – you will start seeing the thing everywhere, but in reality, red Minis are always there and you only start noticing them because they are uppermost in your mind. Like the Grail quest, you only start seeing the clues because you're intent on the quest.'

'Sounds logical.'

'Sure – but just as he says this, a red Mini comes round the corner, just like my rose. The more he gets involved in the mystery, the more synchronicity he experiences.'

Jennifer leant in towards me as if she was about to tell me a secret; her blue eyes were twinkling. 'I've been coming here for years, Gerard, and I've never seen a rose-seller pass by before.'

'OK, but I still don't get why the rose is synchronicity,' I said.

'Its petals are fractal. They unfold along the golden ratio, and it just happens to be the symbol of Mary Magdalene – the church in Rennes-le-Château was dedicated to her. Some researchers believe that it was built on top of an ancient Roman temple dedicated to the goddess Isis. The Isis cult was widespread in Gaul in Roman times – the Christians just reinterpreted Isis as Mary Magdalene. The star Venus is also associated with Isis and Mary Magdalene. Every eight years, it makes five conjunctions with the sun which trace a five-pointed star in the heavens, which mirrors the pentagram on the ground below around Rennes-le-Château.'

'Sustainable geometry designed by God.'

'Hey, you've really got it,' said Jennifer, smiling. 'Both pentagrams are real, and in one sense hidden, but not to the ones who knew about the so-called secret of the geometry. I would say that the area around Rennes-le-Château has been considered a sacred place of spiritual and religious significance for thousands of years.'

Jason took our empty mugs and noticed the long-stemmed rose on the table. He took it inside and returned with it in a vase of water.

What I did not tell Jennifer, not yet anyway, was that back in 1994 I had started a little printing venture making gift cards from my photos of microspheres. My brand was the Estelle Collection. Estelle is French for 'star' and my logo was a stylised graphic using several triangles arranged to make – 'coincidentally' – a rose.

33

Fractals, portals and pine cones 'kissing noses'

We ordered a light snack for lunch.

'What do you know about the Templars, Gerard?'

I thought for a moment, smiling to myself and anticipating that Jennifer was about to tell me something from left field. Most of what I knew came from orthodox historical accounts that the Knights Templar were a religious military order founded in 1118 by Hughes de Payen, ostensibly to protect pilgrims travelling to Jerusalem. Their headquarters in Jerusalem was located in a wing of the king's palace near the destroyed Temple of Solomon. They were fearless fighters in the Crusades, answerable only to the pope. Individual knights took a vow of poverty, donating their wealth to the order when they joined, but the order itself was immensely wealthy, receiving vast donations of money, goods and land, from wealthy landowners. At their height, they held a large fleet. The Languedoc was a Templar stronghold with a number of castles and commanderies. They were also bankers, holding wealth in trust for rich pilgrims and merchant traders. Travelling was a risky business. In a precursor to modern-day banking, travellers gave a sum of money to the Templars before departing on their journey, similar to buying travellers cheques. On arrival, they recovered the equivalent in value from the Templars at their destination. However, many wealthy pilgrims never reached their destination and their money and land defaulted to the order.

Over time, the Templars' power and influence grew across Europe and the Middle East. They lent vast sums of money to many European monarchs, notably Philip IV, King of France from 1285 to 1314, also known as Philip the Fair, whose royal treasury was kept in the Temple in Paris at one time. On Friday 13 October 1307, he charged the order with heresy. At the time, France was in severe financial crisis due to the wars with England and many researchers believe that the king's actions were more likely motivated by his desire to get his hands on the order's wealth, as well as eliminating their power base in the south of France. Thousands of Templars in France were simultaneously arrested and tortured, many were executed and the order was officially dissolved in 1312. Some Templars fled overseas, including to Scotland, supporting Robert the Bruce at the Battle of Bannockburn in 1314. On 18 March 1314, Jacques de Molay, the last grandmaster of the Templars, was burned to death on a scaffold on an island in the River Seine, in front of Notre Dame de Paris. There are many theories about what happened to their great wealth, including that it was hidden in the south of France and was the source of Saunière's wealth. Some believe that it may have been taken out of the country, to Scotland or Nova Scotia, but according to the history books, it has never been found.

'Yes, all very interesting,' said Jennifer. 'But William Mann takes it much further. He believes that the Templars were also accessing the most advanced technologies of their day at the leading edge of scientific thinking, including surveying, map making, road building and navigation. In *Templar Meridians*, he suggests that they had access to ancient knowledge about the earth energy grid and that their settlements were deliberately located at powerful vortex sites and they knew how to activate the ancient ley lines.'

Ah, my intuition was right.

'Author Patrice Chaplin was given information that indicates Saunière was involved with a secret society in Girona. The initiates practised rituals to open an ancient portal on Mount Canigou, which is at the halfway point between Girona and Rennes-le-Château. Apparently, they were able to access another realm where they experienced the Grail. They were also awaiting or invoking the Messiah. According to Chaplin,

Saunière based the Magdalene tower in Rennes-le-Château on the Magdala Torre at Girona, which by the way no longer exists. Dan showed us how the geomantics between Girona and Rennes-le-Château form pine cone shapes naturally, which focus the highly charged waves of energy from the "twin towers" and project it through the land. This energy collides at a point on Mount Canigou, implodes, and creates a doorway or a portal to another realm of experience. Chaplin saw evidence that Saunière was aware of the energy that existed between the two towers.[58] He must have known that both towers are sited at locations of strong vortex energy.'

I thought of the sightings of UFOs over Mount Canigou. 'That was the mountain where you swam in the rock pool, wasn't it?'

'I know, Gerard, this is really freaky stuff, but bear with me. Dan helped us to visualise it as two pine cones kissing noses. The pine cone is a metaphor for a standing wave of energy. The point on Mount Canigou where the two standing waves meet is called the Phase Conjugate point. It's where all the waves gather at one place in golden ratio. The charge is compressed by Phi ratio, and then accelerated at this point. Initiates who had prepared themselves appropriately were able to access this energy to project themselves into other realms of reality with greatly heightened perception. Their DNA charge was compressed then accelerated. This would have been interpreted as a way of achieving immortality, of rising from the dead – a sort of resurrection. Of course, anyone who hadn't prepared themselves properly would, as Dan says, end up as toast.'

I had read reports of near-death experiences where people describe spiralling upwards into another realm of reality, where they received all sorts of information about the meaning of life before returning.

'I saw a fabulous double spiral detail on a huge wooden door at the Abbey of Saint Michel de Cuxa, which is located at the foot of Mount Canigou about eighty kilometres south of Rennes-le-Château,' said Jennifer. 'The monastery is located on the axis facing Rennes-le-Château. That may be an indication that they knew about the vortex energy in that location. Boudet wrote that the cromlech around Rennes-le-Château and Rennes les Bains was a special place where ancient sages gathered to carry out scientific functions amongst other things. Pretty wild stuff, hey, Gerard. In *Foucault's Pendulum*, Umberto Eco suggests that the Templars knew the secret of an immense source of telluric energy, which they were planning to use to conquer the world, and that they are still around today. He suggests that the maintenance of this secret was worth the sacrifice of the whole Temple quarter in Paris.'

'*Foucault's Pendulum* is fiction, isn't it?' I said.

'Yes, I know, but Henry Lincoln did suggest that the Templars discovered something of immense importance in the Holy Land that was only revealed to an elite group of noblemen who were involved in some sort of clandestine activity. He said that it had something to do with secret knowledge, but he did not know what. There are numerous conspiracy theories that a powerful elite is trying to harness telluric energy in order to control the world. What greater treasure, and what greater secret could there be than the power to communicate with Mother Earth and the stars. However, there's more: you are going to love this, Gerard. If you look at a map of known locations of gold panning in the south of France at the time of the Templars, they coincide remarkably with Templar castles and commanderies. Mann suggests that the Templars may have discovered information relating to minerals exploration and mining techniques along with mapping techniques that enabled them to navigate the globe and search out valuable mineral resources in the New World, including copper and gold.

34

White Lady Rock

The afternoon sun set a warm glow over the yellow roses. My original plan for a chat over coffee had developed into one of those magical days where the body and mind feel truly alive with the pleasure of sharing knowledge and information with a kindred soul.

'Did you know that Canberra was originally designed on the principles of sacred geometry?' said Jennifer.

'Canberra, really?'

'Yes, when I was working in Canberra in 2000, someone told me that I should read a book called *The Secret Plan of Canberra.*'

'Well, there's a lot of secrets in Canberra but I've never heard of that one,' I said.

'Walter Burley-Griffin, the architect who initially designed the city, kept it quiet at the time. He didn't want to be labelled a nutter. However, those in the know knew about it. I went to several second-hand bookshops but couldn't find it, so I made notes from the copy in the National Library. Burley-Griffin and his wife were inspired by the ancient spiritual belief in the unity of all life. Their design used the natural formation of five mountains: Black Mountain, Mount Ainslie, Mount Mugga Mugga, Mount Pleasant and Capitol Hill. I don't think that many people realise that Canberra has affinities with Stonehenge, Glastonbury, ancient Egyptian temples and pyramids. The spooky thing is that while I was searching for a copy of the book, Enzo came across the exact same book in a second-hand bookshop in Adelaide – I hadn't even mentioned it to him.'

'Wow, I can see why you would say that's synchronicity,' I said.

'The other interesting thing is that lots of sacred sites around the world have red soil.'

'That would be because of the high iron content.' I said. 'Some authors have commented on the red earth around Rennes-le-Château, but as far as I've been able to determine, no one has made the connection with the geology, with the fact that iron-rich red earth can be an indicator of gold if associated with quartz, hematite and magnetite. However, finding gold in pure white quartz is very rare. The quartz will have a dirty appearance with reddish or brown stains.'

'So red earth equals iron-rich, magnetic force, blood, sacredness and native gold,' said Jennifer.

I thought of the ochre red earth in parts of outback Australia. I knew that in Aboriginal Dreaming it represents the blood of Dreaming spirits and is a critical part of many ceremonies. The red ochre mined by the Adnyamathanha people to the north of Mt Chambers Gorge in the Flinders Ranges is particularly prized, as it sparkles with hematite.

'I assume that where there's iron there's a magnetic field,' said Jennifer. 'Maybe that's what draws us in and reacts with the iron in our body. Rat Scabies compares the red soil around Rennes to the colour of rich, deep, dark blood. The Hebrew word *Adamah*, Adam, means red clay or earth. Jennifer Priestly told Scabies that going to Rennes-le-Château has an impact on a person's karma. That whatever is going on with you at the time, whether it's positive or negative, it brings it to the surface and gets you through it faster.'

'Well, it was the patch of red earth I saw on the way to Rennes-le-Château in 2003 that started this whole journey for me. Maybe it is my karma.'

'People can have all sorts of intense emotional experiences at sacred sites,' said Jennifer. 'Some people can have revelations and increased clarity into their destiny. Jean Luc Robin was very down to earth but even he said that if you come to the country with good intentions, it certainly increases them. So I guess the reverse would hold true as well.'

I remembered a strange experience I had back in 1991 on a gold prospecting trip to a remote part of New South Wales with a mate of mine – something I could never quite explain. 'I wonder if that's what I experienced at White Lady Rock.'

Not that long after Suzie and I divorced, I met David, an English barman who worked with me at the Centennial Hotel in Sydney. We got on well and decided to go on a prospecting trip to two locations near Mount Poole, where the explorer James Poole discovered gold in the 1840s. The locations had unusual names: Good Friday and Easter Monday and were located within a radius of about fifty kilometres from Milparinka, the closest town. Milparinka is off the Silver Highway, towards Cameron Corner on the way to Birdsville. This is where three states meet: New South Wales, South Australia and Queensland. The closest town to Cameron Corner is Tibooburra, about a hundred and fifty kilometres south-east.

It was an eleven-hundred-kilometre drive from Sydney. I had sold the old Go Devil and bought a new Suzuki four-wheel drive, the cheapest four-wheel drive on the market, with a short wheelbase and very light. The only drawback was that you could not carry much; but it was a good performer on sand, especially creek beds.

We arrived at Milparinka around three p.m. and headed straight for the old pub for a cold beer. We met the town's population – the man and his wife who ran the pub. In these parts, Australia is still a rough, tough, pioneering country. The pub, and a fully restored courthouse used as a tourist information office, made up the town – that was it. Drinks finished, we went in search of a good camping spot so we could relax for the rest of the afternoon. We found one about twenty kilometres out.

'This is desolate county, Jennifer. Imagine the ground covered with rocks and more rocks, very hard on the back when sleeping on the ground. It didn't matter, though. We were there on a mission, to do some detecting to find only one thing: gold.

'I've never been in the outback. The furthest north I've been is Whyalla,' said Jennifer.

'You must go one day. Being in the isolation of the outback is one of the best feelings. I love it – no distractions, no TV, radio, telephone – it really heightens your senses. Anyway, as we began to set up camp for the night, I imagined what it must have been like for the first European explorers venturing into the area in the boiling summer and terrible drought of 1845. Captain Charles Sturt's expedition party camped for several months at Depot Glen, near a waterhole in granite country. When the rains finally came in July, James Poole, Sturt's second in command, was very ill. He died a few days after the expedition broke camp to continue their fruitless search for an inland sea. Not far from Depot Glen, they buried Poole's body beneath a beefwood tree, and marked it with his initials. The tree is still living,' I said.

'It was a beautiful clear night and we were looking forward to the next day. David made Billy tea with eucalyptus leaves tossed in at the end for extra flavour. We were ready to settle in for the night and relax. We started to chat about the trip, friends, family and work. Then something strange happened. We both started to feel uneasy, as if something was not quite right, but we didn't know what. It's hard to explain, but it was like a malaise descending on us for no apparent reason. At first, I started feeling out of sorts, and then it progressed to a general bodily weakness, tightening in my chest and finally a feeling of despondency and dejection. David was feeling it too. It was as if we were going through a total emotional withdrawal. At one stage, we were even crying and we didn't know why. It was as if we had been struck by some mysterious illness. As the night wore on, the feeling worsened. All we wanted to do was to get away from the place, but it was the middle of the night, in the middle of nowhere. We got into our swags but didn't get much sleep. Morning couldn't have come fast enough. David made a cup of billy tea and we packed our gear feeling sorry for ourselves. However, we hadn't gone all that way to have a sleepless night then turn around and head home the next morning empty-handed.'

'So what did you do?' said Jennifer.

'Well, with great difficulty, we unpacked our detectors in silence and each tied a scarf around our mouth and nose because of the millions of flies, then we started walking. The feelings of despair and desolation were hanging on, our spirits were low and we still couldn't understand why. It took maybe half an hour to reach the wire fence some three hundred metres away. We were wearing our headphones for better audio accuracy, but I think at that time it didn't matter at all. We jumped the fence, and spotted a small hill surrounded by scrubby flat land. On top of the hill was an unusual natural feature, a small outcrop of quartz, sparkling like snow and surrounded by other small broken rocks. I approached the outcrop, swinging the coil of my detector. The closer I got, the more dazzling it became, and then I noticed something attached to it. I was stunned. A tiny plaque was screwed onto the quartz just a couple of centimetres above the ground, as if someone had put it there not to be seen. It read White Lady Rock Sacred Aboriginal site do not trespass. David was a good fifty metres from me. I called out and he rushed over. I guess he thought I had found a nugget. When he read the plaque all he could say was "Bloody hell, mate, what's this?"'

'Did you know there was a sacred site in that vicinity?' said Jennifer. 'I think you have to have permission to be on a sacred site, don't you?'

'No, we didn't know it was there, and yes you need permission to visit a sacred site. We had been camping right in the middle of one without realising it and clearly without permission to be there. We looked around – nothing. There was only this dazzling white quartz rock and us. We immediately turned back, loaded everything in the car, left and never looked back. The further we travelled away from the site, that immense feeling of depression and desolation went, like a heavy weight being lifted. About an hour later, we were back to our normal selves. The strangest thing was that we were at the location called Good Friday on Easter Monday and at the location called Easter Monday on Good Friday. We hadn't planned it that way – was that just coincidence?'

'That's fascinating, Gerard. Let's see what we can find out.' Jennifer opened her laptop and Googled White Lady Rock. 'Have you ever been back there?'

'No, I haven't, but I'd like to.'

'Here it is – there's not much information about it.' Jennifer studied the screen. 'Apparently, it is important to Indigenous communities throughout western New South Wales because many of the families who lived along nearby Thompson's Creek were forced by the Aboriginal Protection Board to leave the area in 1935. It says that White Lady Rock was a sacred place of healing. If people were very sick, their relatives would travel to the rock to ask the White Lady to make them better.'

'It seems that the White Lady had the opposite effect on us,' I said. 'It's not something that I'll ever forget.'

'The Indigenous people of those regions have recognised sacred places for thousands of years,' said Jennifer. 'Healers say that the natural earth energies at these sites can help spontaneously push up transformational forces in people who are particularly sensitive – were you going through any emotional issues at the time?'

'No, not really – only my divorce from Suzie.'

'There you are. Maybe you were suppressing your feelings about the divorce and the White Lady helped you express them. Interesting that it's called White Lady – I guess because of the colour of the quartz,' Jennifer leant in towards the screen. 'This is interesting. It says that the local Aboriginal people believe that the rock is the body of the White Lady, the "queen". Both Isis and the Virgin Mary are sometimes referred to as the White Lady or La Reine Blanche, the White Queen. There are White Lady churches in the south of France. The Cathars used that term for Mary Magdalene. According to legend, the white ladies of the Corbières and the Ariège lived near water or in caves – close to the earth, places representing the mother's womb. Some people believe that the Notre Dame statues found throughout the south of France are actually of Mary Magdelene, not the Virgin Mary, and are probably a rebranded, miracle-working ancient local goddess.'

Jennifer's brow furrowed. 'Listen to this: it says that the White Lady's head was believed to be made of gold. It was removed in the 1800s and hidden underground somewhere in a nearby creek to protect it from white prospectors. Mmm, I would want to double check that information with the local Indigenous people. The story of the gold head may be a prospectors' legend indicating that there was real gold to be found in this area.'

'There is – that's the reason David and I were there.'

'Clearly it must be an area of strong telluric energy,' said Jennifer. *'Terribilis est locus iste.'*

'You know that *terribilis* can mean awesome,' I said.

'That's exactly what I mean.'

After lunch, I dropped Jennifer at the Central Market in the city. We agreed to meet again with Enzo in a couple of days. However, what should have been a ten-minute trip back to Enzo's house at Norwood turned into a one-hour trip around the eastern suburbs trying to get my bearings. My GPS decided to give up the ghost – gremlins at work again?

35

Out of the blue

To make a big fire all you need is a tiny spark.

Someone tells you a story that sounds like a fairy tale – no verified facts, observable evidence, witnesses or dates. Then out of the blue, a very important piece of information knocks on your door to show you the way. Most of the time when a problem requires a solution, it is necessary to think outside the square to find it. A small clue, overlooked by most, may prove critical in leading you in a completely different direction. Perhaps trying to solve one mystery can help you to solve another one.

Since our meeting at the café, Jennifer had emailed me an article about pyramids written in 2011 by Philip Coppens, a well-known investigator of ancient mysteries and a dedicated Rennie. Philip cited French scientist, Joseph Davidovits's theory that the ancient Egyptians did not carve the blocks used to create the pyramids from stone then hoist them into place, but created artificial blocks from a slushy form of limestone. He proposes that the Egyptians knew how to make a 'geopolymer cement' by dissolving soft limestone, which they quarried on the damp south side of the Giza Plateau, and mixed with lime and tecto-alumino-silicate-forming materials such as kaolin clay, silt, and the salt natron (sodium carbonate). According to Davidovits, they carried the limestone concrete mix by the bucketful and then poured it into moulds placed on the pyramid sides, where it hardened into blocks. The knowledge of this technology was later lost.[59] Davidovits's theory is disputed, but no one really knows how the pyramids were constructed.

I was familiar with Philip Coppens's work. Years earlier, I had emailed him about some information I was given by Leon Creswell, a rig-driller from Broken Hill, who I met when I was passing through Wilcannia, a small town about two hundred kilometres north-east of Broken Hill. Wilcannia is known for its stunning sandstone buildings. The post office, courthouse, customs store, school and other private buildings were constructed in the late 1800s, around the time that gold was discovered at Mount Browne on the Albert goldfield in 1880. Leon told me that when he was a boy he wondered where the source of sandstone was, as he had never heard of a quarry in these parts, the nearest hill being thirty kilometres way. His grandfather told him that the locals used a silica gel-like material to make the blocks and took him to a large sandhill where the gel had been found. Apparently, the locals poured it into moulds, where it set hard like concrete, which they could cut into perfect blocks using crosscut saws. Some evidence is still visible on some of the door strips and window ledges of non-government buildings.[60]

Leon drilled for gas, oil and water – it's tough work. He told me that he discovered an eleven-metre-deep deposit of gel in some of the holes he drilled. According to Leon, water bore records show that in that area there is a three-hundred-metre deposit of pure white silica sand covering several thousand square kilometres. The gel is located on top of the sand and is covered by eight metres of gypsum then three metres of top soil. Naturally, if this technology was being used in Australia a hundred and thirty years ago, in the middle of nowhere, I was keen to find out more.

A year later, I met with Leon again. He wanted to show me the location his grandfather had shown him forty-four years earlier but needed to ask directions because it had been such a long time since he last went. We stopped by a homestead owned by fifth-generation landowners to ask directions. The farmer's wife confirmed that the story was indeed true.

Sometime later, Leon emailed me details of his correspondence with Alf Mostler, professor of geology at Innsbruck University of Austria, with whom he had contact through the professor's brother Halmar

Mostler, a friend of his. The professor confirmed that silica gel is known to form in ancient seabeds, but is very rare.[61] I emailed Philip about the story – he was very interested and asked if I could reveal the location. Unfortunately, it took time for me to reply and, sadly, Philip passed away in the meantime.

Several years later, travelling on the Tanami Track on my way back from Halls Creek in Western Australia, I stopped to see the world-famous sandstone sculptures of Broken Hill located at the peak of Sundown Hill, in the Living Desert reserve. In 1993, the council engaged sculptor Lawrence Beck to develop new sculptures. After admiring Wilcannia's beautiful sandstone buildings, Beck had gone looking for the source of the sandstone – but couldn't find it. Imagine my surprise when I discovered that a local contractor had transported fifty-three tonnes of huge free-floating sandstone blocks from the MacCulloch Ranges to the Broken Hill site. Was Leon's story an outback legend? Did something else lay beneath Wilcannia beside the sparkling white silica sands? Leon passed away some five years ago. The location of his find remains a mystery.

Sundown Hill is a very significant sacred site in much the same way as Uluru. The twelve sculptures are located at the physical end of twelve song lines which come together to create a harmonic node which connects to a similar point at Machu Picchu.[62] Looking now at my photos of the sculptures, I noticed how remarkably reminiscent many of them were of ancient menhirs. The interesting thing is that in order to determine the location for the new sculptures, Beck sought spiritual guidance from an eagle. What did that eagle know and where could I find him?

I thought of my conversation with Jennifer about the earth energy grid and the location of powerful vortex points on the globe. The suggestion that the Templars may have been manipulating the earth grid with ancient esoteric knowledge was certainly at the far end of the conspiracy theory spectrum and something I had not heard before. I imagined that many would dismiss it as lunacy. However, I knew that Henry Lincoln was captivated by the pentagonal geometry in the landscape.

He observed that various medieval churches and chateaux were aligned to the Paris Meridian in a predictable geometric pattern, long before the Meridian was officially established in the sixteenth century. There even appeared to be a significant connection between the layout of Boudet's cromlech and the Paris Meridian. This was more than coincidence or even synchronicity; it was observable and verifiable.

Several Rennes-le-Château researchers highlight the Paris Meridian as being significant, notably David Wood, an expert in large-scale mapping techniques and the author of *Genisis*. He proposes that a gigantic 'temple', covering more than 103.6 square kilometres and marked by churches, mountain tops or rock outcrops, was laid out across the Languedoc landscape with mathematical intelligence. He suggests a connection with ancient Egyptian creation legends, and possibly the origins of the human race. He even suggests that the universe could be recorded in the geometry of the landscape. I was intrigued to find out that, coincidentally, the Paris Meridian goes through my old home town of Mazamet, the gold mine of Salsigne, Arques and the infamous Poussin tomb, then Rennes les Bains and Mount Bugarach.

In his article on pyramids, Philip also cites historian Livio Catullo Stecchini (1913–1979), who suggests that there is evidence showing that the ancients accurately mapped the lands from western Europe to Asia.[63] Stecchini identifies that a number of locations throughout the ancient world are located in exact geodetic relation to the longitude meridian of the Great Pyramid of Giza. The Paris Meridian fits perfectly in Stecchini's 'Pyramid Grid System', as do the megalithic standing stones, dolmens and menhirs around the village of Carnac. Stecchini also noted that there was a connection with certain latitudes and the sighting of ancient oracle centres. What really got me thinking was that Stecchini believed they were also associated with mineral resources, mostly from mines or 'man-made wells', invariably located on hills overlooking rivers. If, as Boudet believed, the cromlech was a special place to the ancient sages, could it also have been an oracle centre and the site of mineral deposits known to the ancients?

I had read dozens of theories about the purpose of the ancient pyramids of Giza. Notable among them is the theory that the pyramids, along with other megalithic structures, were part of a worldwide system for harnessing and transmitting energy, that the Great Pyramid was a geo-mechanical power plant that responded sympathetically with the earth's vibrations and converted that energy into electricity. Some go further and suggest that the great pyramid of Giza was a node in a giant global energy system. There are even theories about pyramids in Australia.

It wasn't only the ancients who were experimenting with earth energies. The famous inventor Nikola Tesla (1856–1943) was forced underground after he gave public demonstrations of how to tap 'free telluric energy' from the oscillating earth field. I imagined how the vested interests of the day reacted – no money to be made from electricity meters or fossil fuel. Tesla was experimenting with technology that could wirelessly transmit power from the inexhaustible energy that flows naturally around our planet via a network of 'capacitors' located at nodes on the earth grid. A pyramid capstone made of gold would have been an excellent conductor of electricity. I couldn't help thinking of White Lady Rock and the curious legend that her head was made of gold. A gold capstone on a quartz outcrop would certainly make an excellent conductor.

According to author Robert Howells, a member of the Priory of Sion told him that full knowledge of the secret at Rennes-le-Château confers a very real and potentially 'world-shattering power' were it ever in the 'wrong hands'. Given the strategic advantage of such information, I could understand why such a secret would only be available to 'initiates'. It was the hot intellectual property of the day, but also dangerous, as much of it would have been classed as alchemy, which was condemned by the Church – another excellent reason for keeping it hidden. I thought of Giordano Bruno, tried for heresy and burnt at the stake in 1600 after daring to suggest that the earth revolved around the sun.

I have spent hundreds of hours examining the microscopic world of crystals. I looked back through my photos of microspheres. Changing my perception slightly, I could see how they could be viewed on a macro level. I imagined the Earth itself as a huge crystal, criss-crossed with energy grids that somehow align with bigger grids on a cosmic scale in mathematically precise ways, creating a giant fractal capacitor that ticks over for eternity. Could this be the secret 'sacred knowledge' brought back to the south of France by the Templars? Knowledge of the earth's natural energy pattern would have given them enormous advantage not only in surveying and mapping but also in exploring the mineral riches of the land.

If Dan Winter is right, and there is a connection between native gold and the earth's energy grid, I could see why, at a time when mining techniques were relatively unsophisticated, this knowledge would have been well hidden and available only to a few, including those with the skill to dowse the energy lines. Winter, along with thousands of others who dare to challenge mainstream scientific views, has come in for his fair share of the usual criticism of 'mad scientist' and 'pseudo-scholar'. However, throughout history, many 'mad scientists' have made incredible discoveries.

Whether Saunière stumbled across the secret knowledge of the earth energy grid or simply stubbed his toe on a nugget, in my view, he discovered native gold and the clues are there for all to see.

36

Gold and roses: Norwood

'*Bonjour mes amis, ça va?*' said Jennifer, beaming at Enzo and me. The smell of warm apple and almond cake wafted from her basket.

Kisses and hugs were exchanged all round, then Jennifer sliced the freshly baked cake into chunky pieces – delicious dunked into our coffee.

'There's something niggling at the back of my mind,' said Enzo. 'I don't think that we can completely rule out the treasure theories.'

There was an audible sigh.

'I have no doubt that the references to treasure in the novels by authors like Jules Verne and his contemporaries are allusions to a treasure around Rennes-le-Château. They used the "green language" to conceal secret messages or an alternative meaning in the narrative, like a story within a story.'

'And the green language is?' said Jennifer.

'It's a symbolic language that has a surface meaning but conveys a message to those who understand the code. Nostradamus used it in his quatrains and Jules Verne in his fiction stories – all of which were based on his knowledge of a secret. Michel Lamy writes that Verne used wordplay as an allegorical language. Take for instance anagrams, where letters in words or entire phrases are rearranged to reveal a new meaning.'

'Like in *The da Vinci Code*,' said Jennifer. '"So dark the con of man" became *Madonna of the Rocks*, da Vinci's famous painting in the Louvre.'

'Exactly,' said Enzo. 'Remember Leigh Teabing, the Holy Grail expert: his name is an anagram of the names of two of the authors of *The Holy Blood and the Holy Grail*: Baigent and Leigh. Lamy also says that any time Verne uses the letters "or" in a word or a name, it's a reference to gold.'

'Of course it's a reference to gold,' I said. 'That part of France is full of place names that include the letters *or*, or *au*. As far as I am concerned, they are obvious references to native gold. Like the ancient Celtic town of Ausch, about seventy-eight kilometres west of Toulouse. The Auscii were there at the time of the Roman conquest in the 50s BC. They were very skilful in working in gold. Boudet wrote that the phonetic pronunciation of *Auch* in English is "Aoutch", which he says means "gold necklace".[64] They sourced the gold from an area where it was nearly flush to the surface as if you could walk on it, like in Burraga, New South Wales. The Greeks and the Phoenicians used gold from the Pyrenees as ballast for their ships when they returned to their countries. To put it simply, if reading between the lines, there must have been plenty.'

'In *Clovis Dardentor*, Verne introduces a character called Captain Bugarach,' said Enzo.

'Didn't Stephen Spielberg base the mountain in *Close Encounters of the Third Kind* on Mount Bugarach?' said Jennifer.

'He was inspired by it just like Verne,' said Enzo. 'But I think the final version in the film was based on the Devil's Tower in Wyoming.'

'Verne's novel *Journey to the Centre of the Earth* is based on Bugarach,' I said. 'He suggests that a mythical race lives in an underground world full of gold and there's a secret entrance near Rennes-le-Château. It is obvious to me that he was alluding to the presence of native gold. Lamy makes a brief reference to the gold mine at Salsigne and so does Gerard de Sède in *Rennes-le-Château: Le dossier, les impostures, les phantasms, les hypotheses.*'

'Lamy makes a curious reference to the relationship between salt and gold,' said Enzo. 'In esoteric terms, salt characterises one of the stages of the alchemical process. Is there a connection between the presence of salt and native gold, Gerard?'

'Not with the knowledge of gold mining today. However, the "salt route" could be referring to the river Sals, which originates in Mount Bugarach and flows through Rennes les Bains. Perhaps he is telling us to follow the "salt river" to get to the gold.'

'I wonder if there were gold mines around Rennes les Bains,' said Jennifer.

Enzo reached for a pile of books tottering on the edge of the sideboard and with deft hands extracted *Refuge of the Apocalypse: Doorway Into Other Dimensions*. 'I've been going back over Elizabeth van Buren's work.' He flicked to a photo of the bas-relief of the *Sermon on the Mount* that graces the back of the church. 'Do you remember the Terrain Fleury?'

'Of course,' I said. 'The one with the sack of gold nuggets.'

I remembered how strangely out of place the sack looked – tied at the top with a rope and with a hole in the side revealing what some say are corn cobs, but what appear to me to be yellow rocks that looked suspiciously like gold nuggets. The bag bore a remarkable resemblance to the drawstring bag associated with La Sanche, the mysterious death cult. There was also a girl holding what again looked like gold nuggets in her apron and, in the first station of the cross, a Jewish priest appears to be holding a gold nugget in one hand and pointing to a location with the other. Given what I had read about the mysterious clues throughout the church, this seemed a bit too obvious. We don't usually associate Jesus with a sack of gold in the literal sense. Maybe it all had some deeper significance or did it mean something else altogether? As Sir Arthur Conan Doyle once said, 'There is nothing more deceptive as an obvious fact.'

'There is a phrase at the bottom – *Venez a moi vous tous qui souffrez qui etes accables et je vous soulagerai* – Matthew 11:28,' said Enzo. 'The King James version reads, "Come unto me, all ye that labour and are heavy laden, and I will give you rest." According to Henry Lincoln, the word *accables* has been used instead of *affligues*. It doesn't change the sense of the phrase, but van Buren suggests that it creates a code in the phrase.'

'Another code,' I said. 'Well, I suppose this one is more tangible than the parchments.'

'The first two letters in the word *accables* are smaller than the others. If you look closely you can see it.'

Jennifer put on her glasses and peered at the picture. 'Oh yes ,I can see it. I didn't notice that when I was there – intriguing.'

'You can't see it in this photo but van Buren says that they are linked by a faint line to the previous "s" in the word *etes*, making the phrase *sac ables*, or more precisely *sac à blés*. She says that *bles* means corn, which is slang for gold in French, so *sac à blés* means sack for gold, a *sac* for putting gold in. She interprets gold in this sense as secret knowledge.'

'Actually, *blé* means wheat,' I said. 'And in slang it means money or *fric* or *oseille*. They all mean money – like bread in English. *sac à blé* means bag for money, a money bag.'

'Even better,' said Enzo. 'Whichever way you look at it, is Saunière telling us that whatever he found has given him access to a sack full of money?'

'It sounds like he's having a laugh,' said Jennifer. 'Come unto me and I will give you a bag of money. There is a report that the Marquis de Fleury discovered sepulchral urns containing pieces of gold. Maybe Saunière is alluding to de Fleury's finds.'

'That's possible,' said Enzo 'The really interesting thing is that the hill is centred between two distinct features in the landscape shown in the bas-relief, which van Buren writes have been identified as Rennes les Bains on the right and Rennes-le-Château on the left – features reported to have been painted by Saunière himself.'[65]

Enzo flicked to an image of what is purported to be the engraving on Marie de Negri's tombstone and another of the Dagobert parchment. 'There are four words on Marie de Negri's tombstone: *Redis Regis* and *Cellis Arcis*. The Latin word *redis* means you return or you restore, and *regis* means royal. *Cellis* means a basement or cave, and *arcis* means a fortress, or an ark, in the sense of a box or enclosure. So the statement could mean return to, or restore, the cave of the royal ark. Then there are the words *Redis Bles* and *Solis Sacerdotibus* written beside the main message of the Dagobert parchment. *Solis* means solely, and *sacerdotibus* means initiated, or it could also mean priests.

'Ah, so if *ble* means money,' I said, 'the words *Redis Bles* and *Solis Sacerdotibus* could actually be translated as "Return the money to the priests", instead of the esoteric translation "Return the corn to the priesthood of the sun".'

'That's not as funny as it sounds,' said Enzo. 'During the French Revolution, the government confiscated Church property, abolished the Church's authority to levy a tax on crops and cancelled special privileges for the clergy. Revolutionaries seized gold and silver crosses, melted bells and even converted some churches into warehouses or stables. They destroyed statues, relics and works of art. The Church considered the revolutionaries to be thieves. I'm sure that retrieving their property would have been high on the Church's list at some point in the future Then in 1905, the French government passed the law of separation of church and state. Church property was confiscated and churches stripped of most of their property rights. At one stage, the church had been the largest landowner in the country – no one could prospect on their land. Congregations had to submit an annual list of members, property, and financial status to government authorities on request. In 1906, Saunière refused to sign the inventory of the Church of St Mary Magdalene. Abbé Jean Rivière, the *curé* of Espéraza, signed it instead. Pope Pius X condemned the law in two encyclicals.'

Enzo stood up and placed van Buren's book on top of the pile. 'More coffee, anyone?'

There were three pieces of cake left – we both nodded. Enzo set about making the coffees using the machine I brought on my last visit. I cast my eyes across the bookshelves crammed with books in his kitchen. Enzo had the knack of easily locating any title as if he had a cataloguing system in his head. Jennifer helped him with the cups and we settled back at the little table.

'Did you know that originally Saunière called the Magdala tower the Tour de l'Horlodge, the clock tower?' said Jennifer.

'I think Baudelaire wrote a poem titled "*L'Horlodge*",' said Enzo, searching on his smartphone.

'Phonetically, the word *l'horlodge* sounds like *l'or lodge*,' I said. '*Lodge* in old French is the word for a box seat at the opera and *or* means gold of course. Was Saunière playing another little trick naming the tower the seat of gold? A bit too obvious?'

Enzo stood up triumphantly. 'Here it is: "*L'Horlodge*" written in 1857.' He began reciting the poem with the exaggerated delivery of a Shakespearian actor. '*Horloge! dieu sinistre, effrayant, impassible / Dont le doigt nous menace et nous dit: Souviens-toi!*'

'Is there a translation?' said Jennifer, rolling her eyes.

Enzo scrolled down, eyes flicking back and forth across the screen. 'Yes, oh this is interesting, listen to this: I'll read the fourth verse in English. "'Minutes, blithesome mortal, are bits of ore that you must not release…'" He looked up, smiled, then paused for extra dramatic effect. "'…without extracting the gold".'

'Ha,' I said. 'There you have it.'

'Red Minis again?' said Jennifer.

'Red Minis?' said Enzo frowning.

'It's an in-joke,' said Jennifer, glancing at me with a smile.

'The French love all these little word and letter games, Enzo. My nickname at school was *mille cent onze*, one thousand one hundred and eleven – four ones when written as numerals. Spoken quickly in French, my surname, Catherin, sounds like *quatre un*, forty-one. Therefore, G41 is my code name – when needed.'

Jennifer smiled. 'Ah, very clever, G41.'

'Thank you, 99.'

'Just call me the Baron,' said Enzo.

'Some researchers suggest that Boudet used cryptic codes to conceal a secret known to the Hautpouls,' said Enzo. 'At the time, a priest wrote that Boudet was the keeper of a secret that could be the cause of major upheavals.'

'Believe me, Enzo, the people who live around Salsigne can tell you about major upheavals,' I said. 'Have either of you ever seen an actual gold vein?'

Enzo and Jennifer shook their heads.

'Jim Shanahan, one of the CEOs of Hill End Gold Limited, sent me an amazing photograph of Bob Fraser, the manager for the underground operations for Northern Gold, a company mining gold at Hill End, Hargraves and Maitland Bar. Bob is standing inside a cave that is literally gleaming with gold covering the walls and ceiling. It should be named the Golden Room. The site was closed in 1917 and only reopened in 1986.'

'Wow, said Jennifer. 'I can imagine how legends about a great treasure or a room of gold could arise from someone finding something like that.'

'A friend of mine owns fourteen hundred acres of land at Maitland Bar, right in the middle of the goldfield,' I said. 'The famous eleven-kilo Maitland Bar nugget was discovered in 1887 on the Meroo Creek, about four hundred metres from where his house now stands. Hill End has many leases around Maitland Bar. Paul and I have our plan C, if you know what I mean.'

'What are plans A and B?' said Jennifer.

'Plan A is finding the diamond pipe and plan B is finding the source of Saunière's wealth of course.'

Silence fell over the room.

Enzo pursed his lips. 'I wonder if that could be an explanation for the story that de Sède tells of Ignace Paris, the shepherd of Rennes-le-Château. In 1645, Paris lost one of his sheep. He decided to go looking for it and thanks to the animal's bleating he spotted it in the bottom of a hole. He descended into the hole and found himself in a cave – standing on gold. He filled his pockets, and went to tell his story to the villagers, but refused to reveal the location of his find.'

'Was it real gold?' said Jennifer.

'Well, there are several versions – some refer to treasure, some to gold coins and some just to gold. It's anyone's guess. One version says that the people were puzzled by his story of rapid fortune and they stoned him. Something to do with trading with the devil, I think. There's another version that says the local lord had Paris tortured and he died of his injuries without revealing his secret.'

'Dying prematurely seems to be a running theme throughout the mystery,' said Jennifer. 'Who was the local lord?'

'One of the Hautpouls.'

I was travelling back to Canberra in a couple of days. I hoped to hear about the diamond exploration licence soon. Enzo, Jennifer and I agreed to continue our research over the next couple of months until I returned to Adelaide before Christmas.

Not long after I was back home, I received a call from Jennifer.

'I've found him.'

'Who?'

'The guy who discovered gold at Salsigne in 1892. His name is Louis Marius Esparseil.'

'Wow, what did you find out about him?'

'Not much. Apparently he was a member of the Société des Arts et des Sciences de Carcassonne.'

'Eighteen ninety-two is around the time that Saunière hit the jackpot,' I said.

'Exactly. See what you can find out on French sites,' said Jennifer. 'Oh, by the way, I think you should read Rat Scabies's book. I can post it to you – what's your address?'

Following my divorce from Rebecca, I had moved into a share house – the street number was 18.

'Eighteen,' she said. 'You're joking.'

'No, why?' I said.

'I live at number 18. It's the number of the goddess Isis.'

37

Mining the French archives

A quick search revealed that Louis Marius Esparseil was born on 9 September 1841 at 11 Rue de la Gaffe in Carcassonne, and died on 6 June 1900 in the same city. At the age of seventeen, after graduating from high school, he moved to Paris with his mother to attend the School of Fine Arts, the Conservatory of Arts and Crafts and the School of Mines and Works. When the Franco-Prussian war broke out in 1870, his mother was concerned for his safety and they returned to Carcassonne. He was a member of various organisations, including the Société des Arts et des Sciences de Carcassonne, and wrote the *Régime minéralogique du département de l'Aude* (Plan of mineralogical regime of the Department of Aude). He also donated a county mineral collection to the city.

In 1892, Esparseil was carrying out research of iron cap ores north of Carcassonne in the Montagne Noire at a location called the Roc de Cors, in the iron concession of Limousis less than two kilometres from Salsigne and Villanière.[66] He sent some rock samples for testing and to his surprise discovered that they contained gold. The gold was disseminated in quartz, and associated with arsenopyrite, pyrite and pyrrhotite. Mining began on the site of the present pit from 1893.[67]

Bérenger Saunière was assigned to Rennes-le-Château in 1885, but it was not until 1892 that he began accumulating his wealth. I wondered if there was a connection between Esparseil and Saunière, and began searching through the online archives of the Société des Arts et des Sciences de Carcassonne. The membership was a mix of professionals from the arts and sciences including doctors, architects, lawyers, artists and musicians. The clergy was represented, with a number of abbots and priests. I carefully scanned the names, hoping to find Saunière's amongst them. Bingo: Henri Boudet, Saunière's friend and fellow priest, was listed as a member in 1888. Allegedly, Boudet gave money to both Saunière and his housekeeper Marie Dénarnaud and was perhaps the 'brains' behind the 'secret'.

My goal was to present the mystery of Rennes-le-Château through the lens of geology; a lens that up until now has remained obscured. Geologists look through scientists' eyes. However, sometimes there is a feeling, call it an intuition, a hunch, something that simmers away at the back of your mind and will not let you go. Chuck Fipke calls it an adventure into the unknown – informed intuition at best. I had the same feeling when I read Tony MacNevin's book about diamonds and the elusive diamond pipe, which I believe lies undiscovered in the outback of New South Wales, and I had the same feeling about Rennes-le-Château. But I needed more than my intuition and thirty-eight specks of gold to put forward a new theory.

Any prospector worth his or her salt reviews the history of a location before setting out to sample the area. One of the first things I did when I selected the land at Kandie Peak to search for diamonds was to review the previous mining explorations in the area. Just because a mob abandons an area does not mean the minerals are exhausted. Finding out who was there, what techniques they used, what they found and why they left is important. There are always clues to possible future sources of gold. The only difference with Rennes-le-Château was the timeline, the access to information, and the skill to sort fact from fiction. History, as they say, is not what happened, but the reports of what happened, usually by the people who 'won'. It can be full of propaganda, originally compiled to suit the political, social, religious and cultural needs of an era rather than being an accurate record of events.

I looked at the map I had downloaded from the web showing the anticline and syncline formation at the southern end of the Montagne Noire. Next to this, I placed the map showing rivers and creeks around Rennes-le-Château; the one I used in 2010 when I found the thirty-eight specks. Now it was a matter of analysing the history of minerals exploration in the region, the known locations of ancient and more recent mines and the history of the ownership of the land – all the time looking for clues.

Over the next few weeks, I continued my research, following the thread of geology. The Internet is an amazing tool. What would have taken years of research in libraries and municipal archives was now available in digitised form at the press of a button. The more I searched, the more references I found to the Montagne Noire. Salsigne is on the southern edge of this range. De Sède's treasure story was based on the theory that the Hautpouls were privy to important information that had something to do with a secret hidden in the land around Rennes-le-Château, Rennes les Bains and the Montagne Noire. The same land was the subject of stories of hidden treasure protected by demons or the devil. The mystery was pulling me back to the region where I had lived in the 1960s with Taty. Back to Mazamet and the little village of Hautpoul on the rocky outcrop above Mazamet named after the noble family who established the village and whose estate seemed to hold secrets that were central to the Rennes-le-Château mystery.

38

'There's gold in them hills'

We know that mining and prospecting for gold and other precious minerals in what is now the Languedoc-Roussillon region goes back to pre-Roman times. The gold-bearing locations in the departments of the Aude, Tarn, Ariege and l'Hérault are well documented, including the presence of alluvial gold in the rivers and creeks such as the Aude, Ariege, Sals and the Orbiel. Historian Guillaume Catel (1560–1626) wrote of the existence of rich gold and silver mines in the mountains of the Languedoc near Rennes les Bains in the Diocese of Alet, not far from Rennes-le-Château. He noted the big caverns and quarries that were dug by the ancients.[68]

France has seen gold rushes since the time of the ancient Celts; then periods when mines were abandoned and knowledge lost. Some explorations resembled archaeological digs as the remains of ancient excavations attributed to the Gallo-Romans guided prospectors in their explorations.[69] The state resumed mining in the twelfth and thirteenth centuries.[70] During the fourteenth century and the first half of the fifteenth century, the state abandoned mining and few or no mines appear to have been worked by the Crown.[71] Then in 1548, under Henry II, King of France from 1547 to 1559, a 'gold mining fever' broke out which lasted until 1602 and possibly longer. Gold mines were opened or reopened, including in the Pyrenees.[72]

In the early part of the seventeenth century, Henry IV, King of France from 1589 to 1610, revived minerals exploration and mining as part of his plan to reactivate the economy following the devastation by the Wars of Religion (1562–1598). He engaged Jean de Malus to research the mineral wealth of the Pyrenees and commissioned the Baron and Baroness of Beausoleil to survey France for mines.[73] He brought in a large number of engineers and miners from the surrounding Germanic countries, as they were more skilled than the locals. Malus reported that there were 'all kinds of metals and minerals in these mountains', including rich gold and silver mines.[74] Gobet wrote that Henry's reign was 'glorious for mineralogy'.[75]

During the Middle Ages (AD 476–1498) most mines were controlled by local lords who diverted royalties into their own pockets and away from the king's and litigation was frequent.[76] Much of Henry's reign and those of kings who followed him – Louis XIII, who reigned from 1610 to 1643, and the early years of Louis XIV, from 1643 to 1715, – were focused on administrative centralisation. As the French kings moved the country away from feudalism, they increased their control of mining operations. The reason was simple – they needed to get their hands on huge sums of cash in order to fund their plans for territorial expansion, to wage various wars, and to control internal conflicts in the country. Finding strategic mineral resources, in particular gold, would help fill the coffers.

Mining laws were based on the Regalian Doctrine under which all mineral wealth was the prerogative of the state, represented by the king, or the feudatory lord. Almost all mining countries of the world, except the United States, follow the Regalian Doctrine, including Australia. Over time, there were various edicts, decrees, legislation and statutory orders controlling the exploration, fossicking and mining of gold and other precious minerals. This included laws controlling the movement of gold out of the country, reforming the administration of mines, encouraging mining development and sponsoring research. The kings tasked intendants with the job of undermining local control by regional nobles.

Under this system, the state could grant concessions or leases to landowners and mining operators at discretion and subject to certain restrictions.[77] Concessions were sometimes permanent and conditional upon uninterrupted mining activity. Mining could be undertaken without the consent of the surface owner who was only entitled to compensation for surface damage. Landowners could explore to a depth no greater than 30.5 metres. However, many had little or no mining experience and this often resulted in shallow unproductive mines. Landowners did, however, have priority in obtaining a concession to mine deeper if they met certain conditions.[78] To obtain a minerals exploration licence in Australia today, you need to demonstrate that you are genuine and have the necessary finances, knowledge and experience in the field and the equipment to run the project.

However, the concession system did not work well. Litigation was frequent and 'unbridled speculation' was widespread. The King's Council heard mining cases and there was much 'favour and intrigue'. The constituent assembly was convinced that mines had become the prey of courtiers gambling with the rights of the surface owners as well as the ones of the inventors.[79] In the world of minerals exploration, scams still occur today. It is not unknown for some small companies listed on the Stock Exchange to apply for a licence with very little intention of looking for minerals. The scam involves raising money for the 'next big find' and selling shares in the business then creating shock waves when money vanishes and they file for bankruptcy.

In 1661, Blaise d'Hautpoul went to court against Nicolas Pavillon(1597–1677), the Bishop of Alet, complaining that the king's people were exploring his grounds and mines.[80] What followed was a legal battle between Blaise d'Hautpoul, Pavillon and Nicolas Fouquet, the king's superintendent of finances from 1653 to 1661, that lasted until 1666. Interestingly, Pavillon had assisted Blaise to restore the church at Rennes-le-Château in 1646. In a curious twist of fate, it would not be long before I experienced my own battle regarding access to land for my diamond exploration project.

Minerals exploration in the Languedoc continued during the sevententh century. In 1666, Jean-Baptiste Colbert (1619–1683), who had taken over from Fouquet in 1661, set up the Compagnie Royale des

Mines et Fonderies du Languedoc, the Royal Company of Mining and Smelting of the Languedoc, to restart the exploitation of the region's mines. He was aware of the mineral wealth in the heart of the Aude, which includes the area around Salsigne, and knew that the limitations of mining techniques of the day and that lack of expertise and poor practices resulted in a proliferation of unproductive mines that were later abandoned. In 1667, Cesar d'Arcons, an engineer from Bordeaux, advised Colbert on the cost-benefit of exploiting the mines in the Languedoc, including those in the Montagne Noire.

In 1678, Colbert created the Compagnie de Mines Blanchefort to prospect on Hautpoul lands.[81] In March 1734, the company Guillaume Roussel, also called Company of the Mines of Languedoc, obtained the concession of the mines of the dioceses of Alet and Narbonne.

Historian and mineralogist Nicholas Gobet (circa 1735–1781) wrote of the existence of abandoned gold and silver mines in the Pyrenees, which had been 'neglected for a long time' and noted that little had been written about this 'important material'.[82] Nicolas Lamoignon de Basville (1648–1724), an intendant over the Languedoc between 1685 and 1718, wrote that the Romans had gold mines in these mountains and that they were perhaps so well hidden they could no longer be found. It is possible therefore that the mines were not exhausted. He observed that the fact that peasants collected large quantities of gold flakes from the streams coming from the mountains was 'certain proof' of the existence of gold higher up.[83]

According to Phillipe de Chérisey, when Louis XIV came to the throne in 1643, the Beausoleils persuaded him that there was a gold deposit in Black Rock near Rennes les Bains on Blaise d'Hautpoul's land. His estate included Rennes-le-Château, and Rennes Les Bains. I assumed that the documents that François-Pierre d'Hautpoul deposited with a lawyer in Esperaza in 1644 contained information about what was of value on and under his land. These documents did not resurface until 1780. What did these documents reveal and who had access to them between 1644 and 1781 during the minerals exploration revival?

In 1767, Rennes-le-Château passed to Paul François Vincent, Marquis de Fleury (1735–1794) when he married Marie de Negre's youngest daughter Gabrielle d'Hautpoul-Rennes (1739–1790). He became the Marquis of Fleury-Blanchefort.[84] In 1794, the Marquis de Fleury came into an unexpected 'fortune', which enabled him to buy up all of the land around Rennes les Chateau that had belonged to the Blanchefort family. Later, he became mayor of the commune.[85] Was the 'bag of gold' in the Terrain Fleury a clue to the source of de Fleury's fortune?

39

Alchemy and demons

The Beausoleils, Jean du Châstelet (1578–1645), from Brabant (now the Netherlands), and his French wife Martine de Bertereau (c. 1601–1642) were geologists, mining engineers and alchemists. They had travelled extensively in Europe and compiled a list of hundreds of potentially financially feasible mines, including gold, silver, lead, copper and iron. They identified that gold is found in association with pyrite but most of all with mispickel, also called arsenopyrite, which just happens to be the main source for the gold at Salsigne. Gobet published their list of mines and included their work in his anthology of French mineralogists published in 1779.[86] The list shows the location of feasible mines – unfortunately, some of them could not be found.

I had no idea that at that time mineralogists practised alchemy and astrology-based mining and prospecting techniques. The Beausoleils believed that metals were living entities, growing inside the Earth's 'womb' from different exhalations and under the influence of the planets.[87] They also believed in a certain 'sympathy' between minerals and metals on the one side, and the Sun, Moon and the seven planets on the other. They developed a set of sixteen prospecting instruments made according to the celestial arrangements of the sun and the planets. This included divining rods made from wood and the mineral they were prospecting for. They believed that minerals and metals exuded vapours and there was a hidden matrix or sympathetic attraction between them. For example, to divine for gold, they used a rod made by joining a piece of wood to a section of gold, both weighing the same. The rod was held at the joint. In the hands of someone who knew the technique and in the presence of native gold, the gold section of the rod would be charged with particles coming from the native gold, and the rod would lose its equilibrium, indicating the presence of gold.

Once when I was prospecting, a driller showed me how he used dowsing technology to find water – he swore by it. He made his dowsing rods from two coat hangers, each one bent at a 90° angle. When I saw the rods moving, without him moving his hands, I was very curious and asked him how it worked. He told me that it was simple, that anybody could do it with a bit of practice, but the most important thing was faith. He showed me how to hold the rods pointing forward, one in each hand, loose enough to be able to move freely. The rods will open to either form a V, or close to form an X – it is that simple. For the rod to be useful, of course, you need to ask a yes/no question.

Picture yourself facing north, standing with your rods pointing forward, then ask a question to which you know the answer is yes. If the rods open, you know that every time you ask a simple yes/no question and the rods open, the answer to your question will be yes. It is similar to calibrating a lie detector. If the rods make an X, the answer is no. I told the driller that it seemed like 'bloody magic'. He agreed, but told me that for it to work, you need to believe in it; that in life you can achieve anything if you put your mind to it, all you need is practice and faith.

Dowsing is commonly used to locate water, especially when people want to dig a well. Less well known is that oil companies also employ dowsers to locate oil for drilling. Sometime later, I read that the dowsing rods are actually responding to changes in electrical conductivity in the earth. It seems that the earth energies are in control here.

The Beausoleils used scientific and practical advice derived largely from the Roman engineer Vitruvius's book on architecture, *De architectura*. Some of their practices were considered to be magic and associated with witchcraft, which was punishable. In 1627, a provincial provost broke into their home and confiscated all of their instruments, papers, documents and personal belongings, and they fled to Germany. Some suggest that the provost's motivation was more about his own interests and an attempt to limit the Crown's explorations. The couple returned to France in 1630 to continue their work under Louis XIII.

The Beausoleils had never received payment and in 1640, Martine wrote the 'Restitution of Pluto', a Latin poem seeking Richelieu's permission to benefit from the mines they discovered in France. They received no reply, but were charged with sorcery and died in prison, she in the Castle of Vincennes in 1642, and he in the Bastille around 1645. It has been suggested that the charges of alchemy and dabbling in the occult were not the reason the couple were interned by Richelieu, as he himself was interested in alchemy and occultism. The Languedoc is thought to have been a centre for alchemy in the middle ages under the Counts of Toulouse. Jean de Chastelet's first treatise on alchemy was printed in Béziers in Provence in 1627.

I recalled the theories that Saunière may have practised alchemy in a secret room in the church. There was also a room for alchemy in the Château d'Hautpoul. Most people associate alchemy with attempts to create gold from other substances; but could Saunière have been practising the alchemical techniques used by the Beausoleils in order to find gold?

An account of an alleged dinner party conversation between Saunière and his guest Antoine Beaux, the Abbé of Campagne-sur-Aude, could be alluding to this. The abbé remarked, 'My friend, to see you doing so well, one would think you found a treasure.' Saunière allegedly responded in the dialect of the Langue d'Oc, '*Me l'an donat, l'ai panat, l'ai parat é bé lo teni*. In modern French it means, *Ils me l'ont donné, je l'ai pris, je l'ai apprêtré; eh bien, je le tiens bien*. They gave it to me, I took it, I made it work and I will hold onto it.'[88] Did this conversation take place? It seems to be confirmed by Patrice Chaplin, who writes that she received a letter in which the author gives an account of something that Saunière is alleged to have said, 'They showed it to me, I laid my hand on it, I made it work and I'm holding it firmly.'[89]

40

Devils, demons and dragons

Fear has its uses.

Mario told me the old Italian tale of *la mano lunga*, the mysterious long hand, told to small children to frighten them into not putting their hands into small spaces where snakes, spiders, and other venomous creatures frequently made their homes. It worked – Mario remembers it to this day.

Danger from devils, demons and even dragons are central to the myths and legends of hidden treasure that have circulated in the south of France for centuries. According to the story, Ignace Paris, the shepherd of Rennes-le-Château, found gold on Blaise d'Hautpoul's land in 1645, a year after Blaise's father, Françoise-Pierre d'Hautpoul, lodged his will and important documents. In 1661, writer Jean Loret, who worked for Nicolas Fouquet, wrote in his weekly gazette *La Muze Historique* about a 'treasure' found in the diocese of Alet les Bains.[90] This was the same year that the king arrested and imprisoned Fouquet on a charge of embezzlement. More coincidence?

Writer Auguste de Labouisse-Rochefort tells a similar story after visiting Alet les Bains in 1803.[91] He describes a treasure protected by the devil not far from the ruins of Blanchefort a few miles from Rennes les Bains. In this version, a shepherdess surprises the devil counting out his gold coins. By the time the villagers were called to see the spectacle, the devil and the treasure had disappeared. Farmers appealed to a sorcerer in Limoux to enter into a relationship with Satan to recover the treasure, which he accepted only on the condition that his fellow citizens assisted him. However, they fled after hearing the noise made by the demon. The devil's treasure was 'nineteen and a half million gold coins', which was close to the amount of 'treasure' in Corbu's story.

Incredibly, at that time mineralogists believed in the existence of demons in the mines. The Jesuit priest Athanasius Kircher devoted a whole chapter of his *Mundus Subterraneus,* published in 1665, to discussing the presence of demons in the underground 'metal mines'[92]. As well as demons, he believed that dragons and 'underground men' inhabited the 'inner world'. Sometimes, demons are described as disturbing the miners' labours, but more often, their presence is taken as an indication of good luck in finding rich veins. However, fear of demons was one of the reasons that mines in the Pyrenees were abandoned in the sixteenth century. In reality, the loud noises heard in the mines resulted from the emission of toxic gases.

I thought of the strange devil statue at the entrance to the church in Rennes-le-Château. Some likened him to the demon said to have guarded the gold in King Solomon's temple. No doubt, the possibility of encountering a demon or a dragon, or entering into a relationship with the devil, was a serious disincentive to treasure hunting exploits.

I recalled the scene in *Close Encounters of the Third Kind* when authorities announce that seven tankers filled with a deadly nerve gas had overturned at a junction in a remote part of the country – not unlike the 'great danger' at the site of the treasure of Lava. A complex hoax was hatched to evacuate the 'red zone' and keep people away. In reality, there was no accident or nerve gas; the authorities knew that an alien mothership was about to land at that location.

There is a legend that a female dragon inhabits Mount Bugarach protecting an egg. Dragons protecting caves and castles filled with gold and treasure are a common theme in many European myths and legends.

The export of gold and silver, whether from a treasure or from a natural source was banned. Gold from a treasure trove belonged to the king and according to the Regalian doctrine, all mines producing gold or silver belonged to the Crown, unless the landowner held a concession.[93] Even then, the landowner was required to pay a royalty to the king. Finders might be lucky to sell a few items from a stash of treasure, but, as with the treasure of Lava, it does not take long for sellers to be found out. Melting old gold coins and jewellery would result in a great loss in value. However, there was another way to benefit from native gold, but it was risky.

41

The counterfeiters of Bezu

Counterfeiting gold coins is not an easy task, or so they tell me. You need gold, tools for the production process, skilled workers and, most importantly, a die tool to create the imprint – not easy to come by unless you have certain connections. As in prospecting, you also need eyes in the back of your head. It is a dangerous occupation – get caught and at best you end up in prison and at worst you end up at the bottom of a cauldron of boiling water.[94] Counterfeiting coins was a common practice in France dating right up until the eighteenth century. It involved making coins that did not contain the required weight in gold or metal, or making correct coins without authorisation.

Charles II (king 823–877) established the king's mint, the Monnaie de Paris, in 864 under the Edict of Pistres. It included the central mint and eight royal provincial workshops. Over the centuries, the French kings authorised nobles and bishops to mint their own coins. In times of war or political unrest, when there was often a lack of currency, feudal lords were known to issue coins directly imitating those of the king. Some produced coins inferior to royal ones, while others minted coins of good quality, but were nevertheless considered as forgers by the king. At the same time, local monetary workshops minted exact replicas of royal coins without authorisation, thus collecting the seigniorage to the detriment of the king's mint.[95]

Counterfeiters were often persons of a high social rank. Counterfeiting was something of an elite crime, requiring very considerable skills, capital and organisation. Its practitioners tended to be goldsmiths or locksmiths, members of the lesser nobility, or priests.[96] In the reign of Henry III (king 1574–1589), many of the French nobles openly employed coiners to forge German coins.[97]

Kings were active in limiting the privileges of the local lords. Louis IX (king 1226–1270), Blanche de Castille's son, limited the privileges of local lords, and the royal mint gained ground. The provincial workshops gradually disappeared and, by 1878, only the Monnaie de Paris was still in operation.

In the fourteenth century, Guillaume de Cathala, along with one or more co-lords, was caught manufacturing counterfeit gold coins in the castle of Jacques de Voisins at Bezu, a few kilometres south of Rennes-le-Château. The counterfeiters were imprisoned then released several years later.[98]

Most counterfeiting scams were relatively small-scale involving lightweight or low-quality coins, described as being *de mauvais aloi or de bas titre*, of doubtful quality. The curious thing about the coins of Bezu was that they were not cheap rip-offs but contained a higher gold content than the official currency. There are three possible sources for the gold used by the counterfeiters: gold from a treasure such as gold coins, jewellery and antique items, 'clippings' of gold from the coinage of the day (a common practice), or native gold. Rennies cite this story as evidence that the counterfeiters were recycling old gold from a treasure – perhaps Templar or Cathar treasure, or the treasure of Blanche de Castille. Blanche's grandson, Philip III (king 1270–1285) and her great grandson Philip IV (king 1285–1314) had both unsuccessfully searched for hidden treasure in the region. However, Phillip IV also knew that there was native gold in the Languedoc. Deposits in what is now known as l'Hérault were actively exploited at the end of the thirteenth century during his reign. Let's assume that the counterfeiters had discovered a source of native gold waiting to be collected. They were faced with the problem of how to make money from the gold – how to sell it without being found out. Making coins of the realm with the gold may have been the answer.

Several years earlier, in 1339, four monks from the Cistercian Abbéy of Boulbonne heard the rumours that were spreading in the Languedoc about a mysterious mountain near Limoux that covered an infinite treasure guarded by a fairy. Bored with cloister life, they dreamt of hidden gold bars and enchanted caves, harbouring immense riches.[99] They used alchemy and witchcraft, common practices of the day, in a plot to capture the fairy and force her to reveal the secret. When the plot was revealed, the monks were tried and imprisoned. Benedict XII (pope 1334–1342), is said to have taken a keen interest in the case and intervened so that the 'sacred deposit of the Razes' would remain secret. Benedict XII was born Jacques Fournier in Saverdun, a small town in the Ariège, and had entered the monastery of Boulbonne whilst still young.[100] He became the Bishop of Pamiers in 1317. Otto Rhan writes that Bishop Fournier had been told the 'secret' of the caves in the mountains of the Ariège from the inquisitor Bernard Gui, who had tortured Cathar secrets from the heretic Pierre Autier.[101] The Cathars had used these caves as places of refuge during the terrible time of the Inquisition. Coincidentally, Benedict XII was Guillaume de Cathala's uncle. Is it possible that uncle and nephew were well acquainted with Cathar secrets, 'treasure stories' and the geology of the mountains of the Ariège? Limoux is only forty-five kilometres south of Salsigne.

42

Fouquet's letter

The Beausoleils were active in France around the same time that Richelieu commissioned Nicholas Poussin's painting *The Shepherds of Arcadia*, thought to have been painted some time between 1638 and 1640. They were imprisoned under Richelieu's orders. I recalled Enzo's comment about Poussin and Teniers having access to secret information handed down by initiates. Had the Beausoleils found something that would bring great wealth to whoever owned it, something that needed to be kept so secret that it would eventually cost them their lives?

Many Rennies refer to a letter that Abbé Louis Fouquet sent to his brother Nicolas after a meeting with the painter Nicholas Poussin in 1656. Most interpret this letter as a reference to the existence of a physical treasure, an important political or religious secret, or some other advantage, such as access to antiquities. The letter reads,

> I have given to Monsieur Poussin the letter that you were kind enough to write to him; he displayed overwhelming joy on receiving it. You wouldn't believe sir the trouble that he takes to be of service to you, or the affection with which he goes about this, or the talent and integrity that he displays at all times. He and I have planned certain things of which in a little while I shall be able to inform you fully; things which will give you, through M. Poussin, advantages which even Kings would have great difficulty in obtaining from him, and which, according to what he says no one in the world will ever rediscover in the centuries to come; and, it would be achieved without much expense furthermore and could even be turned to profit, and there are matters so difficult to inquire into that nothing on earth at this present time could bring a greater fortune nor perhaps ever its equal.[102]

There is another way to look at this letter. Poussin had a secret, something of great value, which even kings would have trouble getting out of him; something that was known to some and which had been recovered. What could bring such advantages or riches 'nothing on earth at this present time could bring a greater fortune nor perhaps ever its equal'? What else in the world's financial system has better value besides native gold? Gold is still the world's greatest monetary asset; its value remains stable regardless of inflation or deflation. The matter 'would be achieved without much expense…' Certainly if stumbling on a gold vein or even a reef, all you need is a pick, a shovel and a bag. '…there are matters so difficult to inquire'. Could we really assume again that it may have been the mineral, knowing the lack of understanding of geology at that time? Yes, unless someone stumbled upon it, it would be difficult to discover – especially if it had been hidden not by man, but by Mother Nature.

Poussin painted an earlier version of *The Shepherds of Arcadia* in 1627. Art historians believe that Cardinal Camillo Massimo commissioned this earlier version as one-half of a pair of paintings; the other painting is *Midas washing at the source of the Pactolus*. In this well-known ancient Greek legend, everything that King Midas touched turned to gold, until he washed his hands in the river Pactolus. If Poussin's paintings did in fact represent the original tomb of Arques, was he giving us a clue that the river Pactolus was actually the river Sals, which passes nearby? Poussin had to know about the gold. In 1685, Louis XIV acquired Poussin's painting and it hung in his private chambers until his death.

The geological evidence is clear. Certain geological locations favour the formation of gold. The discovery of gold in Australia in 1851 was so huge that all eyes were turned down under for good reason. Obviously, there was and there still is gold in France.

Boudet wrote that his book *The true Celtic language and the cromlech at Rennes les Bains* was really about penetrating the 'secret' of the local history. He includes a curious quote from the French philosopher Joseph de Maistre:

Les dialectes, dit J. de Maistre, les noms propres d'hommes et de lieux me semblent des mines presque intactes et dont il est possible de tirer de grandes richesses historiques et philosophiques.[103]

The dialects, says J. de Maistre, the proper names of men and places, seem to me mines almost intact and from which it is possible to draw great historical and philosophical riches.

Could the 'great historical riches' include native gold? In 1779, Nicholas Gobet wrote that the 'inexhaustible' gold mines, which were the source of great wealth for the Romans, were an enterprise that could 'procure advantages' that could not be found in any other kind of work the country could imagine.[104]

Andrews and Schellenberger propose several alternative translations of the coded message in the Dagobert parchment. One reads, 'To Dagobert II, King, and at Sion is this treasure and it is there dormant.' In the world of minerals exploration, undiscovered mineral deposits, whether they be in the earth, below riverbeds, in caves, or on mountainsides, can be described as being dormant. Regardless of the provenance of the parchments, it is on the cards that whoever coded them had knowledge of a source of dormant native gold in the Languedoc.

Was it possible that the story of a lost mine or an undiscovered gold vein was the 'immeasurable treasure'; the big secret handed down through the generations of certain families in the region, certain members of the clergy and a network of select people in the know? Could it be that the legends of treasure were fabrications, or even hoaxes, designed to divert attention away from what was really going on? I did not discount that there were significant religious and political intrigues at the time, but perhaps the source of Saunière's 'fortune' was far less mysterious than everybody thought.

November 2014, not long to Christmas and everything attached to it: the children, the eating and drinking. For me, it was always one of the most stressful times of the year. I had emailed my research to Jennifer and Enzo and was sorting out some photographs on the computer when an email came in from Eden: 'Great news – it's been approved.' Eden works for UTM Global, a company that sells its services to the little guys like me, and companies that don't want the hassle of lodging an application for a minerals exploration licence themselves. They take care of all the paperwork and pay the fees.

The Department of Mineral Resources in New South Wales had granted me a minerals exploration licence for the Diamond Project, my fifteen-year search for the elusive diamond pipe. This was fantastic news; but it meant that the next two years of my life would be almost totally focused on exploration and collecting samples from an area about four hundred square kilometres – the size of a small suburb. The first year would involve intensive loam sampling – a job done by hand. Finally – I could not believe it after so many years – the site was secured and all we needed to do was start sampling and find those diamonds. We could not start work until April of 2015. Temperatures from December to March would be too hot in that part of the country – over 48°C – hot enough to fry an egg on the bonnet of my ute. I have gone fossicking in barren outback country in 48°C – that is, 48°C in the shade. It was not something I wanted to repeat.

I sent a text to Jennifer. 'Fantastic' was her response. That gave me two weeks to drive to Adelaide and work flat-out with Jennifer on the book, and then be back in Canberra just in time for Christmas.

Murphy's Laws:[105]
1. If anything can go wrong, it will.
2. If there is a possibility of several things going wrong, the one that will cause the most damage will be the first one to go wrong.
3. If anything just cannot go wrong, it will anyway.

43

The best-laid plans: Canberra, November 2014

'Rolf, mate, I feel funny in the chest.'

My housemate Rolf had invited a few friends for dinner at a local Turkish restaurant. After dinner, we went back to the house; the friends left just before midnight. I was talking to Rolf when the pain started; it was not so much a pain but a strange feeling in my chest, like nothing I had experienced before. I sat with it for about five minutes, hoping it would go away – but it persisted.

Rolf studied me for a moment with a worried expression. 'Mate, let's go.'

'Let's go where?' I said.

'Bloody hospital, what do you think? It's only two minutes away.'

We were at Canberra hospital in a few minutes. As soon as the nurse at reception saw me put my hands on my chest, ready to say that I had a pain, she came out from behind the desk, took me by the hand and ordered me to sit still and relax. Within a few minutes, I was on a gurney being whisked to the third floor – coronary emergencies. Mind you, by then I was feeling great.

They wired me up to various monitors, took blood and urine samples and told me I would be admitted and the specialist would see me in the morning. I told Rolf not to wait.

Next morning I met Walter, the cardiologist, a great guy.

'Mate, we're going to fix you up,' he said shaking my hand. 'The test results show that some of your arteries are clogged. We considered a stent but we believe you need a triple heart bypass – you'll be brand-new.'

I could not believe it; I was lucky not to have had a heart attack.

'We'll keep you here for another three days to monitor you, and then you'll be on the waiting list. I would say another two weeks before surgery. When a bed is available, the hospital will give you three days' notice. After surgery, you'll be in hospital for about a week, followed by a six-week period when you can't drive or lift anything more than about two kilos. You'll be back to normal in about three months.'

I was stunned. Heart bypass surgery is common – but it happened to other people, not me.

'Do you smoke?' he said.

'Yes.'

'Well, give it up.'

The first thing I did was text the family, Rebecca and my friends. The answer was always the same: 'Oh, My God…when, where, how long in hospital…do you need anything?'

I sent a text to Jennifer: 'Guess where I am.'

Back came her response: 'In the outback?'

I wished. 'No, in bloody hospital having tests for chest pain.'

'Oh my God etc…'

Everything was cancelled or on hold – the trip to Adelaide, the sampling, the diamonds, the book, Rennes-le-Château, chocolate, Camembert cheese and smoking. There was only one question on my mind – why me?

I had the heart bypass surgery in early January 2015. For the first week of recovery, it felt like two double-decker buses had hit me. Four weeks later, my doctor was amazed at how well I was healing and he cleared me to drive. The trip to Adelaide was back on the agenda. This time, I planned to take a different route, heading north through Narrandera and Hay, with a detour via the high plains to check out Mungo National Park, almost eight hundred kilometres from Canberra.

In the late1960s, early 1970s, geologist James Bowler discovered the skeletal remains of two ancient humans, a male and a female. They were buried on the south eastern shore of Lake Mungo beneath the Walls of China, a series of strangely fluted dunes called lunettes, formed by the action of wind and erosion over millions of years. Mungo Lady is dated at twenty thousand years old and Mungo Man at about forty thousand years, when the basins were full of water teeming with life. Bowler's discovery confirmed that Indigenous Australians belonged to the world's oldest continuing culture.

I was more than ready to hit the road; excited as a little kid. The good thing about retirement is that life is not so much controlled by time; I do what I like to do when I want to do it. I was going to sleep where Mungo Man and Mungo Lady slept so many moons ago.

What else could possibly happen?

Murphy's Laws continued:[106]

4. If you perceive that there are four possible ways in which something can go wrong, and circumvent them, then a fifth way, unprepared for, will promptly develop.

44

Mungo Lake

If you have ever seen your gearbox sitting on a mechanic's bench and flooded with oil, in other words stuffed, it is not a pretty sight.

I had topped up my tank at Balranald – the last spot for fuel before you head out on the hundred-and-seventy-kilometre stretch past Penarie and Turlee to Mungo National Park. Ninety kilometres of it is dirt road, nice and wide with patches of bulldust, very fine sand, like talcum powder. There is a real skill to driving on it; you need to press harder on the accelerator to preserve road speed. All the while, great clouds of fine red dust billow up around the vehicle.

Around five p.m., I checked in at Mungo Lodge, the only decent caravan park. Being the only guest, I had the pick of the beds.

'Next time, make a reservation, mate. It's the busy time of the year,' said the owner, with typical Aussie humour. He told me that if I wanted to take some good photos of the Walls of China I should go straight away, because it was ten kilometres away – he did not tell me that access was restricted.

I felt great when I jumped in the ute. I arrived at the designated parking area, walked about three hundred metres when the signs hit me. The dunes were about five hundred metres further on but access beyond that point was strictly prohibited. Disappointed, I walked back to the car, drove back to the lodge, had dinner, took a shower and went to bed. However, I could not sleep.

The following morning I paid my bill of $25 and left. Next stop Mildura for fuel and lunch – a burger with the lot and a coffee. With any luck, I would be in Adelaide in about seven hours. About seventy kilometres out from Mildura, heading for Renmark, I started to hear a clunking sound – not good. Then the clutch went – no gears. I pulled over and got out. To my horror, the oil from the gearbox was gushing onto the road creating a puddle under the truck. I had blown the transmission.

I have been a gold member of the NRMA for over forty years, and was well insured against any breakdown; I was going to make good use of the membership.

An hour and a half later, the tow truck arrived and took the truck and me back to the NRMA garage in Mildura. The next day, I found out the damage: a spacer in the gearbox had gone through the casing, and oil from the transmission had flooded the clutch. I needed to replace the clutch, gearbox and transfer case – all of which were transported from Adelaide to Mildura. The total cost was nearly $6,000. Luckily, my NRMA insurance covered the five days I spent in a motel in Mildura.

I had to look on the bright side, though. If I had broken down on the dirt road heading to Mungo Lake, I would have been lucky to see one car a day; or, even worse, it could have happened in April on the field trip sampling for diamonds in the middle of nowhere with no phone network. In a way, if it was destined to happen, I was glad that it happened there.

I took off on Friday morning. The ute was like brand-new and I arrived in Adelaide that afternoon, happy to see two smiling faces – Jennifer and her wonderful husband Mario.

Mario helped me bring in my gear from the truck. I set my computer up in the dining room, which would become my office over the next ten days. In between cups of coffee, home-cooked meals and long walks, Jennifer and I trawled our way through the geological and historical information I had printed from my online searches of the French archives. Google Translate is an amazing tool. What would have taken me hours was completed in a few seconds, albeit with a few quirky translations.

45

Bloodlines and bones: Adelaide

'There's something I want to show you, Gerard,' said Jennifer.
She got up from the kitchen table and disappeared down the passageway, returning a minute later carrying a large brown padded envelope, which she placed on the table opposite me. Without saying a word, she removed a thick computer printout from an old-fashioned printer – one that took a continuous stream of paper, each leaf joined to the next by a row of perforations. Then she pushed the empty envelope across the table to me. 'What do you see?'

I looked at the postage stamp on the top right-hand corner of the envelope, and then glanced at the address label.

'*Mon Dieu*, Jennifer, who is this?'

'*Mon Dieu* indeed,' said Jennifer, cheeks flushed pink. 'He's my father. After he died, my sister and I found this envelope in his papers. I had no idea. I don't know whether it's real, or a fantasy, but with the synchronicity that's happening to us, I figured maybe it might be important.'

The envelope was addressed to Jennifer's father at a street address in Canada – nothing unusual. However, typed beneath the address label was Baron de Valanjou.

'You didn't tell me you were nobility. This is incredible, really. I don't believe it.'

'Well, I'm not sure whether to believe it, Gerard.'

'How could you not know, Jennifer? Didn't he tell you?' I said, gently probing for more information.

Jennifer sighed.

'My father moved to Canada years ago and we lost touch. When I eventually attempted to contact him, unfortunately it was too late.'

'You didn't have any clues earlier?'

'When I was young, he used to joke that we were from royal Stuart descent, from the wrong side of the pillow, if you know what I mean.'

'We have an expression for that: *mauvais cote de l'oreiller.*'

'He told me that there were deliberate mistakes in official registers of nobility. Apparently, the House of Stuart came under particular attack in order to justify the German succession in Britain. According to some researchers, the legitimate Royal House of Stuart still exists today. Oh, and he was a Freemason, like his father, and a member of a couple of orders. My sister arranged for my father's papers and other items to be returned to South Australia. There were boxes of material. It was a treasure trove of amazing things: medals, photographs, awards, even an old metal tea chest full of military uniforms and his Freemason regalia, and of course this genealogy. It's funny, because I only became fascinated by the mystery of Rennes-le-Château and the sangreal when I started working with Enzo on *The Poussin Enigma.*'

'His version of *The da Vinci Code.*'

'Indeed, that was when Enzo told me about my Sinclair heritage – it was like a trigger, I guess.'

'Sinclair or Stuart heritage?'

'Both, actually. I am a Sinclair on my mother's side. There is a strong connection with the Knights Templar. You could say it's a double whammy of the so-called bloodline. The Stuarts are regarded as the source of the Scottish Rite, and the Sinclairs are said to be the guardians of the secrets of the Holy Grail. Historically, there has been a strong connection between the Stuarts and the Sinclairs, including a history of marriages.'

'More synchronicity, hey,' I said.

'I guess so. Have a look at this.' Jennifer carefully flipped a few pages of the computer printout until she came to the twenty-third generation.

One name jumped out.

I stared for a moment. 'You mean that you're descended from the King of Scotland?'

'Well, according to this genealogy, it seems so. Robert Stewart was born in 1316, the son of Walter Stewart, the sixth High Steward of Scotland and of Marjorie Bruce. He was the first monarch of the House of Stewart and reigned as Robert II, King of the Scots from 1371 to his death in 1390. Marjorie was the daughter of Robert the Bruce and his first wife Isabella of Mar.'

'Incredible. Did you know that Templars who escaped from France fought with Robert the Bruce at the Battle of Bannockburn in 1314, along with members of the Saint Clair family?'

'Yes, I did. Sinclair or Saint Clair means holy light and the family motto is "Commit thy work to God".'

'Seems appropriate, hey, Jennifer.'

'Apparently, one branch is related by marriage to Hughes de Payen, the founder of the Knights Templar. William Mann writes that in 1398 the Scottish prince Henry Sinclair sailed to what is today Nova Scotia along with approximately five hundred of his trusted knights and established a secret Grail settlement at Green Oaks for the Templars fleeing persecution.'

'That's almost a hundred years before Columbus arrived in the New World,' I said.

'Sinclair was hereditary Grand Master of the Scottish Knights Templar and some say a direct descendant of the Grail bloodline. Mann believes that they were also seeking refuge for the sangreal in a place called Arcadia.'

'More synchronicity that your father ended up in Canada,' I said.

'Perhaps, but I don't know how much of this is real,' said Jennifer, indicating the genealogy.

'Well, it exists, so it is real, but is it true and could you ever find out for certain?' I said.

'It's almost impossible to go back this far in a person's bloodline with any degree of certainty. I need to find an expert genealogist to look at it.'

'It's in your genes, Jennifer, it must be,' I said. 'A Merovingian bloodline, legitimate claim to the thrones of Europe and all that. Henry Lincoln wrote that the Sinclairs, and various branches of the Stuarts, are two of at least a dozen families in Britain and Europe today who are of Merovingian lineage.'

'I know,' said Jennifer. 'The bloodline allegedly connects the House of David to the Merovingian dynasty through the descendants of Jesus and Mary Magdalene – hence the reason it's called the Holy Bloodline. There is a tradition in French royal families that they are descended from Mary Magdalene. But even if that is all true, Gerard, as Henry Lincoln says, these descendants would not be any more divine, any more intrinsically miraculous than anyone else.'

'So where does the title Baron de Valanjou fit in?' I said.

'All I've been able to find out is that he was given the title by a pretender to the Russian throne, who claimed a connection to the house of Anjou and the throne of Naples. I assume that the title has something to do with this Stuart genealogy.'

'Anjou is in the Loire valley,' I said. 'Today it corresponds to the department of Maine-et-Loire in central France.'

'The title of Count of Anjou was associated with English nobility as well as French,' said Jennifer. 'In fact, the Anglo-Angevin Empire of the Plantagenet dynasty extended from England to the Pyrenees. Richard the Lionheart, King of England, became the Count of Anjou in 1151 when he inherited the title from his father Henry II, King of England. There's a strong link between the Anjou family and the Templars. René d'Anjou was the last ruler of Anjou. He was fascinated with the theme of Arcadia and the legends of Mary Magdalene's life in southern France. The dynasty adopted Mary Magdalene as their saint. He even ordered excavations of key sites to find her tomb. According to the *Dossiers Secret*, René d'Anjou was the grandmaster of the Priory of Sion from 1418 to his death in 1480. According to Wikipedia, two cousins from Spain both claim the title of Duke of Anjou. They each represent different and competing rationales of the Legitimist claimants for restoration of the French monarchy.'

'Here's me thinking of returning to France and buying a small house in St Martys, when we could all return to the family castle.'

'Funny you should say that,' said Jennifer, 'because in 2007, just by chance, I read an article in the May 2001 issue of *Country Life* about the Château de Beynac, a medieval castle in the Dordogne dating from the twelfth century. Richard the Lionheart occupied the castle briefly in the twelfth century. Lucien Grosso, an Italian by birth, bought the castle in 1962. He was restoring it and wanted to pass it on to a worthy successor. Enzo jumped at the chance and wrote to Signor Grosso suggesting that the castle would make a magnificent headquarters for an order of Knights Templar.'

'Wow, did he hear back?'

'No,' said Jennifer. 'The surprising thing is that in 2001, Lucien Grosso, who was in his nineties at the time, asked the British ambassador if he might bequeath the castle to the British Crown.'

'I don't think the French government would be very happy about that,' I said.

'Exactly. Anyway he died in 2008 and left the castle to Alberic de Montgolfier, president of Eure-et-Loire. However, I suggest that you don't get too excited.'

Jennifer reached for another folder and took out several typed pages each topped with a royal-looking crest. I could tell by the typeface that they had been typed on an expensive typewriter.

'There is a problem. Apparently, there are dozens of self-styled orders in France and Italy created by people with *la folie de grandeur* – delusions of grandeur – or as a way to take money off the unwary.'

'Does Enzo know about this?'

'Yes. Now the cynics would say that the Baron de Valanjou is probably one of those worthless titles of nobility granted by pretenders claiming a royal pedigree. However, Enzo told me that there is another side to the story. That it is all part of the Grail Brotherhood's secret master plan to transform a united Europe into the Grail kingdom ruled by divinely appointed leaders, a sort of theocracy like they had in ancient

Egypt. The Knights Templar were planning to create an independent Templar state covering the area from the Mediterranean up to Carcassonne and Rennes-le-Château, free from the oppressive control of both Church and state. But the plan never materialised.'

'I've read about it,' I said. 'Actually, the Languedoc only became part of France after the Albigensian Crusade.'

'Philip Coppens describes the brotherhood as a type of outsourcing company for nobility,' said Jennifer. 'They provide a nobleman in countries where a dynasty had ended. The leader must have a bloodline link to the Grail dynasty and the proper nous or spirit to rule as a sacred king. The master plan is divine rule with the Grail, considered to be the earthly representative of God at its top, the lost king, yet to reveal himself. It's a persistent thread in French history and legend. On the surface, secret organisations like the Priory of Sion appear to be a scam or a hoax – the question is whether it is just a diversion, a layer within another layer. Like in war or espionage, hoaxes can play an important role in diverting enemy attention away from the main game.'

'That's what happened at Argyle,' I said. 'I imagine Enzo fancying himself in the role of *le roi perdu*.'

'The lost king indeed. At one stage, Pierre Plantard claimed that role as his birthright,' said Jennifer. 'He also claimed that he was a Sinclair. Apparently, the name on his passport was Pierre Plantard de Saint Clair, et Comte de Rhedae, although Henry Lincoln says that appropriating honoured names associated with the esoteric was a tactic used by prewar anti-Masonic French rightists.'

Jennifer carefully placed the thick computer printout back into the envelope. 'The word for Sion in the Welsh language is John. It means God is gracious. Synchronicity or just coincidence?'

'Why do you say that?'

'My father's name was John.'

46

A sign of good fortune ahead: Adelaide, March 2015

'Are you ready, Gerard?' said Jennifer.

'Ready for what?' I said.

'We're going to the market in town. Are you coming?'

'Ha, fantastic. I haven't been to the market since I lived here with Suzie and the kids. We used to go every week. Yes, I am definitely ready.'

Outside, Mario was warming up the car.

'What are you doing in the car?' said Jennifer. 'We're taking the train. It's more fun and we won't have to worry about parking.'

We walked the short distance to the local train station, enjoying the warmth and the cloudless blue sky and chatting about the big houses which years ago were cheap to buy but now cost a mint. We admired the sandstone-fronted houses complemented by well-tended gardens, some with huge old gum trees and native bushes and flowers, and others with perfectly manicured lawns edged with bright white pebbles. Within no time, we were at the station. Stepping onto the train, I was surprised to see less than ten people travelling. We arrived at the central station in less than seven minutes, crossed the street and hopped on the free tram.

'Shall we have lunch at the market?' said Jennifer. 'There's a little place called Le Souk that sells authentic Algerian food – maybe they sell couscous.'

'What a great idea. What do you think Mario?' I replied.

'*Certo*, of course, mate,' said Mario.

It was a Friday, one of the busiest market days. As we entered the undercover central market, the place was buzzing with activity. There were people everywhere, enjoying the atmosphere, sauntering along the alleyways bordered by open stalls, relaxing over coffee and conversation at little cafés. It was a multicultural melting pot – Chinese shops and stalls, Vietnamese, Lebanese – you name it. The open stalls were stacked with colourful arrays of fruit and vegetables, cheeses, meat and poultry. We passed a big chef in his whites giving a demonstration of cooking with truffles and clutching a huge knife. I sighed with relief, knowing I had hung up my whites for good.

I couldn't wait to eat a good couscous, and as we got nearer to Le Souk, I could smell it. Jennifer introduced me to the owner, who was originally from Algeria and after a good handshake – '*Bonjour, monsieur, comment allez vous?*' – we were done.

The menu was simple: chicken, beef, lamb or merguez, a spicy sausage, all served with couscous. Beef and merguez was my choice – delicious. After a short black and a cake, Jennifer suggested we browse for a while, then we planned to hop back onto the tram and go to the art gallery.

Arriving back at the tram stop, Jennifer and I began chatting, when suddenly the smile on her face dropped.

'Oh, my God, Gerard.'

'What's wrong?'

'Your coin – it's gone.'

My hand instantly went to my neck searching for my precious coin, my two-thousand-year-old Roman coin. My friend Michel found it in France in 1980 using my metal detector, which he had borrowed. Michel had found many coins. I liked the fact that the one I chose had been worn smooth over the centuries; I had been wearing it around my neck ever since. Now it was gone, all I was left with was the empty silver setting.

We looked at each other for a moment in stunned silence. What could we do?

'We have to go back and retrace our steps,' I said, close to tears.

We spread out, each of us carefully scanning different spots on the might have stopped. Back in the market, we each took a different alley, scanning the ground and trying to avoid people.

'My God,' I said, looking at the sea of people.

I saw Jennifer in the next alley; we made eye contact, but nothing.

We kept on searching. Then coming around the corner of another alley, I saw Jennifer – this time she was smiling. She came towards me, gave me a big hug then opened her hand triumphantly and there it was. I have had some happy days in my life but nothing like that day. Jennifer had found the coin lying in the middle of an alley near the southern entrance where we had stopped to chat for a brief moment. A tiny insignificant-looking piece of copper with a magnificent history. Incredibly, nobody had picked it up.

My Roman coin was in someone's pocket two thousand years ago. It had been through so many hands and been around my neck for over thirty years. I lost it for a moment, but it came back to me. If that is not a sign of good fortune, what is? In my book, it was a miracle.

47

The Hand of Faith

'OK, chef, let's cook!' Jennifer bounced into the kitchen wearing a frilly red apron over her yellow smock dress and a pink scarf wrapped around her head. 'Enough of Rennes-le-Château and Saunière for today,' she said. 'I'm making dinner.'

I was relieved; my head was spinning with all the different interpretations of various codes, signs and symbols. I respected the efforts of the various researchers, but it seemed to me that many were seeing shapes in the clouds.

'What are we having?'

'Salmon, potato mash, carrots and peas with butter and fresh parsley.'

'Great. What can I do?' I said.

'Peel the potatoes and chop the parsley, chef,' she said handing me a large kitchen knife, handle first.

I made swift work of the big bunch of curly-leaf parsley Jennifer picked from the herb garden.

'I expect you're an expert at cooking fish,' said Jennifer.

'*Oui*, but I'd be happy if I never had to cook one again. I must have cooked thousands over the years, especially working at Doyle's.'

'Any tips?'

'Yes, don't fry salmon in olive oil. It gives the fish a strong taste, like cod-liver oil.'

'OK, good tip, I'll remember that.' Jennifer prepped the fish, three succulent salmon steaks. 'You know, I've never been to the Blue Mountains.'

'You must go. I feel really alive when I'm there. I get the same feeling at Kandie Peak. It's a completely different landscape – dry red soil. I can almost imagine dinosaurs emerging from the ancient rock formations.'

Jennifer smiled, 'Would you say they are sacred places? I feel the same in the medieval monasteries in France. I get goose bumps, tingling, and the hairs on my arms stand up. If you're with someone you love in places like this, you might even generate enough charge to send a spark between you. Dan explains that when you start to feel blissful in a fractal field, your whole body begins sucking in its electric environment and that's what energises you.'

'That's how I feel when I'm in gold country,' I said.

The potatoes were mashed and the peas and carrots were glistening with melted butter.

'Do you eat like this all the time?'

'Pretty much, I love to cook – it's like a meditation,' said Jennifer, tossing a handful of the chopped parsley over the vegetables.

We took the plates into the dining room and settled to enjoy the meal.

'When do you think you'll take off for Kandie Peak?' said Jennifer, pouring me a glass of red wine.

'There's a few things still to organise – access to the land, things like that. I'm hoping in April – it's not as hot then.'

We made swift work of the meal – the salmon was pink and succulent and the potato mash was just as good.

'So would you hire me to work in your restaurant?' said Jennifer beaming.

'Of course, chef, first class.'

After washing the dishes, we settled down in front of the TV. Halfway through the news, a report of an old cold case came on. Police believed they had solved the case of murdered family court judge Justice David Opas, who was shot dead at his Sydney home in 1980, just months after he made an adverse ruling against the accused in a family court matter.

'I know this story,' I said, leaning forward in my chair. 'There's a connection with gold.'

We focused on the story, and then Mario turned the sound down.

'What's the connection?' said Jennifer, turning to face me. 'I'm intrigued.'

'I was on a two-month placement working for a temp agency at the Centennial Hotel opposite Centennial Park in Sydney. In my last week there, during a break in my split shift, I went for a walk along William Street in Paddington to kill time. It's a narrow one-way street lined with small shops. An old chair on display in the window of a second-hand furniture shop caught my interest. There's a lot of furniture like that in Jenolan – chairs and garden benches from around the 1860s, very low to the ground, but comfortable. I went into the shop to ask about it. A woman in her forties greeted me. I knew right away by her accent that she was French. As we were talking, her husband Robert emerged from the back of the shop where he restored the old furniture, and joined us. He was away from the shop a lot during the day searching for pieces to buy, making deliveries and pick-ups. Over the next two weeks, we saw more of each other. It was great having someone I could speak French with during my breaks from work,' I said.

'Anyway, they invited me to dinner at their cottage. During dinner, I told them that I was going to the outback to do a bit of detecting for gold. As soon as I said the word "gold", Robert said, "My God, you're not going to believe me." Here we go again, I thought, another gold story falling in my lap. "Well, go on," I said, all excited, wanting to know more. "You must know about the Hand of Faith," he said. Of course I knew about it. Back in 1980, a guy called Kevin Hillier was fossicking for gold using a metal detector. He found a huge gold nugget less than thirty centimetres under the ground. It weighed 872 ounces, that's twenty-seven kilos, and was sold to the Golden Nugget Casino in Las Vegas for over a million bucks. "You're right," he said. "But there's another story attached to it." Well, by now, my excitement was mounting and I was getting impatient to hear his story. Then he told me that he got involved with some dodgy characters who had hatched a plan to steal the Hand of Faith when it was on the market with a price tag of one big one.'

'A big one?' said Jennifer.

'A million bucks,' said Mario.

'He didn't know why he got involved. Maybe he needed some excitement in his life. The guys fabricated business cards, letterheads, a chequebook and identity cards – the works – and he was chosen to do the transaction, in other words the stealing. His job was to give the seller a cheque for one million dollars, take the nugget and disappear. Everything was organised to take place in a room in a bank in the city. Of course, the cheque in his pocket for one big one, which one of the guys from the Mob had given him that morning, was a fake.'

'So which Mob was that then?' said Jennifer.

Mario rolled his eyes.

'You know – the Mob, capital M. He described how at ten-thirty a.m. he went into the room and waited. A few minutes later, two guys walked in, one of them carrying a briefcase, which he put on a small wooden table and opened. There it was, twenty-seven kilos of nearly pure gold. What a sight. Gosh, that's not something you expect to see every day. He told me that he was not really thinking about its value but he felt paralysed and completely hypnotised by the gold. His heart must have been pumping like hell. Nothing mattered at that moment, only gold. He took the nugget out of the briefcase. It felt so heavy because it was. He put it back in its case, got the cheque out of his wallet to give to the guy and then his whole world fell on top of him. The other guy put a hand on his shoulder and said, "Police. You're under arrest." He froze, it was a set-up – they knew everything. I asked him how they found out. He had no bloody idea. He was arrested, questioned and locked up. You are not going to believe this, but on the day he went to court, a family court judge was assassinated – Justice Opas. In a way, the assassination saved him – the murder story made front page. If the judge hadn't been assassinated on that day, his story would have made the headlines. Imagine it: the long arm of the law saves the Hand of Faith. Instead of getting ten or twenty years, he got five and was released earlier for good behaviour. When I asked him why he did it, he couldn't tell me, but I got the impression that he deeply regretted what he did. All he knew was that he paid the price and realised what life is all about.'

'Have you seen them since?' said Jennifer.

'No, but I often think about them. So many unusual stories related to gold seem to pop up from time to time, when really I'm not seeking gold, but looking for diamonds. Rennes-le-Château was miles away from my thoughts at that time. Maybe something was telling me back then that I was on the right path. When people tell me secrets, Jennifer, I listen, and more often than not, it involves gold.'

48

Change of fortune: Mount Airly, New South Wales, 2015

Back in Canberra, it was six months since the exploration licence had been granted and five months since my operation. I felt good, really good, and we were ready to get cracking and go sampling. I should really say I instead of we, because I was the only one who was doing the work, which amounted to collecting at least forty bags of samplings on the first field trip. Collecting the samples is not too bad, but it takes ages to reduce a bag of twenty kilos to less than a kilo by getting rid of the rubbish, leaving only the heavy minerals, especially doing it by hand using a bucket and a garden hose – forget about it. I needed to find someone with a sorting machine.

My friend Peter Temby told me that Col Ribaux, an old mate of mine, had all the right gear at his place near Airly Mountain, about three hundred kilometres from Sydney. Larry Barron put me on to Col back in 1992 when I was learning about diamonds, and he quickly became a friend. A geologist, diamond and gold miner, Col was a legend in the prospecting game. Back in 1961, he climbed a wild, almost inaccessible mountain near Capertee, and picked up a lovely gem diamond. He has been there ever since.

Col's place is about ten kilometres from the Capertee Valley, in the Garden of Stone National Park. He bought his land for about £150; a transportable home set him back another $450. The valley follows the Capertee River as it cuts through the Sydney Basin. It is the largest enclosed valley in the world, and home of the endangered regent honeyeater and many native plant species. Incredibly, new species of plants and animals are still being discovered in this region.

On the following Saturday, I was on my way – a tedious five-hour drive from Canberra going through Goulburn, Taralga, Oberon, Lithgow then Capertee on the Mudgee road, which winds through mountainous country all the way from Goulburn. I shivered at the thought of hauling a transportable along that route.

I reached Col's place at twelve-thirty p.m. and laughed when I saw the sign at the front:

> Wanted good woman
> Must be able to clean, cook, sew, dig worms and clean fish.
> Must have boat and motor
> Please send picture of the boat and motor.

Col hadn't changed much since I last saw him eight years earlier. He had the coffee going and, within five minutes, the conversation turned to diamonds and gold. I showed him the site maps of the land around Kandie Peak and reports done over the years. Then I showed him the rough diamond I found there some years ago, which he confirmed to be boart or bort, sometimes called ballas, if rounded. We spoke about how I should proceed with sampling at the site and how to process the samples I would bring back.

Then out of the blue he said, 'No worries, mate, I've done thousands of bags. It's a walk in the park. I have the perfect machine for the job. It will process a twenty-kilo bag in less than an hour, with a residue ready to be checked for diamonds. Come for a walk outside. I'll show you.'

The site was a veritable picker's paradise. A treasure trove of equipment and old junk: all sorts of rocks, old car bodies, mining equipment, a bulldozer, a jeep, an old tank, and even an old clapped-out New Zealand Air Force plane that Col got just for the sake of reselling it.

Col showed me the sorting machine. I could not believe it; the processing of the samples was organised. I was jumping with joy.

'Mate, you've been working on your project for a bloody long time,' said Col. 'How long is the drive to Kandie Peak?'

'Two days. Why?'

'Well, I'm going with you. We'll sample for a week, bring back the stuff and process the lot here, not a worry in the world, mate. But I use my own shoes.'

'Your own shoes?'

'I'll take my own car and caravan. The caravan has solar panels and water. I'll feel I'm at home. It'll be much better.'

That was it. Col was going with me. I could not have imagined better help.

Airly Mountain is part of a mesa or tableland, an elevated landform with a flat top and steep sides, characteristic of arid environments. But here it is full of wildlife and covered with trees, ravines and streams. It is pristine country, with a magical feel about it. I imagined that spirits must live there, and the ancestors of the Wiradjuri people, the traditional owners. Definitely a highly spiritual place.

Col's property reached all the way to the sandstone cliffs. As we walked towards the cliffs, Col told me about his chilling encounter with a strange light. One evening, he and his wife were in the house, when they noticed a bright glowing ball of light about two to three hundred feet in diameter coming from the direction of a shed where he had been working on a tractor earlier that day. Col's first thought was that the shed had caught fire, but as he headed towards it, the light disappeared, so he came back to the house. The light appeared again, brighter this time. It seemed to be coming from amongst some old cars in the paddock. Col walked across the paddock to one of the cars and opened the front door. The light shone through the car window, making it bright enough to read a newspaper. He described it as like being inside a neon tube. The focus of the light seemed to be above the ground in a thorny patch of scrub some distance away. He told me that there was something peculiar about it. There was no moonlight; just like the night I saw the orange disc on the way to Jenolan. He has been looking for it ever since, but it hasn't come back.

Col's story was extraordinary. When I worked at Jenolan, the locals told me stories of sightings of the Min Min lights, also called Paddy's Lanterns, that appear out of nowhere and seem to follow travellers, or beckon travellers to follow them. A lot of the old-time prospectors and stockmen who camped out under the stars reported seeing them. I told Col about my experience with the orange disc on the way to Jenolan. Had we experienced the same phenomenon? Something was happening here, but what? By the time we began walking back to the house, it was nearly four p.m., time for me to head back to Canberra – another five-hour drive, which could turn into six or seven hours as the forecast was for rain.

'When are you planning to go, mate?' said Col.

'The sixteenth of June.'

'Why then?'

'Well, that's three weeks away. It gives Sonya time to write to the lessor for access to the land and tell them when we'll arrive.'

'What, you haven't got the land access yet? Mate, this is trouble coming for sure. Just think, they can make your life bloody hard. I know you told me you have a good relationship with them, but that was four years ago. You told me they found gold on their land, didn't you?'

'Yes, they did, the biggest nugget was 1.2 kilos. The landowner even came to Sydney to see me at my work to tell me what he had found.'

'Gerard, that's not the point. You have applied for a Group 6 licence, right. That's for diamonds. But they know that you know they've found gold on that land, if you know what I mean. Maybe they think you are going to look for gold. If they think it is a cover-up, they are going to make your life impossible. They could force you to use certain tracks instead of the one you need to use. There is the dawn to dusk rule where you are not allowed to camp and all sorts of shit. Mate, it's not good. You have to send the letter for access to the land as soon as possible. We will never be ready by the sixteenth. I mean, it's OK by me, one or two extra weeks waiting won't hurt me, but Jesus, mate, watch it.

Two hours later, I was driving back to Canberra with a massive headache. I was right; it rained all the way. As the night drew on, I began to feel an uneasiness that I could not shake. I kept thinking about Col's surreal experience with the Min Min light, or whatever it was. For some reason, it had really shaken me up, and there is a reason for everything, or so they say. With the wind and rain whipping the windscreen, the wipers were working overtime. I switched the headlights onto high beam to cut through the pitch black and hoped like hell I would not be confronted by a kangaroo bounding across the road. Dawn and dusk are usually the time for that, but you cannot be too careful. I glanced up through the windscreen at the night sky, black with storm clouds – no sign of the moon or the stars and, thank God, no strange orange disc following me.

I am the sort of driver who does not take risks. I am always prepared and have never had a serious accident. I was glad when I arrived home safely and hit the sack; it had been a long day, twelve hours driving all up. I slept like a log.

Two days later, Sonya, my company lawyer, sent the letters requesting access to the land affected by the licence. One to the owner of the land, the one who found the gold on his property and with whom I had a very good relationship – or so I thought; the second to the owner of another property, also affected by the licence. We received a reply to our first letter from their solicitors, telling us that under no circumstances were we to write directly to the lessor. We replied to their solicitor's letter but received no response. There was no reply from the second landowner either. What was going on? Then came the waiting game – a war of nerves. That is when I smelt a rat.

They say that when people get deeply involved in the Rennes-le-Château mystery, their karma speeds up. Once, I would have laughed at this statement, but I was starting to believe it might be true, because the fact that I am alive is a miracle. Is it my destiny not to be involved with diamonds. Could it be gold and Rennes-le-Château?

Murphy's Laws continued:[107]
5. Left to themselves, things tend to go from bad to worse.
6. If everything seems to be going well, you have obviously overlooked something.

49

Fortune flips

Several days after I got back from Col's place, like every other morning around ten-thirty, I went to a little café in the Woden shopping centre. The coffee is good, I catch up with other regulars and the barista always greets me with a smile. I think of her as the girl with the dragon tattoo. I am not a fan of tattoos usually, but they suit her.

I spent a leisurely forty-five minutes enjoying the coffee and conversation. I ran through the plans for Kandie Peak in my head, thinking what a lucky break it was to have Col on my team. Like me, he had undergone a triple heart bypass at the Royal North Shore Hospital.

I paid for my coffee.

'You know, you are my favourite Frenchman,' said the girl with the dragon tattoo.

Wow, that was a revelation; a boost to the old ego.

I walked through the shopping mall towards the outdoor car park where I had parked my ute. It was covered with dust from the trip to Col's, but that's the way I like it. The difference between boys and men, as they say, is only the price of their toys.

I stepped up into the cab, put the key in the ignition, tried to turn it to start the engine but it would not budge. Nothing unusual – most drivers will have experienced this. I moved the steering wheel a bit to the right and the key turned. Then before the engine started, I heard a metallic clank. I engaged the reverse gear and started to reverse, but the steering wheel was going round and round like a merry-go-round – I had no steering. I jumped out of the ute. Unbelievable – the shaft from the steering box had snapped flash with the casing of the steering box. The diameter of the shaft is at least three centimetres of solid steel. I got straight on to the NRMA road service.

When the service guy arrived and saw the damage, there was a moment of stunned silence. 'Unbelievable, mate,' he said shaking his head. 'I've never seen a shaft snapped like this, never, mate, never. Do you realise how bloody lucky you are? Bloody hell, go and buy a lottery ticket. Go now, go and buy one, mate, this is your lucky day.'

Only four days earlier, I had driven for about three hundred kilometres on that winding road through the Great Dividing Range returning from Col's place in the middle of the night. With the rain bucketing down, wind pummelling the truck and patches of fog obscuring the bends, with the risk of being hit by a kangaroo that you only see at the last minute – not knowing that the steering column was holding on by a thread. If the steering column had snapped on that road, there were only two places to go – into the mountain, or down the ravine. Either way, I would have been toast. Even if I had made it onto the freeway and the column snapped then, the outcome would have been just as bad. It did not bear thinking about. Steep cliff faces to one side, deep ravines to the other, and oncoming cars. I could see the headline: 'Prospector dies in death plunge'. Then again, it could have happened in the middle of the outback on the way to Kandie Peak, on some remote dirt track where I might have been lucky to see another vehicle every few days.

It took over two hours to get the truck to the local garage. Special rollers were put under the front wheels to steer it out of the car park.

My mechanic was as stunned as everyone else was. 'Mate, you're bloody lucky. Go and buy a lottery ticket.'

I did, but won nothing. I had already won the first prize – my life. I started to wonder if there was a flip side to Murphy's Law after all.

Four days later, a steering box arrived from Darwin. Bob's your uncle, another day in paradise; I was back on the road.

Several more days passed and there was still no response from the landowner. After two weeks of the war of nerves, I had had enough, I was not going to spend any more money just to feed their lawyers. I thought about Col's advice: when solicitors are involved, it is often best to cut your losses and get out. I gave the order to Eden to lodge an application to cancel the licence.

Col's advice to expect the unexpected was right. In the last week of June, I resigned as the main director and shareholder of the company I had registered for the exploration. I was not over the fact that the project I had dedicated myself to for so long was dead and buried. All the hours spent studying, travelling, writing, talking and dreaming had come to nothing. However, I was not going to cry over spilled milk. Putting a positive spin on the situation, I realised that I had more spare time to go places, to see friends, and more time to work on the book. But I needed some new excitement. I needed to get away on a long drive to clear my thoughts. I wondered if my business partner would still be interested after so long in getting a new diamond exploration licence. Maybe we could we have a crack at it if we both shared the cost. I decided to give him a call.

I planned to go to Adelaide to work with Jennifer for at least ten days, and then come back to Canberra for two weeks, maybe even return to France and Rennes-le-Château. In the meantime, I decided to go to the races – not just any races, the annual Birdsville races, held at the beginning of September in the tiny town at the edge of the Simpson Desert on the border between Queensland and South Australia. The race is internationally famous; the population of around a hundred grows close to an incredible ten thousand. I had done the trip once before in 2011. From Sydney it took six days driving 2,050 kilometres to reach Birdsville.

With a new transmission, transfer case, clutch and steering box, I was confident the ute was in good order and would get me there and back without any problems. All I needed was my swag, two to three weeks free time, food and fuel, and I would be on the road again. I did not know if anyone would come with me, but a good woman with a boat and motor would be nice, hey. My good friend Joan, who lives at Batemans Bay on the south coast, jumped at the chance to come with me. We left on 30 August. It took us five days to get there; the crowd was incredible.

Joan and I left Birdsville the morning after the race and headed towards Maree, nearly six hundred kilometres away. White Lady Rock was somewhere near Milparinka, another six hundred kilometres after Maree. Twenty-five years had passed since my first experience at the rock. Over the years, I had often wondered why David and I felt the way we did in that location. I was keen to see if the rock had the same impact on me as last time.

It took three days to reach the location where I expected to find the rock. I had entered the coordinates in my GPS, but after two hours driving around, I still could not find it. One and half kilometres from the destination, the GPS kept repeating 'recalculating, recalculating', as if there was some sort of interference. It was weird, and after a while, I had to shut him up. I was disappointed but pledged to return in about a month.

50

The wilderness and the White Lady

Back home in Canberra, I began planning my return trip to White Lady Rock. This time I was determined to find it. I contacted the Australian government department dealing with Aboriginal affairs to find out the protocols for visiting a sacred Aboriginal site on private land. They told me that I needed authorisation from the local aboriginal land council at Tibooburra.

I rang the Tibooburra office and spoke to the administration officer, I'll call him Bill. I explained that I had been there twenty-five years earlier and wanted to know what I had to do to obtain a permit to visit the rock and take a photograph to include in a book I was writing with a friend. Bill told me that I would need authorisation from his department and from the landholder. He would need to accompany me as my guide, at a cost for his time away from the office, plus $100 for fuel if we used the office vehicle. Most importantly, we needed to organise a definite date for the visit. He assured me that my request would be accepted. Sure enough, the email confirmation came through without any problem. We agreed that I would meet him in Tibooburra in three weeks, which gave me enough time to get ready. I decided to take my ute, saving $100.

As usual, the trip to Tibooburra took two days – I loved it. I arrived at the Tibooburra family hotel the day before the meeting, ready for a cold beer, a meat pie and a yarn. I had stayed there so many times over the years that by now my face was recognisable.

It was about a six-hour round trip from Tibooburra to the rock. The best time to leave was early morning, so the next day I picked Bill up at seven. I didn't have far to go, as he lived just across the street. I was surprised that Bill was non-indigenous; I guess I had assumed he would be a local Aboriginal guide.

'Mate, always expect the unexpected,' he said.

I filled the tank, jumped into the ute, put the key in the ignition, felt the engine jump into action, the steering wheel steady in my hands, and we were on the road. The weather as expected was superb – warm, blue sky and not a cloud in sight. What an adventure.

It took us about forty-five minutes to travel the fifty kilometres to Milparinka. I spotted the letter box at the turn-off to a dirt track, the same spot I had reached with Joan. That time, I had taken the track to the right but turned back when my GPS started playing up. After driving at least ten kilometres along the track to the left, my GPS had played up again.

'Take the left one, mate,' said Bill.

I turned left. The land reminded me of the gibber plain on the way to Innamincka, an extensive flat area for as far as the eye can see, covered with nothing but loose rocks. I told Bill about my experience with my GPS on the same dirt track. He thought it was strange, but did not offer any explanation.

He was surprised that I had gone onto the land. 'This is private property here, mate. You need authorisation.'

'Well, I had no idea.'

'Lucky for you, mate.'

The track was rough, really rough; I could not go any faster than twenty kilometres an hour. However, it gave me a chance to memorise any distinctive landmarks, so that I would remember the location in the future. I set up my GoPro camera on the dash, turning it on for about three minutes, then off, then on again.

'If you're thinking about coming back without permission, be careful. One never knows,' said Bill after a while.

Since my last visit to the rock, I had discovered that there are significant penalties for trespassing on or damaging sacred sites, and not just from the law. Indigenous Australians believe that the ancestral spirits still guard these areas, and have the power to harm any person that disturbs, destroys or disrespects them. People can actually become sick from visiting sacred sites.

'I know,' I said. 'If I need to come back, I'll get in touch with you. Trust a Frenchman's word, mate.'

He appeared relaxed and seemed to accept my answer.

As we drove on, the location looked nothing like the one I remembered from twenty-five years ago, and out here, the landscape does not change much.

'Mate, I don't recognise anything.'

'Well, we're not far now.'

'How far?'

'Ten minutes, two kilometres maybe.'

An outcrop appeared in the distance; it was big, nothing like what I remembered.

'I'll get as close as possible with the car,' I said.

'No, mate, stay on the track.'

'Why?'

Bill insisted that I stay on the track. I wondered what the problem was. I parked the ute on the track; we got out and walked to the outcrop, then walked around it. This was definitely not what I saw twenty-five years ago – it was not the same place.

'Mate, there's no plaque here,' I said, pointing to the bottom of the rock. I had told Bill about the plaque when I rang him. 'The words written on the plaque I saw were "White Lady Rock Sacred Aboriginal site do not trespass". That's how I found out what it was called.'

'Maybe someone took the plaque off. I don't know.'

'Mate,' I said, 'the plaque was very small at the base of the outcrop nearly touching the ground. To see it, you practically had to have your nose on it. This is not the rock I saw, I'm sure of it.'

'Well, to me it's White Lady Rock, mate,' said Bill.

'Well, not to me, mate. I can't understand it.'

As I started taking photos, Bill remarked that I should not take too many, which I thought was strange. When I asked why not, his answer was even more puzzling.

'We don't want too many people to know.'

Know what, I thought. Was it the location of a scared site that needed to be kept secret in order to protect it, or was there something else about the location that needed to be kept under wraps?

We drove back to Tibooburra, had a beer at the pub and chatted for some time. I stayed in town one more night then headed back to Canberra early the next morning.

I felt disappointment at not finding the White Lady Rock I had seen twenty-five years earlier. Bill's remarks about not taking too many photos and needing to stay on the track puzzled me. Which was the real 'lady', the one of twenty-five years ago, or the one I saw with the guide?

I thought about my conversation with Jennifer about the White Lady of legends. I was intrigued that the legend of the White Lady is found both in Australian Aboriginal culture and in Europe. It is well known in the mountainous regions around the Corbières and the Ariège. The White Lady is mentioned in the Virgo stanza in 'Le Serpent Rouge', the strange poem in the *Dossiers Secret*: 'Miraculous vessel of the eternal White Lady of Legends'. I wondered if the miraculous vessel was a veiled reference to the land, mother earth and quartz – the 'mother of gold'. It had to be – it was too much of a coincidence. Was there a link between the White Lady legends around Rennes-le-Château and my findings in the north-west of New South Wales? Both locations are gold-bearing.

On my arrival back in Canberra, there was an email from Enzo. He was flat out writing his next book *The Da Vinci Prophecy*, the sequel to the *Poussin Enigma*. He had been researching the painters Poussin and Teniers and in a flash of insight believed he had uncovered another clue that Poussin knew about the gold, and might have represented this in his paintings.

> Hope you have been keeping well, Gerard… The authors of the *Tomb of God* say that Gerard de Sède told Henry Lincoln the reference to 'Poussin and Teniers hold the key' in the parchment refers to the painting of the *Temptation of Saint Anthony* by David Teniers. I disagree. I say he was misled by the Priory of Sion. I believe that the painting referred to is *The Alchemist*. This confirms that Saunière was finding or making gold and this can confirm your theory. I can't find any other writer who has referred to the painting *The Alchemist*. Furthermore, Château d'Hautpoul next door to the church of Mary Magdalene was known to have a room for alchemy. All this fits in with what Marie Dénarnaud said about people walking on gold without knowing it and also the fact that she told a woman she saw Saunière melting gold. What all this means is that you have been on the right track all along…

51

Dead man's bones: Adelaide

Rennies will tell you that the mystery of Rennes-le-Château has a curious effect. It grabs you and won't let you go. Rat Scabies's friend Christopher started out as a complete sceptic but over time he became hooked on the investigation – a fully-fledged Rennie. Scabies had announced that among his father's old papers he had found some 'never before seen' letters, which dated from the late 1800s and appeared to add to the puzzle and mystery surrounding the Rennes-le-Château enigma. The mystery just kept on expanding.

Plans were underway to commemorate the centenary of Saunière's death in Rennes-le-Château on 21 January 2017. Paul Smith advised visitors not to count on 'historical facts' when visiting Rennes-le-Château, stating that 'it's strictly an amusement park for entertainment only', in the same category as Roswell, Loch Ness, Glatonbury and the Face on Mars. In his view, the answer has always been simple – Saunière's wealth came from trafficking in massses and the 'sensational stories' about Saunière's life were 'modern myths and forgeries invented by 'charlatans and conspiracy theorists, none of which could stand the critical test'.[108]

I agreed that the story was 'steeped in lies, fakes and forgeries'.

Most of the story of Saunière's wealth was a composition of conflicting eyewitness accounts and leaps of faith strung together with circumstantial evidence, much of which was impossible to verify. Then again, I had to admit that a significant percentage of recorded history is. Even science ultimately must admit that it deals with hypotheses.

All you have to do is look at a history book or science book written fifty years ago. Something that was considered a fact in one era becomes fiction as more knowledge is gained. What we know about the world is constantly changing. Even observable phenomena can be interpreted differently. We can never know a truth absolutely, especially in the fields of history and religion. There were very few verifiable facts in the mystery; however, as Rat Scabies once observed, in the world of Rennes-le-Château research, it is easy to dismiss new leads as rubbish.

No matter how many times we went over the story, checking and rechecking, going back to original sources when they were available, there was still a feeling in the back of my mind, call it my prospector's hunch, that we were missing something.

'There's something I want you to watch,' said Jennifer, waving a DVD in her hand. 'Mario picked this up the other day at the library by chance. I think you'll find it interesting. A guy called Bill Decarli has a theory about the location of Lasseter's reef.'[109][110]

Jennifer slipped the DVD into the player and we listened intently as Decarli presented his theory. Lasseter said that he discovered the reef in 1887, about 483 kilometres west of Alice Springs. He reported that in 1900 he and a surveyor by the name of Harding located the reef when they were travelling eastward from Carnarvon on the west coast of Australia. Decarli stated that right from the outset he got the idea that the mystery of the lost reef could be explained by a reversal of bearings or a mirror imaging. Following this hunch, Decarli checked his map and found that there is a group of hills called Carnarvon Hills in Queensland towards the east coast of Australia, right on the same latitude as Carnarvon in Western Australia. Reversing Lasseter's directions, Decarli wondered whether the reef could be east of Alice Springs. He marked an X on the map; and in 1991 set out on a road trip to find the reef. He discovered certain landmarks that indicated what he believed to be the presence of a sixteen-kilometre quartz reef containing gold. He was so convinced that he applied for an exploration licence for a hundred and fifty-five square kilometres around the reef, and a syndicate was formed with a plan to mine it. But the search came to nothing, as the Lands Council declared the area sacred. I thought of my recent trip to Tibooburra, my attempt to find White Lady Rock and the feeling that I was not in the same place I had visited all those years ago.

Jennifer gave me a triumphant look. 'What do you say, G41? Some people think that Lasseter deliberately led the party in the wrong direction to create a diversion away from the real location, which he was going back to later, just like the Argyle hoax.'

'I can understand that. It's an old prospector's trick – reverse the map to hide the location.'

'There was also a suggestion that it was a great central Australian gold scam meant to tempt British investors and finance a railway to Alice Springs. Shades of Corbu's marketing strategy to bring business to Rennes-le-Château. They were also adamant that the reef should not pass into the hands of the federal government, something Saunière was determined to avoid when the Church was stripped of most of its property rights.'

'So you are saying that Lasseter's original expedition could have been a cover-up to hide the real location of the reef,' I said.

'Well, all the papers to do with the expedition were conveniently lost,' said Jennifer. 'Sound familiar? So what do you think – is there a gold reef out there somewhere?'

'Well, I've read a lot about it and I'm still inclined to think that Lasseter fabricated the story to secure himself some income during the Great Depression, but you never know. But Jennifer, this is truly synchronicity.'

'It is?' said Jennifer.

'In 1991, I was working with a temp agency in Sydney.'

'French chef for hire,' said Jennifer. 'Ooh la la.'

'Something like that. Anyway, about six weeks after the French woman's husband told me the Hand of Faith story, the temp agency sent me to a nursing home on Parramatta Road, not far from the city. The average age of the residents must have been around eighty-five. On the first morning, nearly everyone welcomed me in his or her best franglais: "Bonjour, monsour, "Comment allez vous?" For two weeks, a French chef was going to cook their lunches and dinners – I was the new king. The place was bubbling with excitement. Two weeks went like a flash. On the last day, I was walking across the foyer when an old guy called me over – he must have been at least ninety. "Mate, sit down for a minute," he said. I walked over to where he was sitting in his wheel chair. He asked me why I was leaving. I told him that the agency needed me to be somewhere else. Let me tell you he was not happy. "Bloody hell, can you tell them you need to stay here?" So I told him that there was no way I could do that and besides I was excited about leaving because a mate and I were going to Tibooburra in about two weeks to do some detecting. "For gold?" he asked. "Yes, for gold," I said and then I told him that actually we were going to Milparinka. He reached up, took me by the arm, and told me to sit down because he had something to tell me. His hand was shaking and he kept a grip on my arm the whole time. "Listen, I need to tell you this," he said. "I should have listened to my grandfather more often. My grandfather, mate, he knew Lasseter." He fixed his eyes firmly on mine as he began to tell me the story. "Yes, mate, he knew him. I was very young and I remember one day he was in the kitchen with Lasseter and they were looking at some nuggets Lasseter brought with him. Yes, mate, I swear. I should have listened, but I didn't. That's how the cookies crumbles.'"

'Wow, that's incredible,' said Jennifer.

'That was it. That is what he wanted to tell me. Something that must have been so precious to him during all those years. Some old guy I knew nothing about telling me such a story. Why? Because I was the French cook king, because of my nice face or because he loved what I was cooking? Was it true? How can I tell? I have absolutely no means of finding out.'

'So what did you do?'

'Nothing back then, but that old guy put a little worm in the apple that I call my brain, because now I will always have an unanswered question. Why was I chosen to hear the story? Did he give me a piece of the puzzle so I could use it later in my journey? Is that moment now and what, if anything, does it have to do with Rennes-le-Château?'

'Red Minis.' said Jennifer. 'Or could it have something to do with White Lady Rock? If the reef is east of Alice Springs, does that bring it anywhere near the Rock?'

'I don't think so. White Lady Rock is located near Mount Poole, which would be about two hundred and fifty kilometres south-east. Still, it's an interesting thought.' I told Jennifer about my unsuccessful search for White Lady Rock with Joan, the strange experience with my GPS and my return trip to the rock with Bill and our discussion about the area being a sacred site.

'So you really don't think it was the rock you saw twenty-five years ago.'

'Absolutely. I had a weird feeling, as if I was being taken to another destination for some reason.'

Jennifer took the DVD out of the player and snapped it back into its cover then pursed her lips. 'What if it's all true, Gerard?'

'What do you mean?' I said.

'Everything – all the theories about Saunière's wealth. That he took money from saying masses, that he did find treasure, that certain nobles gave him donations for whatever purpose. Perhaps the strength with which some authors dismiss various theories has resulted in some of the clues being overlooked. Even Jean Luc Robin suggests that it is entirely possible that all the theories are correct. He was convinced that Saunière did find something explosive that explains his fortune, at least in part. But he doesn't rule out the possibility that there's an "enormous treasure" that has nothing to do with the affair of Rennes-le-Château that someone might stumble on by chance one day. Why did Saunière stay in Rennes-le-Château, why didn't he go somewhere more glamorous? Whether he was compelled to stay there or whether he chose to, obviously whatever he found had something to do with the actual physical location. Rat Scabies once said that trying to solve the mystery is like trying to pin the tail on a huge donkey and unless someone finds a stash of gold with Saunière's name on it, we'll probably never find out how he made his money. What do you think, Gerard?'

'Look,' I said, 'people have forgotten the core of the story that got everyone's attention in the first place – how Saunière became so rich. The story of treasure has been repeated so many times over the years that people take it to be true. Even de Sède said that the imaginary is something that tends to become true. To get cash, you need a commodity to exchange for money. It could be treasure, diamonds, silver, gold, information or even a winning lottery ticket. Treasure won't work – think of Lava. The sale of information means more than one person is involved – not good. Diamonds – wrong geological location. Silver – the ratio of volume/weight for cash price it too big. If you compare the sale of one ounce of gold to silver, you need much more silver to get the same money and you cannot fill your pocket with it. A lottery win – forget about it. I know you have to be in it to win it but not in those days. When I saw the gold mine of Salsigne in 2006, I was stunned that I had never heard of it. Each year, thousands of tourists and students visit the old gold mining regions in Australia. But at Salsigne and Villaniere there is nothing on offer – no sales of mineral specimens or gold, or any documentation regarding the history, the technology, the mining, the geology, the mineralogy or anything else for that matter. The area could be a real gold mine for tourists and students and anyone passionate about such an incredible find. After all, in its day Salsigne was the biggest opencast gold mine in western Europe.'

'Perhaps they're keeping it under wraps because of the controversy over the serious land degradation and the pollution,' said Jennifer.

'Possibly,' I said. 'But I wouldn't be surprised if it's designed to discourage people from being interested in gold. We don't want another gold rush, do we?'

'I'm surprised that no one's exploring that area now,' said Jennifer.

'Give it time, Jennifer. All the evidence points to native gold as the answer, or at least part of the answer to the mystery. What is required now is for someone to do professional sampling and trace the gold back to the source.'

'Lunch is ready.' Mario popped his head around the door. 'It's a beautiful day. Let's eat on the front veranda.'

Mario had prepared a magnificent spread: a selection of cheeses, prosciutto, a garden salad with slices of home-grown avocado, crusty rolls and a bowl of huge home-grown black olives glistening with an olive oil and oregano dressing. We sat in cane chairs overlooking the broad front garden. One half featured a circular vegetable plot divided into the five segments of a pentagram. After doing a permaculture course, Mario decided to pull out all the roses in the plot and create a magnificent vegetable patch. In the centre of the wheel, a persimmon tree completed the picture.

Mario offered me the Kalamata olives. 'See what you think of these, Gerard.'

I popped one in my mouth. It was firm-fleshed and salty – delicious. 'Magnificent, Mario – you should sell them at farmer's markets. You have a paradise here, you know.'

Mario beamed and popped an olive into his mouth. 'Have you ever thought of returning to France, Gerard – to live?'

'No, not seriously, but if I did maybe I could buy a house in Saint Martys. Perhaps I could do some digging in the backyard, with Enzo as my willing helper, if you get my drift. There are some real bargains, but unfortunately, the lawyers' fees in France are astronomical. I feel that I belong here – in some ways, I feel more like a true blue Aussie than many Aussie-born city dwellers. I'm itching to do another long cross-country trip in the old Truckasaurus – my 1996 Toyota ute. I've done plenty of east-west trips but this time I'm working on a plan to cross the country from south to north beginning in Adelaide and ending in Darwin. It's been on my bucket list for a long time.'

'Incredible,' said Mario. 'That's the route the Ghan train takes, isn't it?

'Sure is – a six-thousand-kilometre round trip. Sleeping in the open, cooking over a campfire, with only the stars and the track to keep me company – that's my idea of heaven.'

Jennifer's face lit up. 'Or Arcadia.'

'So, Jennifer, where to next? What are your plans?'

'I'm thinking of attending a conference on alchemy in Prague. Dan and his colleagues have a new healing invention called the Therapi.[111] It uses frequency modulated electromagnetic waveforms for healing and pain relief. Apparently, the method has been around for over sixty years. It works by creating a magnetic environment of restored fractality – precisely the definition of healing in biologic tissue. They say it may even help to extend lifespan.'

'Have you ever been to Prague?' I said.

'No. I hear that it's a beautiful city,' said Jennifer. 'The ancient plan of the city is really interesting. It's laid out like the petals of a rose.'

'Well, if you go, don't forget to smell the roses while you're there,' I said, winking.

That night, I logged on to Google Earth to begin plotting a journey that would take me across two deserts and five climate zones, through country that has seen bushfires, flash floods and droughts, past prohibited zones and great stretches of mining land and cattle country. Was I taking a risk? Yes, but it was a calculated one and compared to the early explorers I was well prepared with all the mod cons available nowadays.

The beaten track from Adelaide to Darwin takes you along the Augusta Highway, Horrocks Highway and the Stuart Highway. I was travelling off the beaten track. Some stretches would be rough, even impassable. However, what is an adventure without a sense of the unknown? I wanted to feel the isolation, the vastness of the land, the challenge of extremes of heat and cold and even the flies.

An hour later, I made myself a coffee then settled back in front of the computer to check my emails and the French news.

'*Macaniche, boudi,*' I called out to Jennifer and Mario.[112]

52

The new gold rush

Jennifer and Mario stood behind me, peering over my shoulder.

'What have you found, Gerard?' said Jennifer.

'The French government has granted Variscan permits to explore for minerals across the country and gold is on their list.' I clicked on a map showing the French departments. 'Here, in the Sarthe and Mayenne in the north-west of France, near the old gold mine at Rouez, and here in the Vendée, the Saint Pierre licence surrounds the historic La Belliere gold mine. Look at this – Couflens is also on their list. It's in the Pyrenees in the south-west of France on the border with Spain – about a hundred and forty kilometres by road from Salsigne and Rennes-le-Château or about a hundred kilometres as the crow flies. That's still close in geological terms.'

I continued reading. 'The demand for minerals is on the increase in France…there has not been any significant gold exploration in France for decades, until now…the government is planning to reassess all ancient known mines including silver, copper and gold.'

My eyes skipped across the screen as I began to take it all in. I clicked on a few more links. 'Many professional miners believe that there may still be viable gold to be found, around Salsigne and other old mines…a hundred and twenty tonnes of gold came out of Salsigne…some experts believe there could be more than thirty to forty tonnes of gold and rare earth lying dormant around Salsigne. What did I tell you, hey?'

'Oh, my God, Gerard, that's incredible,' Jennifer. 'Who are Variscan?'

'An Australian mining company, with a subsidiary based in Orleans backed by major Singaporean investment funds – it's led by two former members of BRGM. BRGM has identified that tungsten, antimony and gold have the highest potential for mining development – they know that there are plenty of deposits across the country. The French government is issuing *Permis Exclusif de Recherches*, exclusive exploration licences, and Variscan Mines is one of the first companies to benefit.[113] Apparently, Australia is seen as a very favourable partner.'

'Let's hope they do a better job of protecting the environment than the last mob,' said Jennifer.

'They're also planning to invest up to €400 million in a state-owned mining company, Compagnie National des Mines de France, which will prospect for mineral resources in France, French overseas territories and elsewhere in the world, including Africa, Central Asia and South America. The Minister of Industrial Renewal, Arnaud Montebourg, says it is a renaissance – a move reminiscent of Jean-Baptiste Colbert, the pioneer of French *dirigisme.*'

'What is French *dirigisme?*' said Jennifer.

'*Dirigisme* means direct. It's where the government takes more control and gets directly involved in the country's economic and industrial development,' I said. 'The government wants to gain a grip over strategically important mineral resources at home and abroad. Until now, they have been relying on imports of strategic minerals such as tungsten, lithium and germanium, and rare earth elements increasingly used in modern industrial technologies. Remember how Colbert founded the state-owned Compagnie Royale des Mines et Fonderies du Languedoc in 1666 when he took over from Nicholas Fouquet. At that time, the economy was on the brink of bankruptcy because of the king's excessive spending. Here, look, Montebourg says that the government is an intelligent economic actor serving the interests of the nation. Colbertism is coming back and that is good. My guess is that the 2008 financial crisis has something to do with the government's decision. Gold is a safe haven investment during crises. Patrice Christmann of BRGM says that there is good mining potential in France for anyone who takes the trouble to look. He thinks that with luck they might find a world-class deposit. Incredible. I wonder what my friend Pierre Jezequel thinks.'

We were witnessing the revival of exploration and mining in France, led by an Australian company. Clearly Variscan, and most probably others, are, as we say in French, *'en gardant un œil sur le poisson et un autre sur le chat*, keeping one eye on the fish and another on the cat'.

'Wow,' said Mario. 'I say we all head to France – with shovels.'

France was no longer reluctant to issue exploration and mining permits, but it was definitely reluctant to see its gold or any precious metals leaving its territories. Legislation enacted in May 2013 made it illegal to ship precious metals, including jewellery, out of the country. At the time, the government did not announce it, and it was barely reported by the media. Some have suggested that the decree is designed to limit what is known in France as the 'anonymous' or black market, in which no taxes are paid and people are free to trade without the supervision of banks and government. However, euro coins, notes, gold bullion coins and bars attract no tax in France and therefore it is more likely that this initiative is a form of capital control, designed to discourage the ownership of gold bullion and cash outside of the banking system. It is also illegal to send currency out of the country by mail, including coins and notes. As far as any 'treasure' is concerned, we were back to square one – whatever is found still belongs to the state.

I thought of what Marie Dénarnaud allegedly told Noël Corbu: '*Les gens du coin marchent sur de l'or, mais ne le savent pas*. People are walking on the gold, but they don't know it. *Avec celui qu' a laisse le monsieur*. There is some left, there is the possibility to go back and get more. *Nous aurions de quoi nourrir Rennes pendant cent ans et il en resterait*. We could feed Rennes for a hundred years and there would still be some left.'[114]

I thought of Burraga in New South Wales, where gold was found in 1901, so close to the surface that people were literally *marchant sur de l'or*, walking on the gold.

What secrets was Marie keeping for all those years she was Saunière's housekeeper and the thirty-nine years from the time of his death in 1917, to her own in 1956? It seems that the only inkling she gave about the 'secret' was that it was something to do with 'gold'. If Bérenger knew about, or stumbled upon a gold vein, he and Marie must have accumulated a fair amount over a number of years. If all the gold was converted into cash, it is possible that there is a stash of cash hidden away in a bank account or somewhere else. In 1899, after suspending works for two years, Saunière signed a contract for substantial building works. According to Jean luc Robin, he must have spent the preceding two years converting whatever he may have found into cash – hence his frequent travelling.[115]

The accounts of what happened to Marie after Saunière's death on 17 January 1917 vary. She received permission from the local commune to continue living in the presbytery. Documents show that she borrowed money to pay property taxes and maintain the estate, which Saunière had put in her name to keep it out of the hands of Church and state. It must have been a terrible situation for her. Some speculate that she had no money even to pay for Saunière's coffin or for any other incoming bills. However, the evidence clearly shows that she paid for the coffin on 12 June 1917.[116]

At the end of World War II (1939–1945), circumstances worsened. The French government issued a new currency. Anyone could exchange old francs for new ones. However, there was a catch: as a means of apprehending tax-evaders, collaborators and wartime profiteers, French citizens were required to disclose the source of their wealth to the authorities when exchanging their old francs for new. There was much mistrust of the peasant classes, who were suspected of having considerably enriched themselves thanks to the black market.[117] If Marie had tapped into any hidden savings, she would have had to reveal the source. This was a risky situation in post-war France. There were two choices – exchange the money and reveal the source, or live in poverty. It seems that she lived in poverty until Noël Corbu settled all her debts. I assume that she lived comfortably for the remaining years of her life.

Jean Luc Robin believed that it was highly likely that Saunière's capital remained largely untouched at the time of his death and that only the interest had been used for all the building works and his lifestyle. The place to dig is not at the bottom of his garden but much rather in a bank account in a safe country.[118]

53

The 'stone' of Avols

On 14 December 1911 at 3.15 p.m., Albert C. Burrage, an industrialist from Boston Massachusetts, sat in room number 8 of the Hotel des Ventes, the Auction House at 9 Rue Drouot, eagerly awaiting the lot he had travelled to Paris to acquire. Auctioneer M.F. Lair Dubreuil surveyed the audience keenly, secure in the knowledge that mineral dealer and expert M. Alexandre Stuer had authenticated the collection of gold minerals, remarking on the sumptuousness of the specimens. When the auctioneer finally dropped his ivory gavel, Mr Burrage became the new owner of the Bouglise collection.

This is how I imagined the scene, when by chance I came across the *Catalogue de la collection des minéraux de l'or réunie par Georges de La Bouglise*. The catalogue listed over five hundred and forty-one gold specimens collected by prominent French mining engineer, Georges de la Bouglise (1842–1907), a consulting engineer for mines in Europe, America and Mexico. Bouglaise was a serious mineral collector, specialising in native gold specimens at the genesis of their mineralisation. With specimens from Siberia to Australia, Bouglise believed that his collection was the most comprehensive and 'curious series' in any public museum or in any 'particular collection'. There was even a specimen from Gundegai in New South Wales, the site of a gold rush between 1858 and 1875.[119]

When I reached entry number 410 on page 55, my jaw dropped. 'Weight 540 grams. Native alluvial gold [known as] the *Pépite des Avols*, Avols nugget. This large nugget fully rolled and rounded by friction was found in the Ardèche department.'

The find was reported in *La Nature* of 6 July 1889.[120] In 1889, in the Ardèche department, in the town of Gravières near the hamlet of Avols, a shepherd named Clement Trouillas found a large gold nugget measuring ninety-four by fifty by eight millimetres. I read the sentence several times. A large gold nugget found by a shepherd. The story of Ignace Paris sprung to mind. Its size did not compare to some of the huge nuggets found in Australia, but at five hundred and forty grams, it was still an impressive find and it was native gold.

Clement had thrown what he thought was a heavy stone at one of his animals, which had moved away from the herd. Several days later, his brother-in-law Adrien Noël was collecting wood when he found the unusual 'shiny stone' in the shape of a crushed potato on the ground. Clément recognised it as the projectile. I imagined Adrien's dilemma: what to do, who to trust, who to tell. I imagined the excitement as whispers of the find no doubt made their way around the hamlet. Was it really a nugget? Was it really from these parts? Perhaps a French prospector returning from the Californian gold rush had lost it; or was it part of a hidden treasure. Most importantly, were there more to be found? After all, mineralogists had never spoken of similar finds.

Noël took the nugget to the watchmaker in Vans, who wanted to buy it for 1,200 francs. However, people advised that it would be wiser to keep the nugget as an exhibit for scientific purposes. The nugget survived intact and eventually made its way to the Harvard Mineralogical Museum as part of the Bouglise collection.

The Chassezac river is the main tributary of the Ardèche river. It drains the Avols sector where the nugget was found. Like the rivers in the Languedoc-Rousillon region, the Chassezac is a popular river for gold panning today. It flows in a deep schist valley; quartz veins are visible everywhere in the mountains. Finding nuggets on the ground in these locations means one thing – more gold is to be found – and that is exactly what came to light. The priest of Gravières, Father Canaud, had a particular interest in the find. He reported three other known finds to the Academy of Sciences in Paris supplying a drawing of the location of the finds and details of the geology of the region. In 1860, M. Pellet found a nugget about the size of the tip of his thumb whilst picking a vine. It was sold to a goldsmith for sixty francs. In 1830, Joseph Merle discovered a nugget in the bed of the little brook of the fountain below the village of Les Avols. Wedged between two stones, it resembled a small knife handle, and was sold to the goldsmith in Vans for three hundred and eighty francs. In 1810, Father Henri Robert discovered a nugget in Monjoc while he was planting a chestnut tree. Its size is unknown. Four nuggets found in the same sector – all by chance. Had other nuggets been found and kept secret?

1887 Saunière begins renovating the church in Rennes-le-Château with 1,000 francs, courtesy of the Comtesse de Chambord.
1888 Henri Boudet is listed as a member of the Société des Arts et des Sciences de Carcassonne.
1889 The Avols Nugget is found in the Ardèche.
1889 An article about the gold nuggets found in the Ardèche is published in *La Nature*.
1891 Saunière finds 'something'.
1892 Gold is discovered at Salsigne.
1892 Saunière's finances improve dramatically.

Are these events coincidences – red Minis – or are they a series of synchronicities, with a message for those who think outside the square?

French scientist and adventurer Gaston Tissandier first published *La Nature* magazine in 1873 with the aim of popularising science. It is not beyond the realm of possibility that Boudet subscribed to the magazine – or perhaps even Saunière. We know that Saunière had an impressive collection of periodicals that he had been collecting for years. Did this article provide further inspiration for Boudet's explorations and Saunière's 'rock collecting' activities?

Italian researcher Mariano Tomatis reports Laurent Buchholtzer's research into Saunière's accounting books and correspondence. Buchholtzer had access to eight hundred and fifty pages of records dating from 1897 to 1915. On the July 1902 page, Saunière noted, '*acheté poudre mine et mèche*, purchased mine and wick powder'.[121] According to Buchholtzer, he used it for the making of his vineyards. According to others, the priest used gunpowder to excavate the area, perhaps in some abandoned mine.

From the moment I set foot on the vast continent of Australia in 1967, it was obvious that I was going to encounter a drastic change in my life. In France at that time, the most important things for young people like me were food and having fun. Coming to Australia taught me a lesson. I soon realised that I had landed in a country built by pioneers – there was no limit to what one could achieve. Work was plentiful and so was money. Australia is a very rich country – minerals, food and opportunities – we have it all. I quickly discovered that, at that time, the average Aussie had no idea about food, but as far as gold was concerned, they knew plenty.

When the Australian gold rush started in 1841, people collected nuggets from the ground like potatoes. They were literally tripping over them – hard to imagine, but it's true. Gold was so plentiful that the township set up at the junction of the two creeks where Hargraves had found gold was named Ophir after the town in the Old Testament's Book of Kings. According to the legend, the stones of Ophir's mountains were pure gold and every three years King Solomon received a cargo of gold from the town. Ophir is still a working goldfield over a hundred and fifty years later.

The old diggers knew how to recognise a nugget. Fortunes were made and lost but they knew that gold was 'the thing'. Around the same time, the average French person knew nothing about native gold, reflecting the general lack of knowledge about the existence of gold in France during the modern age, even among some in the scientific community and despite the country's history brimming with descriptions that could match those of Ophir in their brilliance. Jean-Baptiste Colbert is famously quoted as saying that 'Fashion is to France what the gold mines of Peru are to Spain.'[122]

From ancient times to the present day, historians, mineralogists, geologists and even the clergy have documented the presence of precious metals within an area of a few square kilometres around Rennes-le-Château and Rennes les Bains. There is a long history of gold mining in the region. The geology around Rennes-le-Château favours native gold; all you need to do is look at a geological map, which you can download from the Internet. Rennes-le-Château is perfectly situated within the anticline/syncline axis. Significant amounts of gold were mined in the same geological configuration at Salsigne only forty-seven kilometres from Rennes-le-Château, which is close in geological terms. It is clear that the Catholic Church, the French kings and the nobility knew that the region was rich with gold – more gold than meets the eyes.

Some say that every researcher finds evidence to support their theory about Rennes-le-Château. We could be staring at Poussin's painting for days hoping to discover the magic code of the Rennes-le-Château mystery.

Had Bérenger Saunière found native gold? I certainly believe so. From the evidence we have, native gold – the one that anybody can sell in exchange for money anywhere in the world, with no questions asked, is the best bet. All he needed was a vein a couple of centimetres wide and a few metres long – and perhaps a cache of nuggets along the way.

54

The search continues

By early 2017, the French government had granted eleven exclusive exploration permits to mining companies.[123] Variscan Mines alone obtained seven permits concentrated in three main areas: Brittany and the Pays de la Loire in the north, the Limousin in the centre and the Midi-Pyrenees in the south. All of Variscan's permits included gold.

In 1910, *The Mercury* newspaper in Hobart, Tasmania, reported on the gold vein discovered in the late nineteenth century at La Lucette in the North West of France, one of the areas Variscan was exploring. In that year, the company mined approximately seven hundred and forty kilos of pure gold. The paper reported that perhaps someday we might hear of a rush to France, in good old Australian style. Was that day now?

The French government promoted the economic benefits to the country, including jobs and growth, stressing that high copper and gold prices and forecasts for long-term stability in those prices made exploration worthwhile. Advances in technology, geological surveying and mining methods were making minerals exploration easier, cheaper and safer. Drones with electromagnetic sensors could map the subsoil to a depth of five hundred metres.

However, despite reassurances from politicians and mining companies, collectives and communes began mobilising against the resurgence of mining. Protests were fuelled by fears for the environment and for public health and safety, and by philosophical and ideological reasons. Militant protestors targeted Variscan's headquarters in Orleans with an explosive device and warned that worse was to come. One group was concerned that the telluric waves of the Druids between Mont Saint Michel and the Broceliande forest would be disturbed.[124]

The future of the Salsigne gold mine had become almost a daily debate. Despite the government having spent millions of euros on the Salsigne clean-up, some estimated that after a century of intense mining, the region would remain polluted for at least ten thousand years.[125] I could understand the community's concern and imagined how furious and sceptical the waitress I had met in Villanière would be at the news.

On 15 October 2018, flash floods swamped large parts of the southwest of France. The river Aude reached flood levels not seen in over a hundred years. Floodwaters carried arsenic pollution from the old Salsigne gold mine across the Orbiel Valley, polluting rivers and towns. Several children living downstream from the mine were tested as being overexposed to arsenic.

By 2017, Variscan's licenses in France were renounced. In June 2019, the Administrative Court of Toulouse cancelled the Couflens licence in the Midi-Pyrenees. By December 2019, there were only four metal exploration permits left in mainland France, in the Massif Central and in the Loire-Atlantique. The government cancelled its plans to create the public company wanted by Arnaud Montebourg.

Variscan's permits may have been terminated but the corresponding deposits remain 'open to research'. There is an old saying that 'gold opens all locks'. Could the area between Rennes-le-Château and Salsigne become another gold rush? Only time will tell, but it is certainly on the cards.

If you think there is no more gold lying in the ground – think twice.

In August 2016, the Australian Prospectors and Miners Association reported that recent finds were causing excitement around the world. In the same month, a prospector found a massive four-kilo gold nugget only thirty centimetres below the ground in a worked-over area on the southern edge of central Victoria's Golden Triangle near Ballarat.[126] As he scraped away the soil, he initially thought it was an old horseshoe. He was stunned that nuggets of this size could still be found.

By 2019, Victoria was experiencing a gold rush revival. It is believed that more than 2.26 million tonnes of gold remain underground in regional Victoria. In July 2019 a Victorian retiree unearthed a two-kilo nugget worth around AU$130,000 on the outskirts of Ballarat. He was searching on old pastureland when his detector started beeping. At first, all he found was an old bullet, but he persevered and eventually unearthed the nugget, which has since been named 'You wouldn't believe it'.[127] You can be sure that locals will be heading out into the bush.

In October 2020, Manhattan Corporation Ltd, a small Australia minerals exploration company, had the best result for that month as part of their Tibooburra Gold Project, located in the north-west of New South Wales, approximately two hundred kilometres north of Broken Hill. One of their test drillings from the New Bendigo Main Zone showed 20.86 grams of gold per ton – a spectacular high-grade result. This zone, named because of the similarity of the mineralisation to the Victorian goldfields, just happens to be in the vicinity of White Lady Rock.

It does not matter whether you are in Salsigne, Ballarat or Tibooburra, or any part of the world where gold has been found before, even two thousand years ago. It is like the fishes in the sea: there will be some left.

Perhaps one day a lone French fossicker following his or her passion will set out with a pan, a pick, a shovel and probably a detector and stumble upon – something. It won't have Saunière's name stamped on it but, ignoring secrecy – the most important rule in prospecting – he or she may just decide to write the next chapter in the Rennes-le-Château mystery.

Epilogue

Another Christmas was approaching. I was preparing to send greetings to friends and family in France who I keep in regular contact with, when an email came in from Pierre Jezequel, the geologist with BRGM in France, now retired, who I had sent my samples to all those years ago when I was just starting out on my quest for diamonds.

> *Bonjour*, Gerard. I can see that you keep the dynamism and the energy of an explorer/adventurer well alive, even in retirement, meaning that you are not. I am looking forward to reading your book when it is published, especially as the subject of the gold of Rennes-le-Château is a topic on which I worked in my lab at BRGM. There were treasure hunters who were asking us to analyse a lot of items they were finding, in the hope of discovering the secret of his fabulous wealth. I used to tell them that this type of research could not be improvised and as for any similar substance, one needs a good background of scientific knowledge and also some good guidelines regarding such enterprise, when hoping to get good results. But this Cartesian spirit way of thinking is often not compatible with the adventure, which in itself gives great pleasures.
>
> A Merry Christmas to you and your loved ones. Enjoy the end of the year and good luck with your adventures that as life never stops.

Out of the blue, my business partner rang – not everything was lost with the diamond exploration. We started formulating a new plan; all we needed was the cash for an exploration licence – Group 6 – diamonds. The Kandie Peak project was resurrected from the ashes.

Henry Lincoln likens gold fever to a sickness, against which nobody has yet found an effective antidote. In a way, he is right, but in my case, I call it my passion. Fossicking for gold and diamonds is in my blood. Searching for clues, looking outside the square, and putting the puzzle pieces together to make connections overlooked by others. The desire of the search is part of my reality.

I have faced death twice in my life; my heart surgery was a real wake-up call. I do not know if I will make it to a hundred like Taty. However, one thing is for sure – I will never give up. Sometimes you find gold or diamonds, sometimes you find old nails and horseshoes. But desire keeps you going and the dream stays with you.

Perhaps it is my Holy Grail.

Bibliography and further reading

A hundred weight of gold. 1851. *Bathurst Daily Free Press and Mining Journal.* 19 July. Available online at http://trove.nla.gov.au/ (accessed 12 February 2017).

Adams, David & Sonnen, Krista. 2005. Sundown Hill: 'A medicine wheel of song lines.' (Handout at workshop.) 14 May.

Andrews, Richard & Schellenberger, Paul. 1996. *The Tomb of God.* Time Warner: London, UK.

Baigent, Michael; Leigh, Richard & Lincoln, Henry. 1996. *The Holy Blood and the Holy Grail.* Arrow Books: London, UK.

Blanc, Jerome & Desmedt, Ludovic. 2007. Counteracting counterfeiting? False money as a multidimensional justice issue in 16th and 17th century monetary analysis. 11th ESHET Conference. Justice in Economic Thought, July. Available online at https://halshs.archives-ouvertes.fr/halshs-00160880/document (accessed 20 January 2020).

Bord, Janet & Bord, Colin. 1974. *Mysterious Britain.* Granada: Great Britain.

Boudet, H. Msg. 1886. *La vrais langue Celtique et le Cromlech de Rennes le Bains.* (The true Celtic language and the Cromlech at Rennes le Bains.) (pdf) Available online at www.signovinces.fr/PDF/Livre_Boudet.pdf (accessed 20 January 2020).

Boxer, Grant. nd. Argyle diamond mine. Available online at https://grantboxer.github.io/2_Argyle.html (accessed 4 November 2020).

Breizh-info. 2015. Mining projects in Brittany: what is Variscan Mines looking for? Available online at https://www.breizh-info.com/2015/06/01/27071/projets-miniers-en-bretagne-que-recherche-variscan-mines (accessed 15 January 2020).

Brunton, Eric. 1971. *Diamonds.* Chilton Book Company: USA.

Callahan, Philip. 2001. Ancient mysteries, modern visions: The magnetic life of agriculture. cited in Martin Gray. 2020. The round towers of Ireland. World Pilgrimage Guide. Available online at https://sacredsites.com/europe/ireland/tower_of_cashel.html (accessed 20 January 2020).

Captier, Antoine; Doumergue, Christian & Tomatis, Mariano. 2009. Musée Bérenger Saunière. Section 1 Rennes le Château avant Bérenger Saunière. Légende Tresoraires. Panel 8. (Bérenger Saunière Museum. Section 1 Rennes le Château before Bérenger Saunière. Treasure Legends. Panel 8.) Available online at http://www.renneslechateau.it/panel_08.pdf (accessed 20 January 2020).

Cardinaux, Stephane. 2016. *Les réseaux telluriques.* (Earth networks.) Available online at https://www.geniedulieu.ch/index.php/les-dossiers/dossiers/78-genie-du-lieu/168-reseaux- telluriques (accessed 20 January 2020).

Catalogue de la collection des minéraux de l'or réunie par Georges de la Bouglïse Ingénieur des Mines. Paris 1911. (Catalogue of the minerals of gold collected by Georges de La Bouglise Mine Engineer.) Privas, Imprimerie Centrale de l'Ardèche. Available online at https://iiif.lib.harvard.edu/manifests/view/drs:44559212$1i (accessed 26 February 2020).

Catel, Guillaume. 1633. *Memoires de l'histoire du Languedoc.* (Memories of the history of the Languedoc.) (pdf) Arnaud Colomiez: Toulouse. Available online at https://archive.org/details/bub_gb_y5u2F3VpBp0C (accessed 20 January 2020).

Certain, M. 1935. Communication concernant la mines d'or de Salsigne faite par al la Société d'Etudes Scientifique de l'Aude. (Communication concerning the gold mines of Salsigne made by the Société d'Etudes Scientifiques de l'Aude.) *Bulletin de La Société d'Etudes Scientifique de l'Aude.* Quarante Cinquieme Annee Tome XXX1X. E. Roudiere: Carcassonne. Available online at https://gallica.bnf.fr/ark:/12148/bpt6k5410522j (accessed January 2020).

Chaplin, Patrice. 2007. *City of secrets: The extraordinary story of one woman's journey to the heart of the Grail legend.* Constable & Robinson: London.

Charles N., Dupuy J.J., Christmann P., Galin R., & Guillon D. 2017. *Industrie minérale et activité minière en France. Collection La mine en France Tome 1.* (Mineral industry and mining activity in France. Collection: The mine in France vol. 1.) (pdf) Available online at http://www.mineralinfo.fr/sites/default/files/upload/tome_01_industrie_mineraleactivite_miniere_final24032017.pdf (accessed 20 January 2020).

Coppens, Philip. nd. *The Canopus revelation: Dividing Egypt.* Available online at http://www.philipcoppens.com/canopus_art4.html (accessed 10 January 2020).

Coppens, Philip. 2009. *Servants of the Grail: The real life characters of the Grail legend identified.* O Books: Winchester UK.

Corbu, Claire & Captier, Antoine. 1985. *L'Héritage de L'Abbé Saunière.* (The legacy of Reverend Saunière.) Bélisane: Nice.

Corbu, Noël. 1955. *The Corbu tape.* Available online at http://www.cromleck-de-rennes.com/noel_corbu.htm (accessed January 2020).

Coudy, Julien & Nogue, Maurice. 1975. *Qui a tue l'abbé Gelis et pourquoi?* (Who killed the Abbé Gelis and why?) Midi Libre. 3–5 October. Available online at http://rennes-le-chateau-en-quete-de-verite.e-monsite.com/accueil/page-73.html (accessed 15 January 2020).

Courrent, Dr. P. 1934. *Notice historique sur les Rennes connus anciennement sous les nom de Bains de Montferrand leur origine Gallo-Romaine et leur evolution jusqu'a la fin du XV111 siecle.* (Historical record on the Rennes, formerly known as Bains de Montferrand, their Gallo-Roman origin and their evolution until the end of the 18th century.) *Bulletin de la Societe d'Etudes Scientifiques de l'Aude.* Quarante Quatrieme Annee Tome XXXV111. E. Roudiere: Carcassonne. Available online at http://gallica.bnf.fr/ (accessed 29 September 2014).

Crabbé, P.J. 1985. Turgot's brief on mines and quarries: early economic analysis of mineral land tenure in *Natural Resources Journal.* 25(2). Available online at http://digitalrepository.unm.edu/nrj/vol25/iss2/ (accessed 20 January 2020).

Cran, William & Corbu, Claire. 1996. *Timewatch: The history of a mystery.* (film) BBC 2 InVision Productions: London. Available online at https://www.youtube.com/watch?v=qXB3mfHeFIM (accessed 10 January 2020).

Cromleck de Rennes. n.d. *The sought after treasures of Rennes-le-Château.* Available online at http://www.cromleck-de-rennes.com/treasure.htm (accessed 10 April 2020).

Croucher, Shane. 2014. How rich is the Vatican? So wealthy it can stumble across millions of euros just 'tucked away'. *International Business Times.* Available online at http://www.ibtimes.co.uk/how-rich-vatican-so-wealthy-it-can-stumble-across-millions-euros- just-tucked-away-1478219 (accessed 15 January 2020).

Crouquet, Roger. 1948. *Visite a une ville morte: Rennes-le-Château, autrefois capitale du Comte de Razès. Aujourd'hui bourgade abandonne.* (Visit to a dead village: Rennes-le-Château, former capital of the county of Razès, now an abandoned village.) *Le Soir illustré.* no. 819. Available online at http://priory-of-sion.com/rlc/bag/crouquet.html (accessed 20 January 2020).

Dawes, Christopher. 2005. *Rat Scabies and the Holy Grail.* Thunder's Mouth Press: New York.

De Basville, Lamoignon. 1734. *Mémoires pour servir à l'histoire de Languedoc.* (Memories to serve the history of the Languedoc.) (pdf) Pierre Boyer: Amsterdam. Available online at https://archive.org/details/bub_gb_7eQ_AAAAcAAJ (accessed 20 January 2020).

De Beaupuy, François. 2014. Gold diggers revive French exploration as prices drive hunt. *Bloomberg.* 21 July. Available online at https://www.bloomberg.com/news/articles/2014-07-20/gold-diggers-revive-french-exploration-as-high-prices-drive-hunt (accessed 20 January 2020).

De Labouisse-Rochefort, Auguste. 1832. *Voyage à Rennes-les-Bains en 1803.* (Trip to Rennes-les-Bains in 1803.) Achille Desauges: Paris. pp. 469–471 in Smith, Paul. 2017. Priory of Sion. Available online at https://priory-of-sion.com/rlc/devilstreasure.html (accessed 20 January 202)).

De Sède, Gerard. 1968. *Le Trésor Maudit de Rennes-le-Château.* (The cursed treasure of Rennes-le-Château.) J'ai Lu: Paris.

De Sède, Gerard. 1988. *Rennes le Château: Le dossier, les impostures, les phantasms, les hypotheses.* (Rennes-le-Château: The dossier, the impostures, the phantasies, the hypothesis.) Robert Laffont: Paris.

Del Mar, Alexander. 1886. *Money and civilization.* George Bell & Sons: London. (pdf) Available online at http://www.haithitrust.org/ (accessed 4 November 2020).

Del Mar, Alex. 1902. *A history of the precious metals from earliest times to the present.* 2nd ed. Cambridge Encyclopedia Company: New York. (pdf) Available online at https://archive.org/ (accessed 12 February 2017).

Destination NSW. 2020. Gundagai gold trails. NSW Government: NSW. Available online at https://www.visitnsw.com/destinations/country-nsw/riverina/gundagai/attractions/gundagai-gold-trails (accessed 29 February 2020).

Douzet, Andre & Coppens, Philip. 2006. *The secret vault: The secret societies' manipulation of Saunière and the secret sanctuary of Notre-Dame-de-Merceilles.* Frontier Publishing: Netherlands.

Du Roy, Ivan & Chapelle, Sophie. 2013. From Brittany to Limousin, mining companies are coming back to France. *Multinationals observatory*. Available online at http://multinationales.org/From-Brittany-to-Limousin-mining (accessed January 2020).

Dunyach, Jean. 1967. The gold of Rennes once more. *L'Indépendant* 9 December. Available online at http://priory-of-sion.com/rlc/dunyach_translation.html (accessed January 2020).

Esparseil, R. 1935. Origin de l'or dans le Montagne Noir de l'Aude. (The origin of gold in the Black Mountain of the Aude department.) *Bulletin de La Société d'Etudes Scientifique de l'Aude*. Quarante Cinquiemme Annee Tome XXXIX. E. Roudiere: Carcassonne. (pdf) Available online at http://gallica.bnf.fr/ (accessed 29 September 2014.)

Fanthorpe, Lionel & Fanthorpe, Patricia. 1992. *Secrets of Rennes-le-Château*. Samuel Weiser: USA.

Fardone, Enzo. 2007. *The Poussin Enigma*. Starburst: Adelaide, South Australia.

Fardone, Enzo. 2009. Jesus Christ: From Jerusalem to Rennes-le-Château. *New Dawn*. Nov-Dec.

Fipke, C.E.; Gurney, J. J. & Moore, R.O. 1995. Diamond exploration techniques emphasising indicator mineral geochemistry and Canadian examples. Geological Survey of Canada Bulletin 423. Government of Canada: Ottowa, Ontario. (pdf) Available online at https://geoscan.nrcan.gc.ca/ (accessed January 2020).

Frolick, Veronon. 1999. *Fire into ice: Charles Fipke and the great diamond hunt*. Raincoast Books: Vancouver, Canada.

Garcia, Jean Pierre. nd. *Rennes-le-Château or the story of a great secret*. Available online at http://www.rennes-le-chateau-archive.com/ (accessed January 2020).

Gardner, Laurence. 2003. *The secrets of the sacred ark: Amazing revelations of the incredible power of gold*. Element Books: London.

Gardner, Laurence. 2005. *The Magdalene legacy: The Jesus and Mary bloodline conspiracy. Revelations beyond The Da Vinci Code*. Harper Element: London.

Geopolymer Institute. 2006. Are pyramids made out of concrete? Available online at https://www.geopolymer.org/archaeology/pyramids/are-pyramids-made-out-of-concrete-1/ (accessed 1 January 2016).

Girou, Jean. 1936. *L'Itinéraire en terre d'Aude.* (The itinerary in the land of Aude.) Couse, Grail & Castelnau: Montpellier in Smith, Paul. 2017. Priory of Sion. Available online at http://www.priory-of-sion.com/rlc/jeangirou.html (accessed 1 May 2016).

Gobet, Nicholas. 1779. *Les anciens mineralogistes du royaume de France: avec des notes.* (The old mineralogists of the Kingdom of France: with notes.) (pdf) Ruault: Paris. Available online at http://gallica.bnf.fr (accessed 5 Feb 2017).

Goitom, Hanibal. 2013. Napoleon Bonaparte and mining rights in France. (blog) Available online at http://blogs.loc.gov/law/2013/12/napoleon-bonaparte-and-mining-rights-in-france/ (accessed 15 October 2015).

Gough, Andrew. 2012. Andrew Gough's Arcadia Discussion zone. (blog) Available online at https://andrewgough.co.uk/ (accessed 23 March 2015).

Gouin. Simon. 2015. Salsigne: A century of mining, 10,000 years of pollution? Multinationals Observatory. Available online athttp://multinationales.org/Salsigne-A-Century-of-Mining-10-000-Years-of-Pollution (accessed January 2019).

Gourlay, R. 2016. Advanced aerial technology: Technologies validates ley lines and the songlines. *EarthHabitats News,* 14 July. Available online at https://www.facebook.com/Earthhabitats.news (accessed 21 January 2017).

Greenbank, Liz. 2013. Fault lines lead to gold. CSIRO Blog 14 June. (blog) Available online at https://blog.csiro.au/fault-lines-lead-to-gold/ (accessed 17 September 2015).

GuppY Orpaillage Loisir. 2004-2011. Available online at http://pujol.chez-alice.fr/ guppyor/ (accessed January 2020).

Hamilton, H.C. 1903. *The geography of Strabo literally translated with notes.* George Bell & Sons: London. Available online at https://archive.org/stream/MN40035ucmf_2/MN40035ucmf_2_djvu.txt (accessed 1 January 2016).

Henry-Claude, Michel; Peyrou, Joel & Zaballos, Yannik. 1998. *Montsegur: Last refuge, last rampart of the Catharist Church. Fragile: France.*

Hodge, Brian. 1976. *Valleys of gold: The goldfields story 1851–1861.* Book 1. Cambaroora Star Publications: Penshurst, New South Wales.

Hopkins, Marilyn; Simmans, Graham & Wallace-Murphy, Tim. 2000. *Rex Deus: The true mystery of Rennes-le-Château and the dynasty of Jesus.* Element Books: UK.

Howells, Robert. 2011. *Inside the Priory of Sion: Revelations from the world's most secret society – guardians of the bloodline of Jesus*. Watkins Publishing: London.

Jacob, Isaac B. nd. (a). Rennes-le-Château: Fall Out-a classified case, finally closed. Available online at http://isaacbenjacob.com/the-rise-fall-out-2/4574153548 (accessed January 2020).

Jacob, Isaac B. nd. (b). Was Bérenger Saunière a spy in the pay of the central powers? Available online at http://www.isaacbenjacob.com/was-berenger-a-spy-1/4552473303 (accessed January 2020).

James, Samantha. 2016. Argyle sits pretty in pink. *The Australian Mining Review*. June. Available online at http://www.miningoilgas.com.au/the-australian-mining-review-archive/ (accessed 18 April 2017).

Jarnac, Pierre. 1985. *History of the treasure of Rennes-le-Château*. Belisane: France.

Jenolan Caves. 2012. Gundungurra Creation Story of Jenolan Caves. Available online at https://www.jenolancaves.org.au/about/aboriginal-culture/dreamtime-story-of-gurrangatch- mirrigan/ (accessed 29 January 2020).

Lamy, Michel. 1994. *Jules Verne, initié et initiateur: La clé du secret de Rennes-le-Château et le trésor des rois de France*. (Jules Verne, insider and initiator: The key to the secret of Rennes-le-Château and the treasure of the kings of France.) Payot et Rivages: Paris, France.

Lincoln, Henry. nd. Why I am sure that the geometry of Rennes-le-Château is beyond question. Henry Lincoln. Available online at http://www.henrylincoln.co.uk/ (accessed 1 May 2017).

Lincoln, Henry. 1991. *The Holy Place: The mystery of Rennes-le-Château. Discovering the eighth wonder of the natural world*. Corgi Books: Great Britain.

Lincoln, Henry. 1997. *Key to the sacred pattern*. The Windrush Press: Great Britain.

Loeb Classical Library edition Vol. III. 1939. The Library of History of Diodorus Siculus. Available online at http://bit.ly/DiodorusE5B (accessed 20 February 2020).

Loret, J. 1661. *La muze historique ou recueil des lettres en verse. Tome 111 1659-1662*. (The historical muze or collection of letters in verse, vol. 3, 1659-1662.) Available online at https://gallica.bnf.fr/ark:/12148/bpt6k62128826/f160.image (accessed 4 November 2020).

Luke Walker. 2014. *Lasseter's Bones*. 2014. (film) Luke Walker: Australia.

Lumni Teaching. nd. *L'opération d'échange des billets Juin 1945*. (The ticket exchange operation June 1945.) Filmed news: Franc pour Franc. Broadcast: 08 June 1945. Available online at https://enseignants.lumni.fr/fiche-media/00000000327/l-operation-d-echange-des- billets-juin-1945.html (accessed 29 January 2020).

MacNevin, A. and Geological Survey of New South Wales. 1977. Diamonds in New South Wales. Department of Mines: New South Wales.

Malus, Jean de. 1595-1605. Avis des riches mines d'or et d'argent et de toutes espèces de métaux et de minéraux des monts Pyrénées. 1595-1605. Paris. (Notice of the rich gold and silver mines and of all kinds of metals and minerals in the Pyrenees Mountains.) Available online at https://gallica.bnf.fr/ark:/12148/bpt6k1527205v?rk=64378;0 (accessed January 2020).

Mann, William. 2006. *Templar meridians*. Destiny Books: Rochester, VT.

Maron, D. F. 2014. Making babies with 3 genetic parents gets FDA Hearing. *Scientific American* 24 February. Available online at https://www.scientificamerican.com/article/making-babies-with-3-genetic-parents-gets-fda-hearing/ (accessed January 2020).

Mason, Harry. 1997. Bright skies. Part 1 of 6. *Nexus Magazine* April–May. Available online at http://www.cheniere.org/misc/brightskies1.htm (accessed 1 March 2015).

Meisner, Gary. 2012. The universe as a Phi-based dodecahedron. Available online at https://www.goldennumber.net/universe/ (accessed 12 February 2016).

Meunier, Stanislas.1889. Pepite d'or d'un demi-kilogramme trouvee en France. (Half a kilogram gold nugget found in France.) *La Nature* 6 Juillet. pp. 85-86. Available online at http://cnum.cnam.fr/CGI/redir.cgi?4KY28 (accessed: 19 February 2020).

Miles, Daniel. 2019. Retiree finds massive gold nugget outside historic gold rush town of Ballarat. *ABC News* 27 July. Available online at https://www.abc.net.au/news/2019-07-27/gold-nugget-found-in-ballarat-by-retiree/11353044 (accessed 29 January 2020).

Mines du patrimoine dans la Montagne Noire. (Heritage Mines in the Montagne Noire.) nd. Available online at https://www.minespatrimoine.fr/mesparseil (accessed February 2017).

Mundell, Robert A. 1997. Money and the sovereignty of the state. International Economic Association Conference in Trento, 4-7 September. Columbia University. (pdf) Available online at http://www-ceel.economia.unitn.it/events/monetary/mundell14.pdf (accessed 5 February 2017).

New South Wales Department of Primary Industries. 2007. Hill End gold deposits. Primefact 569. (pdf) Available online at https://www.resourcesandgeoscience.nsw.gov.au/__data/assets/pdf_file/0006/109725/hill-end-gold-deposits.pdf (accessed 26 January. 2016).

Patton, Guy. 2009. *Masters of deception: Murder and intrigue in the world of occult politics.* Frontier Publishing: Amsterdam.

Pell, Cardinal George. 2014. We've discovered hundreds of millions of euros off the Vatican's balance sheet, says cardinal. *Catholic Herald.* Available online at https://catholicherald.co.uk/weve-discovered-hundreds-of-millions-of-euros-off-the-vaticans-balance-sheet-says-cardinal/ (accessed 4 November 2020).

Pebernard, M. 1898. Histoire de Conque-sur-Orvieil. Mémoires de la Société des arts et des sciences de Carcassonne. Tome 1X. Premier Partie. (History of Conque-sur-Orvieil. Memoirs of the Society for Arts and Sciences of Carcassonne.) Available online at https://gallica.bnf.fr (accessed 24 January 2020).

Peuchet, J. 1805. Statistique elementaire de la France. (Elementary statistics of France.) Gilbert et Cie: Paris, France. Available online at https:// gallica.bnf.fr/ark:/12148/bpt6k62357845.texteImage (accessed January 2020).

Picknett, Lynn and Prince, Clive. 2006. *The Sion revelation: Inside the shadowy world of Europe's secret masters.* Time Warner Books: Great Britain.

Proudfoot, Peter. 1994. *The secret plan of Canberra.* University of New South Wales Press: New South Wales.

Pujol, Hervé. 2014. Faut-il rouvrir la mine d'or de Salsigne? (Should we re-open the Salsigne gold mine?) *CNRS Le Journal,* 5 September. Available online at https://lejournal.cnrs.fr/billets/faut-il-rouvrir-la-mine-dor-de-salsigne (accessed January 2020).

Quintin, Jonathon. 2012. The golden key. (Youtube) Available online at https://www.youtube.com/watch?v=VkHiV2SvATk (accessed 1 March 2015).

Regie Tourisme. nd. Rennes-le-Château: Its site its mysteries. (pamphlet).

Rennes-le-Château Research and Resource. 2017. Available online at https://www.renneslechateau.nl/mystery-of-rennes-le-chateau/ (accessed January 2019).

Rhan, Otto. 1933. *Crusade against the Grail*. Inner Traditions: Rochester Vermont. (pdf) Available online at https://archive.org/details/CrusadeAgainstTheGrail/mode/2up (accessed 10 April 2020).

Ribaux, Col. 2010. Min Min light AKA Paddy's Lantern AKA Jack-o'-lantern sighting in Australia. (Youtube) Available online at https://www.youtube.com/watch?v=eeyYsVp-5Oc (accessed 12 August 2015).

Ribaux, Col. 2011. Letter from Col Ribaux, miner, geologist, conservationist and keeper of the Airly Mountain, Airly State Conservation Area. Airly Diamond Syndicate. Available online at http://www.airlydiamond.com/media-releases.html (accessed 4 November 2020).

Robin, Jean Luc. 2007. *Rennes-le-Château: Saunière's secret*. Editions Sud Ouest: France.

Smith, Paul. 2017. Rennes-le-Château Celebrations. Available online at https://www.priory-of-sion.com/rlc/bscentenary.html (accessed 4 November 2020).

Société des Sciences Naturelles, Archéologiques et Historiques (Creuse). 1963. Mémoires de la Société des Sciences Naturelles et Archéologiques de la Creuse. Tome trente-cinquième. (Society of Natural, Archaeological and Historical Sciences (Creuse). v. 35. (Memoirs of the Society of Natural and Archaeological Sciences of the Creuse.) Gueret: Imprimerie Lecante. (pdf) Available online at https://gallica.bnf.fr/ (accessed: 18 February 2020).

Sutton, David. 2005. Rat Scabies and Christopher Dawes. Interview with Fortean Times. July. (pdf) Rennes-le-Château/The Grail. Available online at https://ratscabies.com/rennes-le-chateauthe-grail/ (accessed January 2020).

Taylor, Grant. 2016. Massive gold nugget find sparks wealth of intrigue. *The Western Australian* 26 August. Available online at https://thewest.com.au/news/wa/massive-gold-nugget-find-sparks-wealth-of-intrigue-ng-ya-116377 (accessed: 10 September 2016).

Tazewell, S.J. 2013. The Legend of Billy Blue. (Blog) Prospecting Australia. Gold Prospecting and Forum. Available online at https://www.prospectingaustralia.com.au/forum/viewtopic.php?id=2450 (accessed 11 January 2017).

Testa, Angie and Decarli, Bill. 2005. *A dead man's dream: Lasseter's reef found*. Hesperian Press: Carlisle WA.

The Connexion: French news and views. 2014. Permit for a new French gold rush. Available online at http://www.connexionfrance.com/gold-mine-old-variscan-mining-licence-aude- maine-et-loire-15473-view-article.html (accessed 3 January 2016).

Tomatis, Marino. nd. Guida storica all'enigma di Rennes-le-Château. (Historical guide to the enigma of Rennes-le-Château.) Rennes-le-Château.it. Available online at http://www.renneslechateau.it/ (accessed 24 February 2020).

Tomatis, Mariano. 2005. Rennes-le-Château e i documenti segreti. (Rennes-le-Château and secret documents.) Mariano Tomatis Wonder Injector. Available online at http://www.marianotomatis.it/slide.php?folder=slides/docsecret (accessed 28 February 2020).

Tomatis, Mariano. 2008. Analisi completa della 'Grande Pergamena' di Rennes-le-Château. (Detailed analysis of the Great Parchment of Rennes-le-Château.) (pdf) Indagini su Rennes-Le-Château Circolare Informativa del Gruppo di Studio e Documentazione su Rennes-Le-Château Anno 11, 13-24, Giugno2007-Maggio 2008, no. 21, Feb 2008, pp 1039-1052. Available online at https://archive.org/stream/Indagini_su_Rennes-le- Chateau2 #page/n435/mode/1up (accessed 9 March 2020).

Tomatis, Mariano. 2020. Il realisimo fantastic di Gérard De Sède. Valico Festival, Roma 22 Febraio. (The fantastic realism of Gérard De Sède. Valico Festival Rome 22 February.) Available online at http://www.rennesle chateau.it/index.php?sezione=home&id=20200308 (accessed 2 March 2020).

Trading economics. 2017. France gold reserves 2000-217. Available online at http://www.tradingeconomics.com/france/gold-reserves (accessed 1 January 2017).

Treub, Lucien F. 1996. The Salsigne gold mine: A world class ore body in the south-west of France. *Gold Bulletin*. 29(4). Available online at http://www.oalib.com/paper/1307713#.WVIKWWPzljo (accessed 3 July 2014).

Tisseyre, Elie. 1906. Une excursion à Rennes-le-Château. Bulletin de la Société d'Etudes Scientifiques de l'Aude, vol.17. pp. 98-105. (Excursion to Rennes-le-Château. Bulletin of the Société d'Etudes Scientifiques de l'Aude.) Available online at https://gallica.bnf.fr (accessed 1 April 2020).

Valderrama, I. & Pérez-Pariente, Joaquín. 2012. Alchemy at the service of mining technology in seventeenth-century Europe, according to the works of Martine De Bertereau and Jean Du Chastelet. *Bulletin for the History of Chem-*

istry, 37(1). (pdf) Available online at http://acshist.scs.illinois.edu/bulletin_open_access/v37-1/v37-1%20p1-13.pdf (accessed 16 September 2016).

Van Buren, Elizabeth. 1986. *Refuge of the apocalypse: Doorway into other dimensions.* C.W. Daniel: Great Britain.

Vessica Adventures. 2016. *Henry Lincoln speaks 01: Stop looking and start seeing.* (Youtube) Available online at https://www.youtube.com/watch?v=cFbyvHF3M0M (accessed 2 January 2017).

Vessica Adventures. 2016. *Henry Lincoln speaks 02: Rumors of treasure at Rennes-le-Château.* (Youtube) Available online at https://www.youtube.com/watch?v=eECeVQU3Prs (accessed 2 January 2017).

Vickery, Amanda. 2011. 18th-century Paris: the capital of luxury. *The Guardian.* 30 July. Available online at https://www.theguardian.com/artanddesign/2011/jul/29/paris-life-luxury- getty-museum (accessed 5 April 2020).

Vidal, J.M. 1904. Moines alchimistes a l'Abbaye de Boulbonne (1339). Bulletin Periodique de la Société Ariégeoise des Sciences, Lettres et arts. (Alchemist monks at the Abbéy of Boulbonne. Periodical Bulletin of the Society Sciences, and Arts.) Nuevieme v. 1903–1904. pp. 133–137. Available online at https://gallica.bnf.fr/ark:/12148/bpt6k57278962/f7.item.r=boulbonne (accessed 12 April 2020.)

Von Daniken, Erik. 1969. *Chariots of the gods: Was God an ancient astronaut?* Transworld Publishers Ltd.: UK.

Wilson, Wendell E. 2020. Biographical Archive: Georges de la Bouglise (1842–1911). Mineralogical Record. Available online at https://mineralogicalrecord.com/ (accessed 27 February 2020).

Winter, Dan. 2014. Fractal conjugate space & time: Cause of negentropy, gravity and perception. (pdf) Implosion Group: Mullumbimby, New South Wales. Available online at http://www.fractalfield.com/onlinebook/FractalTimeSpaceDanWinter.pdf (accessed 15 January 2017).

Winter, Dan. 2016. What is phase conjugation? Therapi: The revolutionary new healing device. Available online at https://theraphi.com.au/what-is-phase-conjugation/ (accessed 1 December 2016).

Wood, David. 1986. *Genisis: The first book of revelations.* The Baton Press: Kent, UK.

References

1. Jenolan Caves. 2012.
2. Robin, Jean Luc. 2007 (p. 82).
3. Ibid. (p. 42).
4. Rennes-le-Château.it. nd.
5. Howells, Robert. 2011 (p. 314).
6. Girou, Jean. 1936.
7. Crouquet, Roger. 1948.
8. Robin, Jean Luc. 2007 (p. 178).
9. Cran, William & Corbu, Claire. 1996.
10. Corbu, Noel. 1955.
11. https://en.geneanet.org/
12. Corbu, Noel. 1955.
13. Lincoln, Henry. 1997 (p. 11).
14. Fanthorpe, Lionel & Fanthorpe, Patricia. 1992 (p. 27).
15. Baigent, Michael; Leigh, Richard & Lincoln, Henry. 1996 (p. 133).
16. Tisseyre, Elie. 1906 (pp. 98–105).
17. Baigent, Michael; Leigh, Richard & Lincoln, Henry. 1996 (p. 108)
18. Lincoln, Henry. 1991 (p. 42).
19. Ibid. (p. 54).
20. Ibid. (p. 51).
21. Ibid. (p. 110).
22. Lincoln, Henry. nd.
23. Robin, Jean Luc. 2007 (p. 38).
24. Tomatis, Mariano. 2005.
25. Lincoln, Henry. 1997 (p. 37).
26. Dunyach, Jean. 1967.
27. Robin, Jean Luc. 2007 (p. 51).
28. Lincoln, Henry. 1997 (p. 75–76).
29. Ibid. (p. 15).
30. Fardone, Enzo. 2009 (p. 43).
31. Jacob, Isaac B. nd (a).
32. BRGM. Schema structural massif du Mouthoumet. Quillan 1077 Orleans France.
33. Tomatis, Mariano. 2005.
34. Strabo (64 or 63 BC–AD c. 24) cited in Hamilton, H.C. 1903.
35. Pebernard, M. 1898 (p. 23).
36. Peuchet, J. 1805 (p. 350).
37. Greenbank, Liz. 2013.
38. Taylor, Grant. 2016.
39. James, Samantha. 2016 (p. 31).
40. Tomatis, Mariano. 2008 (pp. 1039–1052).

41. Lincoln, H. 1997. (p. 119).
42. Robin, Jean Luc. 2007 (p. 82).
43. Ibid. (p. 60).
44. Ibid. (p. 36).
45. Jacob, Isaac. B. nd (b).
46. Tazewell, S.J. 2013.
47. Coudy, Julien and Nogue, Maurice. 1975.
48. Croucher, Shane. 2014.
49. Pell, Cardinal George. 2014.
50. Maron, D.F. 2014.
51. Mason, Harry. 1997.
52. Quintin, Jonathon. 2012.
53. Meisner, Gary. 2012.
54. Cardinaux, Stephane. 2016.
55. Callahan, Philip. 2001.
56. Gourlay, R. 2016.
57. Boudet, H. Msg. 1886 (p. 225).
58. Chaplin, Patrice. 2007 (p. 246).
59. Geopolymer Institute. 2006.
60. Creswell, Leon. 12 May 2005, personal communication.
61. Ibid.
62. Adams, David & Sonnen, Krista. 2005.
63. Coppens, Philip. nd.
64. Boudet, H. Msg. 1886 (p. 147).
65. Robin, Jean Luc. 2007 (p. 90).
66. Société des Sciences Naturelles, Archéologiques et Historiques (Creuse). 1963 (p. 26).
67. Treub, Lucien F. 1996 (p.138).
68. Catel, Guillaume. 1633 (p. 51) [published posthumously].
69. Société des Sciences Naturelles, Archéologiques et Historiques (Creuse).1963 (p. 15).
70. Del Mar, Alexander. 1886 (p. 190).
71. Ibid. (p.192).
72. Del Mar, Alexander. 1902 (p. 80).
73. Valderrama, Ignacio & Pérez-Pariente, Joaquín. 2012 (p. 2) .
74. Malus, Jean de. 1595–1605.
75. Gobet, Nicholas. 1779 (p. xxvj).
76. Goitom, Hanibal. 2013.
77. Crabbe, P.J. 1985 (p. 286).
78. Goitom, Hanibal. 2013.
79. Matthieu, cited in Crabbe, P.J. 1985 (p. 269).
80. *Rennes le Chateau. Research and Resource.* 2017.
81. *Rennes le Chateau. Research and Resource.* 2017.
82. Gobet, Nicholas. 1779.
83. De Basville, Lamoignon. 1734 (p. 251).
84. Garcia, Jean Pierre. nd.
85. Robin, Jean Luc. 2007 (p. 39).
86. Gobet, Nicholas. 1779.
87. Valderrama, I. & Pérez-Pariente, Joaquín. 2012 (p. 5).
88. Rennes le Chateau. Research and Resource. 2017.
89. Chaplin, Patrice. 2007 (p. 282).

90. Loret, J. 1661.
91. De Labouisse-Rochefort, Auguste. 1832.
92. Valderrama, I. & Pérez-Pariente, Joaquín. 2012 (p. 5).
93. Mundell, Robert A. 1997 (p. 11).
94. Ibid. (p. 15).
95. Blanc, Jerome & Desmedt, Ludovic. 2007 (p. 5).
96. Ibid. (p. 13).
97. Del Mar, Alexander. 1886 (p. 197).
98. Garcia, Jean Pierre. nd.
99. Vidal, J.M. 1904 (pp. 133–136).
100. Rhan, Otto. 1933 (p. 181).
101. Ibid. (p. 185).
102. Fanthorpe, Lionel & Fanthorpe, Patricia. 1992 (p. 80).
103. Boudet, H. Msg. 1886 (p. II).
104. Gobet, Nicholas. 1779 (p. 178).
105. http://www.murphys-laws.com
106. Ibid.
107. Ibid.
108. Smith, Paul. 2016.
109. Luke Walker. 2014.
110. Testa, Angie and Decarli, Bill. 2005.
111. https://theraphi.com.au/
112. *Macaniche, boudi* is a term used in the South of France meaning 'oh gosh'.
113. De Beaupuy, Francois. 2014.
114. Andrews, R. & Schellenberger, P. 1996 (pp. 172–173).
115. Robin, Jean Luc. 2007 (p. 115).
116. Ibid. (p. 171).
117. Lumni Teaching. nd.
118. Robin, Jean Luc. 2007 (p. 191).
119. Destination NSW. 2020.
120. Meunier, Stanislas. 1889 (p. 85).
121. Tomatis, Mariano. 2005.
122. Vickery, Amanda. 2011.
123. Charles N. et al. 2017.
124. Breizh-info. 2015.
125. Gouin, Simon. 2015.
126. Taylor, Grant. 2016.
127. Miles, Daniel. 27 July 2019.

www.ingramcontent.com/pod-product-compliance
Lightning Source LLC
Chambersburg PA
CBHW071805080526
44589CB00012B/688